ALGEBRA
TEACHER'S
ACTIVITIES KIT

150
Ready-to-Use Activities
with
Real-World Applications

Judith A. Muschla • Gary Robert Muschla

D1119627

JOSSEY-BASS
A Wiley Imprint
www.josseybass.com

Published by Jossey-Bass
A Wiley Imprint
989 Market Street, San Francisco, CA 94103-1741   www.josseybass.com

Jossey-Bass books and products are available through most bookstores. To contact Jossey-Bass directly, call our Customer Care Department within the U.S. at 800-956-7739, outside the U.S. at 317-572-3986 or fax 317-572-4002.

Jossey-Bass also publishes its books in a variety of electronic formats. Some content that appears in print may not be available in electronic books.

Library of Congress Cataloging-in-Publication Data

Muschla, Judith A.
  Algebra teacher's activities kit : 150 ready-to-use activities with real-world applications / Judith A. Muschla, Gary R. Muschla.— 1st ed.
      p. cm.
  ISBN 0-7879-6598-7 (alk. paper)
  1. Algebra—Study and teaching (Secondary)—Activity programs. I. Muschla, Gary Robert. II. Title.
  QA159.M87 2003
  512'.071'2—dc21

                                                        2003006235

Printed in the United States of America

FIRST EDITION

For Erin

About the Authors

Gary Robert Muschla received his B.A. and M.A.T. from Trenton State College and taught at Appleby School in Spotswood, New Jersey, for more than twenty-five years. He spent many of his years in the classroom teaching mathematics at the elementary level. He has also taught reading and writing and has been a successful author. He is a member of the Authors Guild and the National Writers Association.

Mr. Muschla has written several resources for teachers, including: *The Writing Teacher's Book of Lists* (1991), *Writing Workshop Survival Kit* (1993), *English Teacher's Great Books Activities Kit* (1994), *Reading Workshop Survival Kit* (1997), *Ready-to-Use Reading Proficiency Lessons and Activities, 4th-Grade Level* (2002), *Ready-to-Use Reading Proficiency Lessons and Activities, 8th-Grade Level* (2002), and *Ready-to-Use Reading Proficiency Lessons and Activities, 10th-Grade Level* (2003), all published by Jossey-Bass. He currently writes and serves as a consultant in education.

Judith A. Muschla received her B.A. in mathematics from Douglass College at Rutgers University and is certified to teach K–12. She has taught mathematics in South River, New Jersey, for over twenty-five years. She has taught math at various levels at South River High School, ranging from basic skills through calculus. She has also taught at South River Middle School where, in her capacity as a team leader, she helped revise the mathematics curriculum to reflect the Standards of the NCTM, coordinated interdisciplinary units, and conducted mathematics workshops for teachers and parents. She was a recipient of the 1990–91 Governor's Teacher Recognition Program award in New Jersey, and she was named the 2002 South River Public School District Teacher of the Year. Along with teaching, she has been a member of the state Standards Review Panel for the Mathematics Core Curriculum Content Standards in New Jersey.

The *Algebra Teacher's Activities Kit* is the sixth book Gary and Judith Muschla have co-authored. They have also written *The Math Teacher's Book of Lists* (1995), *Hands-on Math Projects with Real-Life Applications* (1996), *Math Starters! 5- to 10-Minute Activities to Make Kids Think, Grades 6–12* (1999), *The Geometry Teacher's Activities Kit* (2000), and *Math Smart! Over 220 Ready-to-Use Activities to Motivate and Challenge Students, Grades 6–12* (2002), published by Jossey-Bass.

Acknowledgments

We would like to thank Michael Pfister, principal of South River High School, and our colleagues for their support of our efforts in writing this book.

We would also like to thank Steve Thompson, our editor, for his guidance in bringing this project to completion. Without his efforts, completing this book would have been a far greater task.

Thanks also to our daughter, Erin, who was the first reader of the manuscript and who caught numerous typos and oversights.

Special thanks to Michelle Di Giovanni for her comments and suggestions, which helped us to finalize the manuscript and turn it into a practical resource for teachers.

Special thanks also to Cathy Mallon, our production editor, for her efforts in guiding this manuscript through the production process, and to Diane Turso for proofreading and making the final corrections.

Finally, we'd like to thank our students, who over the years have made teaching challenging, exciting, and rewarding.

Introduction

As math curriculums across the country are being revised in an effort to prepare students for the challenges of the 21st century and reflect the Standards of the NCTM, algebra instruction is gaining great emphasis. It has become clear to educators that algebra is the foundation to learning higher mathematics. Mastery of algebra prepares a student for subjects such as geometry, trigonometry, and calculus; hones a student's problem-solving skills and ability to express mathematical relationships; and fosters a student's overall competence in math.

This book will support your teaching efforts by helping you to provide your students with activities that will expand their understanding and appreciation of algebra. Our best wishes to you in your teaching.

How to Use This Resource

This resource is divided into ten sections, containing a total of 150 activities. Each section also includes Teaching Suggestions and Answer Keys. A brief description of the sections follows.

Section 1, "The Language of Algebra (Using Whole Numbers)" has fifteen activities that address the special terminology of algebra. The activities focus on numerical relationships, operations, and algebraic reasoning.

Section 2, "Integers, Variables, and Expressions," contains fifteen activities, ranging from basic operations with integers to the use of integers with variables and expressions. Along with providing the foundation for solving equations and inequalities, these activities highlight how integers relate to real-world situations.

Section 3, "Linear Equations and Inequalities," offers twenty-four activities that cover the skills and concepts needed for writing and solving linear equations and inequalities. The activities of the section focus on real-life situations and include such topics as direct variation, percents, systems of linear equations, formulas that apply to temperature, and matrices.

Section 4, "Graphing Linear Equations and Inequalities," includes fifteen activities that address a variety of topics and skills. Beginning with the number line, the activities cover graphing solutions of equations and inequalities with one variable, graphing the solutions of combined equations and inequalities, graphing the equation of a line on the coordinate plane, graphing inequalities with two variables, and graphing systems of equations and inequalities.

Section 5, "Basic Operations with Monomials and Polynomials," contains twelve activities. Starting with basic operations with monomials, this section goes on to cover numerous skills and concepts relating to monomials and polynomials.

Section 6, "Factors of Monomials and Polynomials," includes twelve activities. Focusing on the factoring of monomials and polynomials, the activities of this section provide the foundation for solving quadratic and cubic equations.

Section 7, "Functions and Relations," provides twelve activities, starting with T-tables and concluding with piecewise-defined functions. Other topics include finding the values of functions, domain and range, basic operations with functions, the composition of functions, the inverses of functions, and graphs of families of functions.

Section 8, "Complex Numbers," contains twelve activities. Covering various topics, including real numbers, square roots, radicals, conjugates, and using i, this section offers students a thorough review of complex numbers and related concepts.

Section 9, "Polynomial, Exponential, and Logarithmic Functions," contains thirteen activities. The activities cover skills and topics related to various types of functions and also include real-life applications such as calculating monthly loan payments and compound interest.

Section 10, "Potpourri," offers twenty activities that combine many of the skills and concepts covered in the previous sections in a fresh manner. In this section you will find games and puzzles that are designed to stimulate algebraic thinking via unconventional approaches.

Each section begins with Teaching Suggestions, followed by Answer Keys. The Teaching Suggestions offer insight to the effective implementation of each activity and highlight what, if any, prerequisite skills students must have to complete an activity successfully. Detailed Answer Keys reduce the amount of time needed for correcting students' work.

The activities are designed for flexibility and easy implementation. Each is reproducible, stands alone, and is numbered according to section. For example, Activity 1-9, "Simplifying and Evaluating Expressions," is the ninth activity in Section 1. Activity 3-19, "Writing and Solving Inequalities," is the nineteenth activity in Section 3, while Activity 5-8, "Multiplying a Polynomial by a Monomial," is the eighth activity in Section 5.

The title of each activity focuses on the skills or concepts the activity addresses. Thus, the table of contents serves as a skills/concepts/topics list. For example, if you are teaching graphing, specifically the x- and y-intercepts, you should turn to Section 4, "Graphing Linear Equations and Inequalities." Activity 4-7, "Finding the X- and Y-Intercepts," and Activity 4-8, "Using the X- and Y-Intercepts to Graph a Line," would likely support your lesson.

The activities in each section follow the typical algebra curriculum and generally progress from basic to challenging. The activities are suited for various purposes. They can be used to supplement your math program, for reinforcement, for challenges or extra credit, or even for substitute plans.

To reduce your workload, as well as provide students with quick feedback, many of the activities are self-correcting. Correct answers enable students to complete a message or statement about math, which in turn tells them their answers are right.

We suggest that you utilize the activities in a manner that best supports your program. Choosing those activities that satisfy the needs of your students will help them to gain a better understanding and appreciation of algebra.

Contents

Section 5   Basic Operations with Monomials and Polynomials   147

Section 8   Complex Numbers   235

Contents

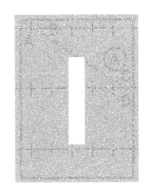

The Language of Algebra (Using Whole Numbers)

Every discipline has its own language. Soccer has its goals, figure skating has its triple axels, and geometry has its polygons. Specialized terminology makes it possible to understand the discipline. How could someone describe baseball without mentioning the words "innings," "strikes," and "outs"?

The fifteen activities of this section focus on the basic terminology of algebra. Understanding this language will help your students to understand numerical relationships, describe operations, and reason algebraically. By becoming fluent in the language of algebra, your students will be prepared to move on to more advanced skills and concepts.

Teaching Suggestions for the Activities

1-1 Using the Order of Operations I

This activity requires your students to simplify an expression. The expressions of the activity focus on the four basic operations—addition, subtraction, multiplication, and division. No grouping symbols or exponents are included. All numerical values are positive whole numbers. The symbols · and × are used to denote multiplication.

Introduce this activity by discussing the rules for the Order of Operations, which are noted on the worksheet. Go over the example on the worksheet together, noting the steps that are taken to arrive at the numerical value.

Review the instructions on the worksheet with your students. Explain that the first column lists the expression and the second column the steps necessary to simplify an expression. Point out that each step on the right can be paired with only one expression on the left and that each step can be used only once. Remind your students to include the numerical values of the expressions in their answers.

1-2 Using the Order of Operations II

This activity builds upon the skills addressed in Activity 1-1 and provides more practice with the Order of Operations. It includes the use of grouping symbols.

Begin the activity by reviewing the Order of Operations with your students. Emphasize that parentheses, braces, brackets, and the fraction bar are all considered to be grouping symbols. Operations within these symbols must be done first. Remind your students that a number directly to the left of a grouping symbol implies multiplication.

Go over the instructions for the activity with your students. Note that, along with identifying the incorrect answer, they are to explain why the answer is wrong.

1-3 Using the Order of Operations III

For this activity your students are to simplify various expressions using the Order of Operations. Grouping symbols, exponents, and fractions appear in the expressions. Unless your students are experienced with simplifying expressions, you should assign Activities 1-1 and 1-2 before assigning this one.

Start the activity by reviewing the Order of Operations. You should also explain the concept of a base and an exponent. For example, in the expression 2^3, 2 is called the base and 3 is the exponent. The exponent means that 2 is used as a factor three times. Thus, 2^3 means $2 \times 2 \times 2$ or 8. Point out that a common error students make when working with exponents is to multiply the base times the exponent, for example, in this case, 2×3, obtaining the incorrect answer of 6.

Depending on the abilities and backgrounds of your students, you may also wish to introduce the concept of a square number, which is a number raised to the second power. For example, $5^2 = 25$ shows that 25 is a square number. Some other examples of square numbers are 9, 16, 36, 49, 64, and 81.

Make sure your students understand the instructions for the activity. Remind them to follow the directions closely when placing their answers in the Code Box.

1-4 Using Square Numbers

The purpose of this activity is to familiarize your students with square numbers. Review the examples of square numbers included on the worksheet. Depending on the needs of your students, you may wish to expand the list.

Start this activity by drawing squares on the board or an overhead projector. Draw: a 1×1-inch square, a 2×2-inch square, a 3×3-inch square, and a 4×4-inch square. Emphasize to your students that the number that represents the area in each square is a square number.

Next, explain the Square Number Theorem, referring to the examples on the worksheet. Remind your students to find the square numbers first, then add. You might mention that this procedure is the same as following the Order of Operations.

Go over the instructions on the worksheet, and emphasize that the last five problems require students to find the four square numbers that add up to the number. This is the opposite of what they have to do in problems 1 through 10. Suggest that guess and check is a good strategy to use in solving the last four problems.

1-5 Translating Algebraic Expressions into Phrases

This activity requires students to complete a crossword puzzle with a word omitted from a phrase. It provides practice in writing expressions.

Introduce the activity by explaining that an algebraic expression is a combination of a variable (or variables) and a number (or numbers). Note the examples on the worksheet. Emphasize that order matters when subtracting and dividing. For instance, $n - 3$ means 3 less than a number and not 3 minus a number. Incorrect order is a common mistake when writing expressions.

Review the instructions on the worksheet with your students. Remind them that this is a crossword puzzle, and encourage them to focus their attention on the clues.

1-6 Writing Phrases as Algebraic Expressions I

This activity is a follow-up to Activity 1-5. For this activity, your students are given a phrase containing an expression. They are to determine if the expression is stated correctly. If it is incorrect, they are to correct the expression.

Note the common errors that many students make with these types of expressions. For example, they may overlook order. $n - 8$ is not the same as $8 - n$. They may also overlook grouping symbols. For example, three times the sum of a number and 10 is 3(n + 10) or 3(10 + n), but not 3n + 10.

Review the instructions on the worksheet with your students. Remind them that half of the problems on the worksheet are correct. Students must correct the incorrect problems.

1-7 Writing Phrases as Algebraic Expressions II

This activity provides your students with more practice using algebraic expressions. In each problem of this activity, your students are to think of a number, do a series of numerical operations, and obtain an answer that the teacher can predict. Your students, with the aid of algebra, are to explain these problems as well as create problems of their own. To complete this activity successfully, your students must be able to translate phrases into algebraic expressions.

Start this activity by reviewing the Distributive Property. Go over the instructions on the worksheet, then do the first problem as a class exercise. Instruct your students to write the number they begin with in the blank in Column I, recording each successive number in the blanks provided. (You may wish to suggest that for problems 1 through 3 students choose a number between 1 and 9 to keep the math simple.) Complete Column II (for the first problem) as a class. The steps are n, which represents the first number the students record, n^2, $n^2 - 4$, $2n^2 - 8$, $2n^2$, n. Point out that in this problem your students end with the number with which they started.

Note that your students should use a variable to represent a number in Column II. If they are asked to use another number, they should choose a different variable.

1-8 Simplifying Expressions by Combining Like Terms

This activity is designed to provide an introduction to combining similar terms. Begin the activity by explaining basic notation: $3 \times 4n$ can also be written as $3 \cdot 4n$ or $3(4n)$, all of which equal 12n. Also, n can be written as 1n. $0 \times n$ equals 0. Review the vocabulary on the worksheet and make sure that your students understand the Distributive Property.

Go over the instructions on the worksheet. Remind your students to simplify each expression completely.

1-9 Simplifying and Evaluating Expressions

In this activity your students will simplify expressions by combining like terms and then evaluate the expressions. The problems on the worksheet do not contain negative numbers or exponents.

Begin the activity by reviewing how to simplify expressions. Depending on the abilities of your students, you may also find it helpful to discuss the Distributive Property. Remind your students that expressions such as 2a can be expressed as $2 \times a$ and that b can be expressed as $1 \times b$. Note that to substitute a number for a variable, your students should write the number in place of the variable. For example, if a = 3, then 2a = 2×3 or 6.

Go over the instructions on the worksheet with your students. Caution them to pay close attention to grouping symbols and remind them to always multiply before adding or subtracting.

1-10 Evaluating Expressions Using Exponents

This activity requires your students to evaluate expressions using exponents. The answers will be positive whole numbers.

Begin this activity by discussing 0 and 1 as exponents. Note that x^1 = x and that $x^0 = 1$. Depending on the background and abilities of your students, you may also find it useful to review grouping symbols.

Go over the instructions with your students and discuss the examples on the worksheet. Remind your students to be sure to follow the Order of Operations where necessary.

1-11 Writing Equations

In this activity your students are provided with information that they are to express in terms of an equation. Although they are not required to solve the equation, they may be curious to find the solution. The equations and their solutions are provided in the Answer Key.

Begin this activity by writing some equations on the board or an overhead projector. Two examples are P = 4s, for finding the perimeter of a square, and A = $l \times w$, for finding the area of a rectangle. Explain that the equal sign means that the number on the left of the equation has the same value as the number on the right. Encourage your students to volunteer examples of other equations, which you may list on the board or an overhead projector. As you do, emphasize the equality and the meaning of the variables. Also review key words such as "variable," "more than," and "product."

Go over the instructions on the worksheet with your students. Caution them to be as accurate as possible in writing equations.

1-12 Writing Equations and Inequalities I

For this activity your students must recall, find, research, and synthesize various facts. (Most facts fall within the category of general knowledge.) Your students are then required to compare numbers and write an equation or inequality.

Since your students may need to conduct minor research to find some of the information necessary to complete this activity successfully, you may prefer to assign this activity as homework. If you have access to the Internet from your classroom, the activity can easily be conducted there. Another option is to reserve time in your school's library so that students may use reference sources. This is a nice approach, because it provides an example to students of how math is linked to other areas.

Start this activity by reviewing the meaning of an equation. Note that the values on both sides of an equal sign are the same, and emphasize that in an inequality the numbers are not equal. If necessary, explain the meanings of the symbols > and <, which appear on the worksheet.

Review the instructions on the worksheet with your students. Encourage them to concentrate on the phrases as they work to complete the activity.

1-13 Writing Equations and Inequalities II

This activity builds on the skills covered in Activity 1-12 and provides more practice with equations and inequalities. Along with the symbols > and <, the symbols ≥ and ≤ are used in many of the equations.

Start the activity by discussing the symbols on the worksheet, then go over the instructions. Depending on the abilities of your students, you may find it helpful to do the first problem together. Remind students to read each problem carefully before writing an equation.

1-14 Identifying the Solution of an Equation

In this activity your students are required to match solutions to equations. They are to substitute a given value and determine whether or not it is a solution to the equation. Obtaining the correct answers will enable them to complete a statement at the bottom of the worksheet.

Begin the activity by reviewing the Order of Operations. Because there are no grouping symbols, your students should substitute, then multiply and divide in order from left to right, then add and subtract.

Go over the instructions on the worksheet. Note that of the five possible solutions above the four equations, only one is not a solution for any of the equations. Your students are to write the letter of each solution in the blank before the equation. After determining the correct solutions, they are to write the letters in order to complete the statement at the bottom of the worksheet.

1-15 Determining the Solutions of Equations and Inequalities

This activity builds on the skills covered in Activity 1-14. For this activity your students are given twenty equations and inequalities for which they are to choose the solutions.

Begin the activity by reviewing the meaning of the equal sign and the four inequality symbols: >, <, ≥, and ≤. Go over the instructions with your students. Emphasize that they are to record the letter of every solution. Some problems have more than one. If no solution is given, they are to record the letter that precedes "none."

Answer Key for Section 1

1-1.   1. $8 - 6 + 5 = 7$ 2. $3 + 8 + 4 = 15$ 3. $3 + 2 + 4 = 9$ 4. $21 - 14 + 6 = 13$ 5. $2 + 9 - 1 = 10$ 6. $48 + 2 - 7 = 43$ 7. $3 + 25 - 2 = 26$ 8. $4 + 12 - 16 = 0$ 9. $5 + 2 - 4 = 3$ 10. $60 - 60 + 2 = 2$ 11. $6 + 18 + 4 = 28$ 12. $1 + 6 - 2 = 5$

1-2.   1. $15 - 2 \times 3 = 39$ is incorrect. Subtraction was done first, then multiplication was done.   2. $16 + 8 \div 2 = 12$ is incorrect. Addition was done first, then division was done.   3. $3[2 + 4] = 10$ is incorrect. Grouping symbols were ignored; multiplication was done first, then 4 was added.   4. $50 \div (5 \times 10) = 100$ is incorrect. Grouping symbols were ignored; division was done, then multiplication was done.   5. $9 + 3 \div 3 + 4 = 8$ is incorrect. Addition was done first, then division was done, followed by addition. 6. $\frac{6 \cdot 4}{2 + 4} = 16$ is incorrect. The fraction bar was ignored. Multiplication was done first, then division by 2 was done, and finally 4 was added. 7. $19 - [3 + 5] = 21$ is incorrect. Brackets were ignored. Three was subtracted from 19, then 5 was added.   8. $\frac{3 + 7 + 12}{3 + 20 - 1} = 33$ is incorrect. $3 + 7$ were added to $12 \div 3$. Then 20 was added and 1 was subtracted. 9. $3 + 12 \div 3 \times 2 = 10$ is incorrect. Addition, division, and multiplication were completed from left to right.   10. $6 \times 10 - 3 \times 4 = 228$ is incorrect. Multiplication, subtraction, and multiplication were done from left to right.

1-3.   1. 9   2. 144   3. 384   4. 325   5. 57   6. 19   7. 104   8. 24,389   9. 22   10. 300   11. 72   12. 30   13. 1   14. 1,296   The numbers remaining are the first thirteen square numbers.

1-4.   1. 177   2. 37   3. 54   4. 146   5. 494   6. 189   7. 245   8. 142   9. 246   10. 269. For problems 11–15 answers may vary; possible answers follow.   11. $1 + 4 + 9 + 9$ 12. $1 + 4 + 9 + 16$ 13. $9 + 9 + 16 + 25$ 14. $9 + 16 + 25 + 36$ 15. $25 + 25 + 25 + 25$

I-5.

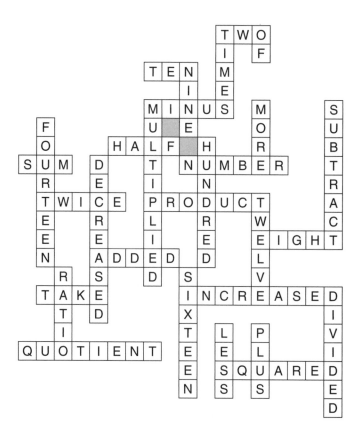

I-6. Twelve problems are incorrect. Problem 2 should be n − 2.   Problem 4 should be 2n + 4n.   Problem 5 should be n ÷ (n + 3).   Problem 6 should be (n + 6) ÷ 12.   Problem 9 should be $(n + 4)^2$.   Problem 10 should be n(n − 8).   Problem 13 should be 7 − n.   Problem 17 should be $5n^2$. Problem 19 should be 8n − 1.   Problem 21 should be 6(n + 3).   Problem 22 should be 3n + 2.   Problem 24 should be $\frac{3n}{3}$.

I-7. Problem 1. The final number is the same as the original number. n, n^2, $n^2 - 4$, $2n^2 - 8$, $2n^2$, n.   Problem 2. The final number is 2. n, n + 5, 2n + 10, 2n + 16, 2n + 4, n + 2, 2.   Problem 3. The final number is the same as the original number. n, n + 7, 10n + 70, 2n + 14, 2n, n.   Problem 4. The final number is the grade followed by the age. n, 10n, 10n + 6, 100n + 60, 100n + 48, 100n + 48 + y, 100n + 17 + y, 100n + y.   Problem 5. Problems will vary.

I-8. 1. V, 11x   2. Q, 12x   3. P, 4x + 5y + 4   4. L, 7x + 3y + 1   5. K, 15x   6. O, 0   7. U, 2x   8. W, 2x + 14   9. A, x   10. N, 6x + 6y   11. I, 10x + 18y   12. E, 17x + 12   13. R, 6y   14. T, 9x + 12   15. S, 18x + 12y + 3 A French mathematician, Francois Viète (1540–1603), introduced the use of <u>vowels to represent unknown quantities</u>.

I-9. U. 4a, 12   F. 5a + 12, 27   L. 2a + b + 3d, 23   P. 4a + 4b, 20   R. 10a + 15, 45   D. a + c + 15, 18   M. 13c + 14, 14   T. 15a + 18, 63   O. 5b + 18, 28

A. 6b + 28, 40   Y. 7a + 2d + 5, 36   N. a + 6b, 15   E. 4d + 6, 26   H. 18a +6, 60   S. 4b + 4d + 4, 32   I. 20a + 12b + 6d + 8, 122   V. 3a + 1, 10
It is easier to simplify first and then evaluate.

1-10. 1. I, 1   2. N, 9   3. H, 49   4. I, 1   5. S, 32   6. B, 100   7. O, 64   8. O, 64   9. K, 512   10. L, 81   11. A, 21   12. G, 29   13. E, 19   14. O, 64   15. M, 218   16. E, 19   17. T, 1,728   18. R, 432   19. I, 1   20. E, 19   21. P, 4   22. U, 22   23. B, 100   24. L, 81   25. I, 1   26. S, 32   27. H, 49   28. E, 19   29. D, 11   René Descartes (1596–1650), a French philosopher and mathematician, first used the modern notation for exponents in his book *La Geometrie,* published in 1637.

1-11. Equations may vary. (Solutions were not required, but answers are provided.) 1. s = 31 − 1; s = 30   2. c = 7 − 3; c = 4   3. l = 44 + 50; l = 94   4. 2p = 16; p = 8   5. $\frac{1}{6}$w = 4; w = 24   6. l = 3,787,319 − 251,041; l = 3,536,278   7. r = $\frac{1}{2}$ × 70; r = 35   8. l = 2 × 7 + 1; l = 15   9. p = 1.9 × 86,560,000; p = 164,464,000   10. f = 2 × 17 + 9; f = 43   11. b = 350 − 206; b = 144   12. g = 2,800 − 400; g = 2,400   13. p = 9 × 8; p = 72   14. t = 1965 − 77 − 21; t = 1867   15. a = 23 × 13 + 12; a = 311

1-12. 1. 3 < 4   2. 5 > 3   3. 12 < 13   4. 16 = 16   5. 100 > 50   6. 42 < 64   7. 9 < 22   8. 48 > 40   9. 5 < 10   10. 89 = 89   11. 4 = 4   12. 12 < 36   13. 8 = 8   14. 4 < 7   15. 16 = 16   16. 32 > 25   17. 4 > 2   18. 100° C = 212° F   19. 2 = 2   20. 9 sq. ft. > 3 sq. ft.   21. $20 < $100   22. 100 = 100   23. 360 > 180   24. 6 < 8   25. 7 = 7

1-13. 1. p ≥ 10   2. a ≥ 18   3. h > 4   4. a < 12   5. t ≥ 25   6. c = $7   7. p ≤ 350   8. t = $120   9. c = $240   10. p ≤ 10   11. t = 15   12. t = 10   13. n ≥ 3   14. d = 390   15. d > 3

1-14. Set 1. B, 5   Y, 8   A, 52   L, 54   Set 2. K, 12   H, 4   W, 36   A, 8   Set 3. R, 7   I, 9   Z, 30   M, 18   I, 85   Algebra comes from the Arabic word "al-jabr," which appeared in the title of a book written around 825 by al-Khwarizmi, an Islamic mathematician.

1-15. 1. none   2. {10, 20}   3. {0}   4. {1, 2}   5. {12, 14, 16}   6. {2}   7. none   8. {9, 34}   9. {3, 6, 9}   10. {4, 8}   11. {1, 2}   12. {6, 7}   13. {8, 12}   14. none   15. {1, 2, 3}   16. none   17. {3, 6, 9}   18. {2, 3}   19. {24, 36}   20. none. It is impossible to list all of the solutions.

Using the Order of Operations 1

Use the following rules to simplify an expression:

1. Simplify products and quotients in order from left to right.
2. Simplify sums and differences in order from left to right.

For example, $12 \div 2 + 2 \times 2 - 1$ can be written as $6 + 4 - 1$ or 9.

Directions: Each expression can be simplified using the Order of Operations. Choose the steps from the list on the right and write these steps below the appropriate expression. Then simplify the expression.

Expression	**Steps**
1. $72 \div 9 - 3 \times 2 + 5 =$	$48 + 2 - 7$
2. $3 + 2 \cdot 4 + 4 =$	$1 + 6 - 2$
3. $18 \div 6 + 6 \div 3 + 4 =$	$3 + 25 - 2$
4. $21 - 7 \times 2 + 6 =$	$60 - 60 + 2$
5. $14 \div 7 + 18 \div 2 - 1 =$	$3 + 8 + 4$
6. $6 \times 8 + 4 \div 2 - 7 =$	$8 - 6 + 5$
7. $3 + 75 \div 3 - 2 =$	$3 + 2 + 4$
8. $4 + 6 \times 2 - 4 \times 4 =$	$6 + 18 + 4$

Algebra Teacher's Activities Kit

Copyright © 2003 John Wiley & Sons, Inc.

Using the Order of Operations 1

Expression	**Steps**
9. $15 \div 3 + 2 - 4 \cdot 1 =$	$21 - 14 + 6$
_____	
10. $6 \cdot 10 - 4 \times 15 + 2 =$	$5 + 2 - 4$
_____	
11. $6 + 12 \div 2 \times 3 + 4 =$	$2 + 9 - 1$
_____	
12. $1 + 2 \times 3 - 6 \div 3 =$	$4 + 12 - 16$
_____	

Using the Order of Operations II

The Order of Operations is listed below.

1. Simplify expressions that are set within grouping symbols such as parentheses, braces, brackets, and the fraction bar.
2. Simplify products and quotients in order from left to right.
3. Simplify sums and differences in order from left to right.

Directions: Each expression below has been simplified in two ways: one by following the Order of Operations and the other by not following the Order of Operations. Circle the equation with the *incorrect* answer, then explain how the incorrect answer was obtained.

1. $15 - 2 \times 3 = 9$ $15 - 2 \times 3 = 39$

_____

_____

2. $16 + 8 \div 2 = 12$ $16 + 8 \div 2 = 20$

_____

_____

3. $3[2 + 4] = 10$ $3[2 + 4] = 18$

_____

_____

4. $50 \div (5 \times 10) = 100$ $50 \div (5 \times 10) = 1$

_____

_____

5. $9 + 3 \div 3 + 4 = 14$ $9 + 3 \div 3 + 4 = 8$

_____

_____

Algebra Teacher's Activities Kit

Copyright © 2003 John Wiley & Sons, Inc.

Using the Order of Operations II

6. $\dfrac{6 \cdot 4}{2 + 4} = 4$ $\dfrac{6 \cdot 4}{2 + 4} = 16$

7. $19 - [3 + 5] = 21$ $19 - [3 + 5] = 11$

8. $\dfrac{3 + 7 + 12}{3 + 20 - 1} = 1$ $\dfrac{3 + 7 + 12}{3 + 20 - 1} = 33$

9. $3 + 12 \div 3 \times 2 = 11$ $3 + 12 \div 3 \times 2 = 10$

10. $6 \times 10 - 3 \times 4 = 228$ $6 \times 10 - 3 \times 4 = 48$

Using the Order of Operations III

Sometimes an expression may contain a number raised to a power such as 2^3, which is read as 2 to the third power, or 8. These expressions must be simplified after the expressions within grouping symbols but before multiplying or dividing. Follow these steps:

1. Simplify expressions within grouping symbols.
2. Simplify powers.
3. Multiply and divide in order from left to right.
4. Add and subtract in order from left to right.

Directions: Simplify each expression in problems 1 through 14. Find each answer in order in the Code Box at the end of the activity, starting in the upper left and moving across each line. When you find an answer, cross it out. (The answer to Problem 1 appears before the answer to Problem 2 and so on.) Each answer will be separated by a number or group of numbers. Some numbers will not be crossed out. Describe the numbers that remain.

1. $6 \times 3 - 9 =$ _____

2. $12^2 =$ _____

3. $6 \times 8^2 =$ _____

4. $(8 + 5)(2 + 3)^2 =$ _____

5. $2^3 \times 7 + 1 =$ _____

6. $1 + 2(4 - 1)^2 =$ _____

7. $2(3 + 7^2) =$ _____

8. $(4 + 5^2)^3 =$ _____

9. $6 + 12 \div 3 \times 2^2 =$ _____

10. $3 \times 10^2 =$ _____

11. $2^3 (7 + 2) =$ _____

12. $\frac{1+3+8}{4} + 3^3 =$ _____

13. $\frac{3^2 + 4^2}{5^2} =$ _____

14. $(3^2 \times 2^2)^2 =$ _____

Code Box

9 1 1 4 4 4 3 8 4 9 3 2 5 1 6 5 7 2 5 1 9

3 6 1 0 4 4 9 2 4 3 8 9 6 4 2 2 8 1 3 0 0

1 0 0 7 2 1 2 1 3 0 1 4 4 1 1 6 9 1 2 9 6

Describe the numbers that remain. _____

_____

_____

Algebra Teacher's Activities Kit

Using Square Numbers

A *square number* is a number raised to the second power. Some square numbers are listed below.

$$1 = 1 \times 1 = 1^2 \qquad 9 = 3 \times 3 = 3^2$$
$$4 = 2 \times 2 = 2^2 \qquad 16 = 4 \times 4 = 4^2$$

Pierre de Fermat (1601–1665), a French mathematician, stated that every natural number can be expressed as the sum of four square numbers. This was proven to be true in 1770 by another mathematician, Joseph Louis Lagrange.

Directions: Find the number represented by the sum of the numbers below.

1. $2^2 + 3^2 + 8^2 + 10^2 = $ _____

2. $1^2 + 2^2 + 4^2 + 4^2 = $ _____

3. $2^2 + 3^2 + 4^2 + 5^2 = $ _____

4. $1^2 + 3^2 + 6^2 + 10^2 = $ _____

5. $2^2 + 11^2 + 12^2 + 15^2 = $ _____

6. $2^2 + 6^2 + 7^2 + 10^2 = $ _____

7. $1^2 + 6^2 + 8^2 + 12^2 = $ _____

8. $2^2 + 5^2 + 7^2 + 8^2 = $ _____

9. $5^2 + 6^2 + 8^2 + 11^2 = $ _____

10. $3^2 + 4^2 + 10^2 + 12^2 = $ _____

Now find the square numbers that have been added to express the numbers below.

11. _____ + _____ + _____ + _____ = 23

12. _____ + _____ + _____ + _____ = 30

13. _____ + _____ + _____ + _____ = 59

14. _____ + _____ + _____ + _____ = 86

15. _____ + _____ + _____ + _____ = 100

Translating Algebraic Expressions into Phrases

This crossword puzzle is like most crossword puzzles. The only difference is that all of the missing words relate to expressions.

Directions: Use the clues to complete the crossword puzzle.

Down

1. 5n means 5 _____ a number.
2. $\frac{1}{3}$ n means $\frac{1}{3}$ _____ a number.
4. 4 more than 5 is _____.
5. 8n means a number _____ by 8.
6. n + 7 means 7 _____ than a number.
7. n – 9 means _____ 9 from a number.
8. 2(3 + 4) equals _____.
10. 10^2 equals one _____.
12. n – 2 means a number _____ by 2.
16. The product of 6 and 2 is _____.
19. $\frac{n}{4}$ is the _____ of a number and 4.
20. 4^2 equals _____.
23. $\frac{n}{7}$ means a number _____ by 7.
24. n – 8 means 8 _____ than a number.
25. n + 2 means a number _____ 2.

Across

1. 3 less than 5 is _____.
3. 2 × 3 + 4 equals _____.
5. n – 5 means a number _____ 5.
9. $\frac{1}{2}$ n means one _____ of a number.
11. n + 10 means the _____ of a number and 10.
13. n is a variable that stands for a _____.
14. 2n means _____ a number.
15. 6n means the _____ of a number and 6.
17. 12 minus 4 equals _____.

Translating Algebraic Expressions into Phrases

18. n + 1 means a number _____ to 1.
21. n − 3 means _____ 3 from a number.
22. n + 10 means a number _____ by 10.
26. n ÷ 7 means the _____ of a number and 7.
27. 3^2 means 3 _____.

Writing Phrases as Algebraic Expressions I

The foundation for solving problems in algebra as well as in life is being able to express ideas clearly. In algebra, for example, a number can be expressed simply as n.

In an algebraic expression, order does not matter in addition or multiplication. For example, 2 more than a number can be expressed as n + 2 or 2 + n. Three times a number can be expressed as 3n or n × 3.

Order does matter in subtraction and division. For example, 4 less than a number is n − 4. The quotient of 10 and 2 is 10 ÷ 2 and not 2 ÷ 10.

Grouping symbols, such as parentheses and fraction bars, must be included if numbers are to be grouped and then added, subtracted, multiplied, divided, or squared. For example, 3 times the sum of a number and 5 is represented as 3(n + 5). The sum is found first, then multiplied by 3. The sum of a number and 8, divided by 16 is written as $\frac{n+8}{16}$ or (n + 8) ÷ 16.

Directions: Each phrase is paired with an algebraic expression. If the algebraic expression is correct, write C (for correct) on the line following the equation. If it is incorrect, correct it. Hint: Half of the problems are incorrect.

1. The sum of a number and 8   n + 8   _____

2. 2 less than a number   2 − n   _____

3. Twice a number   2n   _____

4. The sum of twice a number and 4 times the same number   2(n + 4n)   _____

5. A number divided by 3 more than the same number   n ÷ n + 3   _____

6. The sum of a number and 6 divided by 12   n + 6 ÷ 12   _____

7. The square of the quotient of a number and 7 $(n \div 7)^2$ _____

8. 10 less than a number   n − 10   _____

Writing Phrases as Algebraic Expressions I

9. The square of 4 more than a number $n + 4^2$ _____

10. A number multiplied by 8 less than itself $n \times n - 8$ _____

11. Half the sum of a number and 5 $\frac{1}{2}(n + 5)$ _____

12. 4 more than a number $n + 4$ _____

13. 7 decreased by a number $n - 7$ _____

14. The sum of a number and 5 divided by 6 $(n + 5) \div 6$ _____

15. 6 more than twice a number $2n + 6$ _____

16. A number decreased by 15 $n - 15$ _____

17. The product of 5 and a number squared $5 + 2n^2$ _____

18. One-half of a number $\frac{n}{2}$ _____

19. One less than 8 times a number $8(n - 1)$ _____

20. The product of a number and 22 $22n$ _____

21. 6 times the sum of a number and 3 $6n + 3$ _____

22. The sum of 3 times a number and 2 $3(n + 2)$ _____

23. The product of a number squared and 8 $8n^2$ _____

24. The quotient of 3 times a number and 3 $3n + 3$ _____

Writing Phrases as Algebraic Expressions II

Algebra can be used to explain some "mysterious tricks" about numerical operations. Some people call this "mathemagic," although no magic is involved. Algebra can be used to explain the trick.

Directions: Follow the instructions for each problem. Write the result in Column I. Then complete Column II by using a variable for the number you are thinking of. Be sure to simplify expressions in Column II before you go to the next step.

	Column I	Column II
Problem 1		
1. Think of a number	_____	_____
2. Square the number	_____	_____
3. Subtract 4	_____	_____
4. Multiply by 2	_____	_____
5. Add 8	_____	_____
6. Divide by twice the original number	_____	_____
Problem 2		
1. Think of a number	_____	_____
2. Add 5	_____	_____
3. Multiply by 2	_____	_____
4. Add 6	_____	_____
5. Subtract 12	_____	_____
6. Divide by 2	_____	_____
7. Subtract the original number	_____	_____
Problem 3		
1. Think of a number	_____	_____
2. Add 7	_____	_____
3. Multiply by 10	_____	_____
4. Divide by 5	_____	_____
5. Subtract 14	_____	_____
6. Divide by 2	_____	_____

Algebra Teacher's Activities Kit

Writing Phrases as Algebraic Expressions II

	Column I	Column II

Problem 4

1. Start with the grade you are currently in   _____   _____
2. Multiply by 10   _____   _____
3. Add 6   _____   _____
4. Multiply by 10   _____   _____
5. Subtract 12   _____   _____
6. Add your age   _____   _____
7. Subtract 31   _____   _____
8. Subtract 17   _____   _____

Problem 5

Create a problem so that the answer is twice the original number. Share your problem with another student in class.

Simplifying Expressions by Combining Like Terms

Expressions are sometimes made up of *terms*, which are the product of numbers and variables. (A *variable* is a letter that represents a number.)

Like terms are also called *similar terms*. They have the same variables. For example, 3a and 2a are like terms, but 3a and 2b are not.

Only like terms can be combined by addition or subtraction. The result is an expression in simplest form. Examples:

$$3a + 2a = 5a$$
$$3a + 2b \text{ cannot be simplified}$$
$$3a + 10 + 3b + 2a - 2b + 13 = 5a + b + 23$$

You must follow the rules for multiplication and the Distributive Property to simplify expressions. Examples:

$$2 \times 6a = 12a$$
$$3(4a + 2b) = 12a + 6b$$

Now go to the next page of this activity.

Simplifying Expressions by Combining Like Terms

Directions: Simplify each expression. Find your answer in the Answer Bank at the right, then write the letter of your answer in the blank before the problem number. Write the letter above the problem number in the message at the end of the activity to learn an important fact about mathematics. The first problem is done for you.

		Answer Bank
1. __✔__	$4x + 7x =$	R. $6y$
2. _____	$4 \cdot 3x =$	S. $18x + 12y + 3$
3. _____	$6x + 5y - 2x + 4 =$	P. $4x + 5y + 4$
4. _____	$x + 3y + 6x + 1 =$	I. $10x + 18y$
5. _____	$3 \cdot 5x =$	K. $15x$
6. _____	$4x + 3x - 7x =$	V. $11x$
7. _____	$x + 2x + 3x - 4x =$	N. $6x + 6y$
8. _____	$5 + 2x + 9 =$	U. $2x$
9. _____	$2x - x =$	O. 0
10. _____	$2(x + 3y) + 4x =$	Q. $12x$
11. _____	$4(2x + 3y) + 2(x + 3y) =$	W. $2x + 14$
12. _____	$7(2x) + 3(x + 4) =$	T. $9x + 12$
13. _____	$4(5x) + 2(3y) - 20x =$	A. x
14. _____	$12x - 3x + 2y + 12 - 2y =$	E. $17x + 12$
15. _____	$3 + 6(3x + 2y) =$	L. $7x + 3y + 1$

A French mathematician, Francois Viète (1540–1603), introduced the use of

$$\overset{\checkmark}{\underset{1}{\rule{1cm}{0.4pt}}} \; \underset{6}{\rule{1cm}{0.4pt}} \; \underset{8}{\rule{1cm}{0.4pt}} \; \underset{12}{\rule{1cm}{0.4pt}} \; \underset{4}{\rule{1cm}{0.4pt}} \; \underset{15}{\rule{1cm}{0.4pt}} \quad \underset{14}{\rule{1cm}{0.4pt}} \; \underset{6}{\rule{1cm}{0.4pt}}$$

$$\underset{13}{\rule{1cm}{0.4pt}} \; \underset{12}{\rule{1cm}{0.4pt}} \; \underset{3}{\rule{1cm}{0.4pt}} \; \underset{13}{\rule{1cm}{0.4pt}} \; \underset{12}{\rule{1cm}{0.4pt}} \; \underset{15}{\rule{1cm}{0.4pt}} \; \underset{12}{\rule{1cm}{0.4pt}} \; \underset{10}{\rule{1cm}{0.4pt}} \; \underset{14}{\rule{1cm}{0.4pt}}$$

$$\underset{7}{\rule{1cm}{0.4pt}} \; \underset{10}{\rule{1cm}{0.4pt}} \; \underset{5}{\rule{1cm}{0.4pt}} \; \underset{10}{\rule{1cm}{0.4pt}} \; \underset{6}{\rule{1cm}{0.4pt}} \; \underset{8}{\rule{1cm}{0.4pt}} \; \underset{10}{\rule{1cm}{0.4pt}}$$

$$\underset{2}{\rule{1cm}{0.4pt}} \; \underset{7}{\rule{1cm}{0.4pt}} \; \underset{9}{\rule{1cm}{0.4pt}} \; \underset{10}{\rule{1cm}{0.4pt}} \; \underset{14}{\rule{1cm}{0.4pt}} \; \underset{11}{\rule{1cm}{0.4pt}} \; \underset{14}{\rule{1cm}{0.4pt}} \; \underset{11}{\rule{1cm}{0.4pt}} \; \underset{12}{\rule{1cm}{0.4pt}} \; \underset{15}{\rule{1cm}{0.4pt}}.$$

Simplifying and Evaluating Expressions

To *simplify* an expression means to replace it with its simplest name, being sure that like terms are combined. Example:

$$3a + 2a + 3b + 4 = (3a + 2a) + 3b + 4 = 5a + 3b + 4$$

To *evaluate* an expression means to substitute a given number for each variable and follow the Order of Operations. If a = 3 and b = 2, the above equation would be evaluated as $(5 \times 3) + (3 \times 2) + 4 = 15 + 6 + 4 = 25$.

Directions: Simplify each expression and write your answer in the first blank. Then evaluate each expression for the given values and write this answer in the second blank. After you have finished the problems, write the letter of the problem above its "evaluated" answer on the bottom of the page to complete the statement. The first problem is done for you.

$$a = 3 \quad b = 2 \quad c = 0 \quad d = 5$$

U. 3a + a _____4a_____ ____12____

F. 3a + 12 + 2a _____ _____

L. 2a + b + 3d _____ _____

P. 4(a + b) _____ _____

R. 5(2a + 3) _____ _____

D. a + 12 + c + 3 _____ _____

M. 3c + 2(5c + 7) _____ _____

T. 3a + 6(3 + 2a) _____ _____

O. 12 + 3b + 2(3 + b) _____ _____

A. 2(3b + 14) _____ _____

Y. a + 5 + 2(3a + d) _____ _____

N. a + b(2 + 4) _____ _____

Algebra Teacher's Activities Kit

Copyright © 2003 John Wiley & Sons, Inc.

Simplifying and Evaluating Expressions

E. 14 + 4(d − 2)　　　　　　　_____　　_____

H. 2(3a + 1) + 4(3a + 1)　　　_____　　_____

S. 6(b + d) − 2(b + d) + 4　　_____　　_____

I. 8 + 6(3a + 2b + d) + 2a　　_____　　_____

V. 4 + 3(a − 1)　　　　　　　_____　　_____

‾‾‾‾ ‾‾‾　　‾‾‾‾ ‾‾‾　　‾‾‾ ‾‾‾ ‾‾‾ ‾‾‾‾ ‾‾‾ ‾‾‾
122　63　　　122　32　　　26　40　32　122　26　45

‾‾‾ ‾‾‾　　‾‾‾ ‾‾‾‾ ‾‾‾ ‾‾‾ ‾‾‾ ‾‾‾‾ ‾‾‾ ‾‾‾
63　28　　　32　122　14　20　23　122　27　36

‾‾‾ ‾‾‾‾ ‾‾‾ ‾‾‾ ‾‾‾　　‾‾‾ ‾‾‾ ‾‾‾
27　122　45　32　63　　　40　15　18

‾‾‾ ‾‾‾ ‾‾‾ ‾‾‾　　‾‾‾ ‾‾‾ ‾‾‾ ‾‾‾ ʊ ‾‾‾ ‾‾‾ ‾‾‾.
63　60　26　15　　　26　10　40　23　12　40　63　26

Evaluating Expressions Using Exponents

An *exponent* is a number that appears in the upper right-hand corner of a number or an expression. It represents the number of times the base (which is the number or expression) is used as a factor. Examples:

$$3^2 = 3 \times 3 \text{ or } 9$$
$$4 \times 3^2 = 4 \times 3 \times 3 \text{ or } 36$$
$$(4 \times 3)^2 = 4 \times 3 \times 4 \times 3 \text{ or } 144$$

Note that the placement of grouping symbols makes a difference when using exponents.

Also note that any base to the zero power is equal to 1 and that any base to the first power is equal to itself. Examples:

$$3^0 = 1 \qquad 3^1 = 3$$

Directions: Evaluate each expression. Write your answer in the blank that follows the problem. Then find your answer in the Answer Bank and write the letter of each answer in the blank space before each problem. Finally, write the letters of each problem in order, starting with the first problem, to complete the statement at the end of the activity.

1. _____ a^0 if $a = 5$ _____

2. _____ b^2 if $b = 3$ _____

3. _____ n^2 if $n = 7$ _____

4. _____ $(2a)^0$ if $a = 5$ _____

5. _____ a^5 if $a = 2$ _____

6. _____ m^2 if $m = 10$ _____

7. _____ c^2 if $c = 8$ _____

8. _____ h^3 if $h = 4$ _____

9. _____ $(2h)^3$ if $h = 4$ _____

10. _____ $(c + 4)^2$ if $c = 5$ _____

11. _____ $c + 4^2$ if $c = 5$ _____

12. _____ $c^2 + 4$ if $c = 5$ _____

Algebra Teacher's Activities Kit

NAME _____ DATE _____ SECTION _____

Evaluating Expressions Using Exponents

13. _____ $(n + 1)^2 + n$ if $n = 3$ _____

14. _____ a^6 if $a = 2$ _____

15. _____ $2 + m^3$ if $m = 6$ _____

16. _____ $3m + m^0$ if $m = 6$ _____

17. _____ $(2m)^3$ if $m = 6$ _____

18. _____ $2m^3$ if $m = 6$ _____

19. _____ $3^2 - a^3$ if $a = 2$ _____

20. _____ $5a^2 - a + 1$ if $a = 2$ _____

21. _____ $(x - 3)^2$ if $x = 5$ _____

22. _____ $x^2 - 3$ if $x = 5$ _____

23. _____ $4n^2$ if $n = 5$ _____

24. _____ v^2 if $v = 9$ _____

25. _____ $(8v)^0$ if $v = 2$ _____

26. _____ $8v^2$ if $v = 2$ _____

27. _____ $(2n + 3)^2$ if $n = 2$ _____

28. _____ $2n^2 + 11$ if $n = 2$ _____

29. _____ $n^2 - n - 1$ if $n = 4$ _____

Answer Bank					
E. 19	B. 100	R. 432	K. 512	I. 1	L. 81
O. 64	N. 9	U. 22	S. 32	D. 11	A. 21
T. 1,728	M. 218	G. 29	P. 4	V. 256	H. 49

René Descartes (1596–1650), a French philosopher and mathematician, first used the

modern notation for exponents ___ ___   ___ ___ ___   ___ ___ ___ ___

___ ___   ___ ___ ___ ___ ___ ___ ___ ___,

___ ___ ___ ___ ___ ___ ___ ___ in 1637.

Writing Equations

An *equation* is a mathematical sentence that states that two quantities are equal. An equal sign (=) separates an equation into two parts, which are called sides of the equation.

Directions: Write an equation for each situation described below. Use the given variable. There may be more than one equation for each problem.

1. The number of days in September is one less than the number of days in October. Let s represent the number of days in September. There are thirty-one days in October.

   _____

2. The time in California is three hours earlier than the time in New York. It is 7 P.M. in New York. Let c represent the time in California.

   _____

3. The length of an NBA (National Basketball Association) court is forty-four feet longer than the width, which is fifty feet. Let l stand for the length of the court.

   _____

4. Each player begins a chess game with a total of sixteen chess pieces. This is twice the number of pawns. Let p stand for the number of pawns.

   _____

5. Forty-eight states of the United States are located in four time zones. This is $\frac{1}{6}$ of the number of time zones in the world. Let w represent the number of time zones in the world.

   _____

6. The total area of the United States is the combination of the area of its land and water. The total area of the U.S. is 3,787,319 square miles, of which 251,041 square miles is water. Let l stand for the area of the land.

   _____

7. A rabbit moves half as fast as a cheetah at full speed. A cheetah can run seventy miles per hour. Let r stand for the speed of the rabbit.

   _____

Algebra Teacher's Activities Kit

1-11
(continued)

Writing Equations

8. The average life span of a lion is one year more than twice the life span of a fox, which is seven years. Let l represent the life span of a lion.

   _____

9. The Pacific Ocean and the Atlantic Ocean are the two largest oceans in the world. The approximate area of the Atlantic is 86,560,000 square kilometers. The Pacific is a little more than 1.9 times as large. Let p represent the area of the Pacific Ocean.

   _____

10. It takes about seventeen muscles to smile and about nine more than twice that number to frown. Let f represent the number of muscles it takes to frown.

    _____

11. A newborn baby has more bones than an adult, because bones grow together as a person matures. The typical baby has 350 bones and an average adult has 206. Let b represent the difference in the number of bones.

    _____

12. The number of calories recommended for boys, ages 11 to 14, is 2,800 calories per day. The number recommended for girls, ages 11 to 14, is 400 calories less per day. Let g represent the number of calories recommended for girls each day.

    _____

13. The label on a bag of candy says there are about nine servings per bag, and that the serving size is eight pieces. Let p represent the number of candies in the bag.

    _____

14. The word processor was invented in 1965. The ballpoint pen was invented seventy-seven years earlier, and the typewriter was invented twenty-one years before the ballpoint pen. Let t stand for the year the typewriter was invented.

    _____

15. The first modern Olympic Games were held in Athens, Greece, in 1896. Thirteen countries were represented and twelve more than twenty-three times that number of athletes participated. Let a stand for the number of athletes.

    _____

Writing Equations and Inequalities 1

An *equation* is a mathematical sentence in which the = symbol connects two expressions of the same value. An *inequality* is a mathematical sentence in which the symbols < (is less than) or > (is greater than) are used. In an inequality, the expressions on either side of the equation do not have the same value.

Directions: Each pair of phrases below and on the next page describes a number. Write =, <, or > on the blank between each pair of phrases to show the relationship between the numbers that the phrases represent. Hint: The number of equations < the number of inequalities.

1. the number of singers in a trio _____ the number of singers in a quartet

2. the number of digits in a ZIP Code _____ the number of digits in an area code

3. items in a dozen _____ items in a baker's dozen

4. perimeter of a 4 × 4 square _____ perimeter of a 3 × 5 rectangle

5. the number of U.S. senators _____ the number of states

6. total number of dots on a pair of dice _____ the number of squares on a checkerboard

7. minimum number of players on a baseball field _____ minimum number of players on a football field

8. length of a professional basketball game (in minutes) _____ length of a college basketball game (in minutes)

9. length of a radius of a 10-inch circle _____ length of a diameter of a 10-inch circle

10. the average of 90, 96, and 81 _____ the average of 90, 86, and 91

11. the number of quarters in a dollar _____ the number of quarts in a gallon

12. the number of inches in a foot _____ the number of inches in a yard

13. the number of sides on a stop sign _____ the number of tentacles of an octopus

Algebra Teacher's Activities Kit

Copyright © 2003 John Wiley & Sons, Inc.

Writing Equations and Inequalities I

14. the number of oceans   _____ the number of continents

15. 16 ounces   _____ 1 pound

16. 2^5 _____ 5^2

17. the number of aces in a   _____ the number of red kings in a
    deck of cards   deck of cards

18. 100° C   _____ 212° F

19. the number of players required _____ the number of players required
    for backgammon   for chess

20. one square yard   _____ three square feet

21. the denomination of a bill with _____ the denomination of a bill with
    Andrew Jackson's portrait   Benjamin Franklin's portrait

22. the number of centimeters   _____ the number of cents in a dollar
    in a meter

23. the number of degrees in a circle _____ the number of degrees in a triangle

24. the number of legs of an ant _____ the number of legs of a spider

25. the number of stars in the   _____ the number of stars in the
    Big Dipper   Little Dipper

The Language of Algebra (Using Whole Numbers)   31

Writing Equations and Inequalities II

Common situations can be expressed as equations or inequalities. While the = sign is used to show expressions of equal value, several symbols can be used to express inequalities, including:

<, which means is less than
≤, which means is less than or equal to
>, which means is greater than
≥, which means is greater than or equal to

Directions: Write an equation or inequality for each problem. Use the appropriate variable.

1. The sign on a clearance rack in a store says $10 and up. Let p represent the price of one item.

   _____

2. A person must be 18 years old to vote in the United States. Let a represent the age of a person eligible to vote.

   _____

3. In order to go on some rides in amusement parks, children must be over four feet tall. Let h represent the height required for admittance to these rides.

   _____

4. Children under twelve years of age can order from a child's menu in many restaurants. Let a represent the age at which kids can order a kid's meal.

   _____

5. A minimum charge at a restaurant is $5 per person. Let t represent the total bill for five people.

   _____

6. When ordering from a particular catalog, the shipping and handling charges are $7 for orders less than $20. Let c represent the shipping and handling charge of a $15 order.

   _____

7. The occupancy limit in the school cafeteria is 350 people. Let p represent the number of people that may safely occupy the room.

   _____

Algebra Teacher's Activities Kit

Writing Equations and Inequalities II

8. The admissions fee to a nearby amusement park is as follows:

    Children 2 and under — Free

    Children between the ages of 2 and 12 — $20

    Children over 12 and adults — $40

    Let t represent the total admission fee for a family of two adults, a 3-year-old child, and a 10-year-old child.

    _____

9. The bus company charges $120 per bus to transport up to forty-three passengers to and from the museum for the class trip. Let c represent the charge for transportation for eighty passengers.

    _____

10. Tables in a restaurant accommodate ten people. Let p represent the number of people able to sit at each table.

    _____

11. An aquarium provides one free ticket per eight students. Let t represent the number of free tickets for a group of 125 students.

    _____

12. It takes ten minutes to boil an egg. Let t represent the time it takes to boil a half-dozen eggs.

    _____

13. To qualify for the honor roll, a student must have at least three A's and no grade less than a B on his or her report card. Let n represent the number of A's required for a student to qualify for the honor roll.

    _____

14. A family of five traveled 390 miles to Florida. Let d represent the total distance they traveled.

    _____

15. A student who is absent from school more than three days in a row must bring in a medical excuse when he or she returns to school. Let d represent the number of consecutive absences that require a note.

    _____

The Language of Algebra (Using Whole Numbers)   33

Identifying the Solution of an Equation

A *solution* to an equation is a number that makes the equation a true statement when the solution is substituted for the variable.

Directions: A group of equations is written below a set of numbers. All but one of the numbers is a solution to one of the equations. (One number in each set is not a solution to any of the equations.) Write the letter of the solution in the blank before each equation. Then write the letters in order, starting with the first equation, to complete the statement at the bottom of the sheet.

Set 1:   L. 54   Y. 8   C. 20   B. 5   A. 52

_____ $3a - 2 = 13$

_____ $4x - 1 = 31$

_____ $\frac{n}{4} - 5 = 8$

_____ $15 = 6 + \frac{m}{6}$

Set 2:   K. 12   R. 30   W. 36   A. 8   H. 4

_____ $3n + 29 = 65$

_____ $18 = 4t + 2$

_____ $\frac{x}{3} + 2 = 14$

_____ $3g - 4 = 20$

Set 3:   Z. 30   M. 18   I. 9   R. 7   A. 110   I. 85

_____ $18 + 2b = 32$

_____ $2n + 5 = 23$

_____ $\frac{a}{10} + 3 = 6$

_____ $3x - 4 = 50$

_____ $\frac{2n}{5} - 23 = 11$

Algebra comes from the Arabic word "al-jabr," which appeared in the title of a

book written around 825 ___ ___

___ ___ - ___ ___ ___ ___ ___ ___ ___ ___ ___ ___ ___ , an Islamic mathematician.

Algebra Teacher's Activities Kit

Determining the Solutions of Equations and Inequalities

A *solution* of an equation or an inequality is a number that makes the statement true.

Directions: Circle the letter(s) of the *solution or solutions* for each equation or inequality. If there is no solution to a problem, circle the letter for "none." Then write the letters in order, starting with the first problem, to complete the statement at the end of the activity. A fact about inequalities will be revealed.

	T H E	I
1. $a > 3$	$\{1, 2, 3\}$	none
	M T I	N
2. $c \geq 10$	$\{0, 10, 20\}$	none
	S T H	E
3. $w < 5$	$\{0, 5, 10\}$	none
	O I M	F
4. $0 < x$	$\{0, 1, 2\}$	none
	P O S	T
5. $3x \geq 36$	$\{12, 14, 16\}$	none
	S A T	N
6. $x^2 = 2x$	$\{2, 4, 8\}$	none
	T H E	I
7. $2x = 17$	$\{8, 9, 34\}$	none
	N B L	A
8. $2x > 17$	$\{8, 9, 34\}$	none
	E T O	F
9. $\frac{x}{x} = 1$	$\{3, 6, 9\}$	none
	A L I	T
10. $2x^2 \geq 9$	$\{2, 4, 8\}$	none

1-15
(continued)

Determining the Solutions of Equations and Inequalities

		S T I	N
11.	$x + 7 < 10$	$\{1, 2, 3\}$	none
12.	$3r - 7 > 9$	N A L $\{5, 6, 7\}$	O none
13.	$\frac{n}{4} - 1 > 0$	T L O $\{4, 8, 12\}$	D none
14.	$\frac{h}{14} > 3$	I N A $\{14, 28, 42\}$	F none
15.	$\frac{1}{x} \geq 0$	T H E $\{1, 2, 3\}$	I none
16.	$15 < \frac{a}{5}$	O F A $\{15, 25, 75\}$	S none
17.	$12 \leq 2n + 6$	O L U $\{3, 6, 9\}$	I none
18.	$35 \leq 10x + 20$	N T I $\{1, 2, 3\}$	S none
19.	$s - 9 \geq 15$	D O N $\{15, 24, 36\}$	F none
20.	$\frac{24}{n} < 8$	I V E $\{1, 2, 3\}$	S none

___ ___   ___   ___ ___ ___ ___ ___ ___ ___ ___ ___ ___

___ ___   ___ ___ ___ ___   ___ ___ ___   ___ ___ ___

___ ___ ___   ___ ___ ___ ___ ___ ___ ___ ___ ___ ___.

Algebra Teacher's Activities Kit

Copyright © 2003 John Wiley & Sons, Inc.

Integers, Variables, and Expressions

Integers, variables, and expressions are fundamental to the study of algebra. The fifteen activities of this section range from basic operations with integers to their use with variables and expressions. The section includes numerous activities that lay the foundation for solving equations and inequalities while highlighting how integers relate to some real-world situations.

Teaching Suggestions for the Activities

2-1 Using a Number Line to Graph Integers

This activity introduces students to the number line. Points are described and students are asked to identify the integers that represent specific points.

Begin the activity by explaining that integers are the set of whole numbers and their opposites. Note that zero is neither positive nor negative.

Next, explain that integers can be represented on a number line. Positive integers are located to the right of zero, and negative integers are located to the left. You might also mention that consecutive numbers are the same distance apart, which is often referred to as a unit. Point out that the arrows at the ends of a number line indicate that the number line continues infinitely, and that the number line on the worksheet represents just part of a complete number line.

Review the instructions on the worksheet with your students so that they understand what they are to do. Upon completion of the worksheet, encourage your students to volunteer their responses to the last two problems.

2-2 Representing Integers

This activity requires your students to apply the concept of integers to everyday situations. To complete this activity successfully, your students should be familiar with integers and the number line. If your students need practice with integers, assign this activity only after they have completed Activity 2-1.

Begin the activity by explaining that integers are the set of whole numbers and their opposites. Note how integers are essential to describing real-life situations by referring to the examples on the worksheet. You might ask your students to volunteer other examples of how integers can be used to describe everyday occurrences.

Go over the instructions on the worksheet, and note that in order to complete this activity, your students must pay close attention to the clues they are given. Remind them that after they have completed the puzzle, they are to write an explanation of how the words they found apply to integers.

2-3 Adding Integers

For this activity your students are required to add integers. The activity focuses on a magic square.

Start the activity by discussing magic squares, which are a square arrangement of numbers placed in such a manner that the sum of the numbers along each row, column, and diagonal is the same. This sum is called the magic number of the square.

Offer the example of the magic square below on the board or an overhead projector. Note that the magic number is 3.

4	-3	2
-1	1	3
0	5	-2

Review the instructions on the worksheet with your students, and explain that they are to create a magic square by adding integers. They will verify that their figure is indeed a magic square by finding the sum of each row, column, and diagonal, and then write an explanation of any patterns they observe.

2-4 Adding and Subtracting Integers

This activity provides your students with practice in the addition and subtraction of integers. As they find the sums and differences of integers, they will complete a magic square.

Introduce the activity by discussing the features of a magic square with your students. A magic square is a square arrangement of numbers in which the sum of each row, column, and diagonal is the same. This number is called the magic number. Emphasize that different magic squares have different magic numbers.

Display the following magic square on the board or an overhead projector.

8	−13	
−4		

Tell your students that the magic number is −3. To find the number in the right-hand corner, they should add 8 + −13 and subtract the sum from −3. Write the math on the board or overhead projector. −3 − (−5) = 2. Instruct your students to place 2 in the upper right-hand corner of the square. By following a similar procedure, they should be able to complete the square, which is pictured below.

8	−13	2
−7	−1	5
−4	11	−10

For this activity, your students are to finish the magic square on the worksheet. Tell them that the magic number of the magic square is −20. Caution them to work carefully, for a single mistake will result in numerous incorrect answers.

2-5 Comparing Sums and Differences

This activity requires your students to utilize various skills. To complete the worksheet, your students must add or subtract two or more integers and compare the sums.

Introduce the activity by briefly reviewing the skills required for adding and subtracting integers. You might find it helpful to put the following problems on the board or an overhead projector and let students volunteer the answers.

$$2 + 3 = 5 \qquad -17 + 3 = -14$$
$$6 + -4 = 2 \qquad -4 - (-3) = -1$$
$$-10 + 15 = 5 \quad 4 - (-3) = 7$$

Review the directions on the worksheet with your students. Note that they are to complete both equations for each problem, then write the larger answer in the blank to the right. If the answers are the same, they are to leave the blank empty. After they have completed all of the problems, they are to add the answers to obtain their score, which should be 10.

2-6 Multiplying and Dividing Integers

This activity focuses on multiplying and dividing two or more integers. To complete the worksheet successfully, your students are required to follow the Order of Operations.

Begin this activity by discussing the rules for multiplying and dividing integers. Remind your students that they must simplify any expressions within grouping symbols first. Then they must multiply and divide from left to right.

Write the following example on the board or an overhead projector: $-12 \div 6 \times 2 =$

The answer is –4. Remind your students that they must multiply and divide from left to right.

Now offer this example: $-12 \div (6 \times 2) =$

The answer is –1. Note that, while the numbers are the same, the parentheses change the problem and result in a different answer. If necessary, go over the steps of the Order of Operations and show how the answer is obtained.

Review the directions on the worksheet with your students. Remind them to use the Order of Operations when working out the problems.

2-7 Solving Word Problems with Integers

The word problems in this activity require your students to be able to use all of the basic operations with integers. Not only must your students solve each problem, but they must explain how the integers are used.

Introduce this activity by reviewing the basic operations of integers. Note that the focus of this activity is for students to apply integers to real-world situations.

Explain that a gain of something can be expressed as a positive integer and that a loss can be expressed as a negative integer. When Jack is paid $10 for mowing his neighbor's lawn, Jack gains $10. Jack's gain can be represented as +10. If Jack loses $5, his loss can be represented as –5. Jack has $5 less than he had before he lost the money.

Go over the instructions on the worksheet with your students. Encourage them to think about how integers apply to each situation.

2-8 Simplifying Expressions by Combining Similar Terms

This activity requires students to identify and combine similar terms as well as add integers to simplify expressions. It should be noted that the Commutative and Associative Properties are used in the activity.

Begin the activity by explaining that expressions can be simplified by combining similar terms. Depending on the abilities of your students, you may find it useful to discuss similar terms and how to identify them. Note that terms with unlike variables cannot be simplified. Note that the rules for adding integers also must be taken into account when simplifying expressions.

Go over the instructions on the worksheet with your students, noting that they are to simplify the expressions. Remind them to complete the statement at the end of the worksheet.

2-9 Using the Distributive Property to Simplify Expressions

In this activity the Distributive Property is used in each problem. One number in each equation is omitted, and your students must determine the missing number.

Begin the activity by conducting a review of the Distributive Property. Depending on the background of your students, you might find it useful to write the following example of the Distributive Property on the board or an overhead projector: $a(b + c) = ab + ac$. To complete this activity successfully, your students will also need to be able to combine similar terms and add and subtract integers.

Review the instructions on the worksheet with your students, noting the hint that each number from 1 to 9 is used at least once, but that one number is used twice. Caution your students to analyze each problem carefully before determining their answers.

2-10 Integers and Using the Order of Operations I

In this activity your students will use the Order of Operations to simplify expressions with parentheses. The problems do not contain exponents.

Introduce the activity and discuss the examples on the worksheet. Emphasize the Order of Operations.

Review the instructions on the worksheet with your students. Note that they must carefully follow the instructions and use the Order of Operations to simplify each expression.

2-11 Integers and Using the Order of Operations II

This activity extends the skills and concepts presented in Activity 2-10. It includes exponents.

Begin the activity by reviewing the Order of Operations presented on the worksheet. Next, discuss the examples with your students. Point out that $-5^2 = -25$, while $5^2 = 25$ and $(-5)^2 = 25$. In the first two examples, the base is 5. In the third example the base is -5. Note the importance of parentheses.

Go over the instructions on the worksheet with your students. Emphasize that only one pair of parentheses must be placed in each equation.

2-12 Evaluating Expressions

In this activity a value is assigned to each variable. Your students must substitute this value into an expression and simplify it. A variety of expressions is included.

Start the activity by reviewing the Order of Operations. Explain that the Order of Operations is a set of instructions that governs the evaluation of expressions.

Go over the instructions on the worksheet with your students. Note that a number is assigned to each variable. These values are included in the directions on the worksheet. Your students are to substitute the value for the variable and then evaluate the expression. Obtaining the correct answers will enable them to complete the statement at the end of the worksheet.

2-13 Finding the Absolute Value

This activity focuses on finding the absolute value of an integer or an expression. Since this can be a difficult concept for students to master, you should make sure that your students understand the definitions and examples that are provided.

Introduce the activity by discussing the definition of absolute value, which is the distance of a number from zero on the number line. To illustrate the meaning of absolute value, you may find it helpful to put the following examples on the board or an overhead projector. Emphasize that $|15| = 15$ and $|-15| = 15$, while $-|15| = -15$. Make sure your students understand $|-15 - 20| = 35$ and that $|-15| - |20| = -5$.

Review the instructions on the worksheet with your students. Instruct them to determine the absolute value of each number or expression first, then use the Order of Operations to simplify the expression. Finding the correct answers will enable them to complete the statement at the end of the worksheet.

2-14 Using Scientific Notation

This activity requires students to rewrite a number from standard form to scientific notation. The activity includes both small and large numbers.

Begin the activity by explaining that scientific notation is a practical method for writing very large and very small numbers. It is based on using powers of 10.

Offer your students these examples on the board or an overhead projector:

$$32,000 \text{ can be expressed as } 3.2 \times 10^4$$
$$0.023 \text{ can be expressed as } 2.3 \times 10^{-2}$$

Review the instructions on the worksheet. Note that students are to write only the underlined numbers in scientific notation.

2-15 Reviewing the Concepts and Skills of Integers

The problems in this activity focus on the skills and concepts that have been addressed in this section. Thus, the activity serves well as a review.

Start the activity by explaining that it is a culmination of the study of integers. The activity reinforces many of the concepts and skills associated with integers.

Go over the instructions on the worksheet. Note that by finding the correct answers, your students will be able to complete the statement at the end of the activity.

Answer Key for Section 2

2-1. 1. 0, K   2. 2, M   3. –5, F   4. –10, A   5. 6, Q   6. –8, C   7. –2, I   8. 10, U
9. 8, S   10. 4, O   11. 5, P   12. 3, N   13. –1, J   14. –9, B   15. 1, L
16. –3, H   17. Answers may vary.   18. Answers may vary.

2-2. 1. opposite 2. descending 3. before 4. freezes 5. less 6. credit 7. left 8. without 9. withdrawal 10. Zero 11. below 12. Red 13. colder 14. loss 15. warm 16. deposit 17. line 18. basement 19. negative 20. eight   Explanations may vary. They should convey that integers are not fractions; the three words are <u>perfect</u>, <u>whole</u>, and <u>complete</u>.

2-3.

−4	2	−9	5
−1	−3	4	−6
6	−8	1	−5
−7	3	−2	0

Explanations may vary. The sum along each row, column, and diagonal is −6. The sum of the circled numbers in the four corner squares is −6. This is the same as the sum of the circled numbers in the four center squares.

2-4.

−14	4	18	−20	−8
2	16	−26	−2	−10
20	−28	−4	−16	8
−22	0	−18	6	14
−6	−12	10	12	−24

2-5. 1. −8, −7, −7 2. −1, −13, −1 3. −16, −16 4. −11, 1, 1 5. −8, 8, 8 6. 12, −22, 12 7. −33, 33, 33 8. −13, −13 9. −54, −46, −46 10. −26, −14, −14 11. 8, −32, 8 12. 26, −26, 26 Score: 20

2-6. 1. E, −8 2. V, −108 3. E, −8 4. R, 36 5. Y, −1 6. A, −10 7. N, 3 8. S, 48 9. W, 392 10. E, −8 11. R, 36 12. I, −56 13. S, 48 14. A, −10 15. N, 3 16. I, −56 17. N, 3 18. T, −28 19. E, −8 20. G, 2 21. E, −8 22. R, 36. <u>Every answer is an integer.</u>

2-7. 1. The Bears' 31-yard line   2. 3 strokes   3. 18 games   4. 3,619,000 square miles   5. 45 years   6. 425° F   7. Yes. She was within her limit by 80 calories.   8. About 200 A.D.   9. March 25   10. $16   11. $30   12. Can't be determined. The coins could not be dated B.C.; there was no other time (A.D.) to compare it to yet.

2-8. 1. C, $3a + 3$ 2. O, $4a$ 3. I, $13a - 3b$ 4. N, $-9a$ 5. S, $13a - 5$ 6. T, $11a + 31$ 7. O, $4a$ 8. K, $8a$ 9. E, $6a - 7$ 10. N, $-9a$ 11. S, $13a - 5$ 12. A, $4a + 20b$ 13. N, $-9a$ 14. D, $8a + 11b + 9$ 15. M, $6a + 8b - 1$ 16. O, $4a$ 17. N, $-9a$ 18. E, $6a - 7$ 19. Y, $a - 10$ A numismatist collects <u>coins</u>, <u>tokens</u>, <u>and</u> <u>money</u>.

2-9. 1. 2   2. 7   3. 4   4. 9   5. 1   6. 8   7. 6   8. 6   9. 3   10. 5

2-10. 1. −15   2. −6   3. −24   4. −82   5. −63   6. 44   7. −15   8. 13   9. −8   10. −29   11. 81   12. 31   The final answer is $-146 + 2(73) = 0$.

2-11. 1. $(3 + 2)^2 = 25$ 2. $3 \cdot (4 + 5) = 27$ 3. $2^3 - (7 + 6) - 2^2 + 3 = -6$ 4. $2^2 - 6^2 - (2^2 + 2^3) = -44$ 5. $3 \times (2^3 - 5 \times 2) = -6$ 6. $-12 \cdot (3 - 6) \cdot -3^2 = -324$ 7. $-4^2 \cdot (3^3 - 1) = -416$ 8. $6^2 \div (-2^2 + 2) = -18$ 9. $(-5)^2 + 3^2 = 34$ 10. $3 \cdot 2^4 - (10 - 3^2) = 47$ 11. $-7 \cdot (2^3 - 5) \cdot 3 = -63$ 12. $16 \cdot (13 - 8) - 40 \div (10 - 5) = 72$

2-12. 1. H, −1   2. I, −7   3. S, 1   4. A, 4   5. B, 8   6. A, 4   7. L, 6   8. J, 2   9. A, 4   10. B, 8   11. R, 21   12. W, 0   13. A, 4   14. L, 6   15. M, 16   16. U, −4   17. Q, 9   18. A, 4   19. B, 8   20. A, 4   21. L, 6   22. A, 4   23. H, −1   The word algebra comes from a 9th-century text by al-Khwarizmi entitled <u>hisab al-jabr w' al muqabalah</u>, which means "the science of reunion and reduction."

2-13. 1. 15   2. 4   3. 3   4. 8   5. 15   6. 0   7. −18   8. −20   9. 9   10. 4   11. 14   12. 11   13. 25   14. −2   15. −12   16. 11   17. −6   18. −19   19. 24   20. 12   21. 11   22. 1   23. −6   You are absolutely correct.

2-14. 1. 9.3×10^7 2. 6.6×10^4 3. 8.64×10^5 4. 1×10^{-4} 5. 1.7×10^{-3} 6. 3.6×10^9 7. 5×10^{-2} 8. 3.5×10^7 9. 1×10^{-8} 10. 1.86×10^5

2-15. 1. S, −20   2. U, −5   3. M, 36   4. O, 18   5. F, 12   6. T, −12   7. H, 17   8. E, −40   9. S, −20   10. Q, 112   11. U, −5   12. A, 25   13. R, 11   14. E, −40   15. S, −20   16. O, 18   17. F, 12   18. F, 12   19. O, 18   20. U, −5   21. R, 11   22. I, 20   23. N, −9   24. T, −12   25. E, −40   26. G, −6   27. E, −40   28. R, 11   29. S, −20   Joseph Louis Lagrange, an 18th-century Italian mathematician, found that every natural number can be written as the <u>sum of the squares of four integers</u>.

Using a Number Line to Graph Integers

The points on a number line are associated with numbers. Each point on the number line below represents an integer from –10 to +10. The number paired with the point is called the *coordinate* of the point, while the point paired with the number is called the *graph*. Consecutive integers are spaced the same distance apart on the number line. The distance between consecutive integers is referred to as a *unit*.

Directions: Use the number line to locate the integers described below. Write the coordinate and point that is the graph of the number.

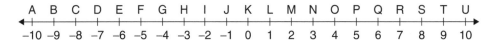

```
  A   B   C   D   E   F   G   H   I   J   K   L   M   N   O   P   Q   R   S   T   U
◄─┼───┼───┼───┼───┼───┼───┼───┼───┼───┼───┼───┼───┼───┼───┼───┼───┼───┼───┼───┼──►
 –10  –9  –8  –7  –6  –5  –4  –3  –2  –1   0   1   2   3   4   5   6   7   8   9  10
```

1. This integer is located in the middle of the number line. It is neither positive nor negative. _____

2. By definition, prime numbers are always positive. This integer is the only even prime number. _____

3. This integer is five units to the left of K. _____

4. This integer is the smallest integer that is represented on this number line.

    _____

5. This integer is located halfway between U and M. _____

6. To locate this integer, move three units to the left of –5. _____

7. To find this integer, move three units to the right of –5. _____

8. This integer represents the distance from K to U or from A to K. _____

9. This integer is halfway between Q and U. _____

10. This integer represents twice the distance from K to M. _____

11. This integer is the opposite of the integer that is paired with F. _____

12. This integer is halfway between J and R. _____

13. This integer is the opposite of the integer that is neither a prime nor composite number. _____

14. This integer can be located by either of these ways: move one unit from A or one unit from C. _____

15. This integer is one-third of the distance from K to N. _____

16. This integer is located six units to the left of N. _____

17. Write a clue to describe the integer paired with E. _____

    _____

18. Write a clue to describe the integer paired with R. _____

    _____

Representing Integers

We use integers every day to represent common occurrences. Gains, losses, and break-evens are everywhere. Stocks go up and down, teams are ahead in the score or behind, and temperatures increase or decrease. All of these situations, and more, can be described with integers.

Directions: The twenty sentences below relate to integers. Complete each statement by filling in the blank, using the grid at the end of this activity as a guide. Then write each answer in the grid, one letter per space. When you are finished, read down the letters in the boxes and break the letters into three words. These words describe the meaning of the Latin term for integer. Write an explanation of how these three words apply to integers.

1. –4 can be read as negative four or the _____ of four.
2. As the number line is read from right to left, the integers are in _____ order.
3. When launching a spacecraft, "T minus one" refers to one second _____ liftoff.
4. Water _____ at 32° F.
5. All negative integers are _____ than zero.
6. Instead of issuing a refund, some stores will _____ your account when you return an item.
7. Moving to the _____ is considered to be moving in the negative direction.
8. Positive integers can be written _____ any sign.
9. In banking, a _____ of $350 is written as –$350.
10. _____ does not represent any change.
11. –300 feet means three hundred feet _____ sea level.
12. _____ ink is often used to show a negative balance.
13. A temperature of –30° is _____ than a temperature of 30°.
14. +8 means a gain of eight; therefore –7 means a _____ of seven.
15. The temperature of a _____ day is about 75° F.
16. In banking, a _____ of $5 is written as +$5.
17. A number _____ is always a straight line.
18. One story below ground level is called a _____.
19. Water is frozen at _____ 1° C.
20. The opposite of negative eight is _____.

Representing Integers

1
2
3
4
5
6
7
8
9
10
11
12
13
14
15
16
17
18
19
20

What are the three words? _____, _____, _____.

How do these three words apply to integers? _____

_____

_____

Algebra Teacher's Activities Kit

Adding Integers

A *magic square* is an arrangement of numbers so that the sum of every row, column, and diagonal is the same.

Directions: Create a magic square by adding the numbers in the vertices of each small square and placing the sum inside the circle. The first sum is done for you. After you have found all of the sums, add the circled numbers along each row, column, and diagonal. Then answer the question at the end of the activity.

−7	−6	−3	−12	−1	−4	2	6
	(−4)		◯		◯		◯
14	−5	11	6	−2	−2	−7	4
10	−6	−4	−10	−12	6	−5	−2
	◯		◯		◯		◯
4	−9	13	−2	15	−5	10	−9
2	−11	−7	9	−5	−9	−1	−2
	◯		◯		◯		◯
8	7	−16	6	−4	19	−1	−1
−8	−4	15	−3	−4	−8	−13	3
	◯		◯		◯		◯
5	0	−1	−8	20	−10	8	2

Describe any patterns you see. _____

_____

_____

_____

Adding and Subtracting Integers

The magic number of the magic square below is –20. Some numbers in the square, however, are missing.

Directions: Find the missing numbers so that the sum of the integers in each row, column, and diagonal equals –20.

–14	4		–20	
2			–2	
20	–28	–4		
	0	–18	6	14
–6		10	12	–24

Comparing Sums and Differences

Comparing values and quantities is a skill we use all the time. Integers enable us to compare things accurately.

Directions: Find the sum or difference for each problem and write your answers in the blanks. Then compare the answers of the equations and write the larger answer in the blank at the right. If two answers are the same, leave the final blank empty. To find your score, add the integers along the right.

Larger Answer

1. $-2 + -6 =$ _____ $-3 + -4 =$ _____   _____

2. $-7 + 6 =$ _____ $-7 - 6 =$ _____   _____

3. $-4 - 12 =$ _____ $-4 + -12 =$ _____   _____

4. $-2 + -3 - 6 =$ _____ $-2 - 3 - (-6) =$ _____   _____

5. $10 - 18 =$ _____ $-10 + 18 =$ _____   _____

6. $-10 - (-22) =$ _____ $-10 - 12 =$ _____   _____

7. $-25 - 8 =$ _____ $25 - (-8) =$ _____   _____

8. $6 - 19 =$ _____ $6 + (-19) =$ _____   _____

9. $-230 + 176 =$ _____ $-50 + 4 =$ _____   _____

10. $-14 - 7 - 5 =$ _____ $-2 - (-8) - 20 =$ _____   _____

11. $-12 + 20 =$ _____ $-20 + -12 =$ _____   _____

12. $34 + -8 =$ _____ $-34 + 8 =$ _____   _____

Score = _____

Multiplying and Dividing Integers

Multiplying and dividing integers is an easy task. Just remember the following:

- The product or quotient of two positive or two negative integers is positive.
- The product or quotient of two integers with unlike signs is negative.
- The product of 0 and any integer is 0.
- An integer divided by 0 is undefined.
- When you work with more than two integers, follow the Order of Operations.

Directions: Solve each problem and write the answer in the space after the equal sign. Find the answer of each problem in the Answer Bank and write the letter of the answer in the space *before* the problem. Then write the letters in order, starting with the first problem, on the lines at the end of the activity to reveal a statement.

1. _____ $2 \times 8 \div 4 \times -2 =$ _____

2. _____ $-36 \div 2 \times 6 =$ _____

3. _____ $-32 \div -4 \div -2 \times 2 =$ _____

4. _____ $3 \times 3 \times 2 \times 2 =$ _____

5. _____ $-12 \div 3 \div 2 \div 2 =$ _____

6. _____ $-100 \div 2 \div 5 =$ _____

7. _____ $-27 \div -3 \div 3 =$ _____

8. _____ $-2 \times 3 \times -8 =$ _____

9. _____ $28 \times 4 \div 2 \times 7 =$ _____

10. _____ $-28 \times 4 \div (2 \times 7) =$ _____

11. _____ $-4 \times 27 \div -3 =$ _____

12. _____ $28 \times 6 \div -3 =$ _____

13. _____ $12 \times 3 \div 6 \times 8 =$ _____

14. _____ $60 \div (4 \times 3) \times -2 =$ _____

15. _____ $30 \div (5 \times 2) =$ _____

16. _____ $-4 \times 2 \times 7 =$ _____

17. _____ $12 \div (2 \times 2) =$ _____

18. _____ $-56 \div (4 \div 2) =$ _____

19. _____ $-16 \div 2 \times 4 \div 4 =$ _____

20. _____ $2 \times 8 \div (4 \times 2) =$ _____

21. _____ $20 \times -4 \div (2 \times 5) =$ _____

22. _____ $-3 \times (24 \div -2) =$ _____

Answer Bank

W. 392	Y. −1	I. −56	S. 48	R. 36
A. −10	N. 3	E. −8	T. −28	G. 2	V. −108

___ ___ ___ ___ ___   ___ ___ ___ ___ ___ ___

___ ___ ___ ___   ___ ___ ___ ___ ___ ___ ___ .

Algebra Teacher's Activities Kit

Copyright © 2003 John Wiley & Sons, Inc.

Solving Word Problems with Integers

Integers relate to real-life situations. Every time you think of a gain or a loss, you are thinking in terms of integers. A loss of five yards in football can be thought of as –5 yards. Finding a $10 bill on the street can be thought of as a gain of $10 or +10.

Directions: Solve each problem.

1. After losing eight yards on a play, the Bears retain possession of the football on their 23-yard line. Where was the ball before this play?

   _____

2. Juan, an avid golfer, used two strokes on a miniature golf hole, which was one stroke below par. What was par for this hole?

   _____

3. Even after a five-game winning streak and winning a total of fifteen games, the Bombers are out of first place by three games. How many games did the first-place team win?

   _____

4. The Sahara Desert covers 3,579,000 square miles. The entire United States is about 40,000 square miles larger. What is the area of the United States?

   _____

5. The average life expectancy for men in Japan is seventy-six years, which is thirty-one years more than the average life expectancy in most developing countries. What is the average life expectancy for most developing countries?

   _____

6. Neptune's largest moon is called Triton, and at –393° F it is the coldest place in the solar system. What is the difference between this temperature and the freezing point of water, which is 32° F?

   _____

Integers, Variables, and Expressions

Solving Word Problems with Integers

7. Sue is watching her weight and tries to limit herself to 1,800 calories per day. Yesterday, she consumed 350 calories for breakfast, 440 calories for lunch, 720 calories for dinner, and 210 calories for a bedtime snack. Was she within her limit? By how many calories was she over or under her limit?

8. Diophantus, a Greek mathematician, developed algebra about five hundred years after Euclid completed writing *Elements* in 300 B.C. (*Elements* is the basis for geometry, and many historians consider Diophantus to be the father of algebra.) Approximately when was algebra developed?

9. The deadline to file a federal income tax return is April 15. Sam wished to file early this year to avoid the stress of rushing at the last minute. His return was postmarked exactly three weeks earlier than the deadline. When was his return postmarked?

10. Three girls chipped in to buy concert tickets for themselves and one additional ticket as a birthday gift for a friend. The tickets cost $37.50 each and each of the three girls paid $50. Since they forgot to add in the $12 processing charge per ticket, they did not have enough money to pay for the tickets. How much more money did each of the three girls have to pay in order to purchase the four tickets?

11. The last check written on a checking account was $125, which caused the account to be overdrawn by $95. How much money was in the account before the last check was written?

12. In 1990 a coin collector found an ancient coin dated 15 B.C. How old was the coin? (Be careful here.)

Simplifying Expressions by Combining Similar Terms

Similar terms are the same expressions except for the number to the left of the variable. This number is called the *numerical coefficient* of the term. Examples of similar terms are x, 3x, and –7x. 3x and 3y are not similar terms. To simplify an expression, add the coefficients of the similar terms and add the integers.

Directions: Simplify each expression and write the answer in the blank after the expression. Find each answer in the Answer Bank, and write the letter of each answer in the blank before the expression. Then write the letters in order, starting with the first problem, to complete the statement at the end of the activity.

1. _____ 3 + 9a – 6a = _____

2. _____ 10a + –4a – 2a = _____

3. _____ 7a + –3b + 6a = _____

4. _____ –16a + 7a = _____

5. _____ 8a + 7 + 5a – 12 = _____

6. _____ –3a + 2 + 14a + 29 = _____

7. _____ 15 + 12a – 18 + 3 – 8a = _____

8. _____ –9 + 9a + 9 – a = _____

9. _____ 17a + 9 – 11a – 16 = _____

10. _____ –13a + 7b + 4a – 7b = _____

11. _____ –12a + 6 + 25a – 11 = _____

12. _____ 5a + 7b – a + 13b = _____

13. _____ 9a – 15 + 12 – 18a + 3 = _____

14. _____ 10a + 15b + 8 – 2a – 4b + 1 = _____

15. _____ 9a + 4b – 5c – 1 – 3a + 4b + 5c = _____

16. _____ 16a – 10a – 2a = _____

17. _____ 12b + 3b – 7a – 5b – 2a – 10b = _____

18. _____ 7a – 7b – a + 13b – 6b – 7 = _____

19. _____ 4a – 2 – 3a – 8 = _____

Answer Bank
N. –9a
E. 6a – 7
A. 4a + 20b
T. 11a + 31
D. 8a + 11b + 9
S. 13a – 5
I. 13a – 3b
K. 8a
M. 6a + 8b – 1
O. 4a
C. 3a + 3
Y. a – 10

A numismatist collects ____ ____ ____ ____ ____,   ____ ____ ____ ____ ____ ____,

____ ____ ____   ____ ____ ____ ____ ____.

Using the Distributive Property to Simplify Expressions

Many people love puzzles. This one requires some careful analysis. It also requires an understanding of the Distributive Property, which states

$$a(b + c) = ab + ac \text{ and } (b + c)a = ba + ca$$

Directions: One number is missing from each problem below. Find the missing number. Hint: Every number from 1 to 9 is used once, and one number is used twice.

1. _____$(18n + 6) = 36n + 12$

2. $-9(n + 3) +$ _____ $= -9n - 20$

3. $38 +$ _____$(5n - 3) = 20n + 26$

4. $15 -$ _____$(3n - 10) = 105 - 27n$

5. $9(n +$ _____$) + 4(n - 6) = 13n - 15$

6. _____$(n + 9) - 18 = 8n + 54$

7. _____$n + 7(3 + n - 4) = 13n - 7$

8. $7n -$ _____$(2n - 5) = -5n + 30$

9. $8n + (n - 5)$_____ $- 9n = 2n - 15$

10. $5(n - 3) - 7n +$ _____ $= -2n - 10$

Integers and Using the Order of Operations I

Although we may not always like to follow rules, in most cases rules are designed to make things easier. Imagine trying to play any game without following rules. When working with integers, we have rules, too. These are called the Order of Operations, which state:

1. Simplify expressions within parentheses and other grouping symbols first.
2. Multiply and divide from left to right next.
3. Add and subtract from left to right last.

Directions: Solve each problem, then follow the instructions at the end of the activity. Be sure to use the Order of Operations.

1. $14 - 10 \cdot 3 + 2 \div 2 = $ _____

2. $(8 + 8) \div -4 - 2 = $ _____

3. $-13 - 4 \cdot 2 - 3 = $ _____

4. $-2 \cdot 3 - 4 \cdot 8 - 22 \cdot 2 = $ _____

5. $-4 \cdot 10 + 3 \cdot -5 - 8 = $ _____

6. $28 - 4(5 - 9) = $ _____

7. $-20 - 25 \div -5 = $ _____

8. $-5 + 3 \cdot 6 = $ _____

9. $2 + 7(6 - 10) + 18 = $ _____

10. $4 - 9 \cdot 3 - 6 = $ _____

11. $-45 - 6 \cdot 3 \cdot -7 = $ _____

12. $15 - 8(-4 \div 2) = $ _____

Find the sum of the first six answers. Add this to twice the sum of the last six answers.

The final answer = _____

Integers and Using the Order of Operations II

It is necessary to follow the Order of Operations when working with integers. Operations in parentheses, for example, must be done first. For example:

$$-7 + 9 \cdot 6 = 47 \text{ but } (-7 + 9) \cdot 6 = 12.$$

The Order of Operations is as follows:

1. Simplify expressions within parentheses.
2. Find the value of all powers.
3. Multiply and divide from left to right.
4. Add and subtract from left to right.

Directions: The equations below are incorrect. Rewrite them correctly by inserting one group of parentheses in each equation to obtain the given answer. Be sure to follow the Order of Operations.

1. $3 + 2^2 = 25$ _____

2. $3 \cdot 4 + 5 = 27$ _____

3. $2^3 - 7 + 6 - 2^2 + 3 = -6$ _____

4. $2^2 - 6^2 - 2^2 + 2^3 = -44$ _____

5. $3 \times 2^3 - 5 \times 2 = -6$ _____

6. $-12 \cdot 3 - 6 \cdot -3^2 = -324$ _____

7. $-4^2 \cdot 3^3 - 1 = -416$ _____

8. $6^2 \div -2^2 + 2 = -18$ _____

9. $-5^2 + 3^2 = 34$ _____

10. $3 \cdot 2^4 - 10 - 3^2 = 47$ _____

11. $-7 \cdot 2^3 - 5 \cdot 3 = -63$ _____

12. $16 \cdot 13 - 8 - 40 \div (10 - 5) = 72$ _____

Algebra Teacher's Activities Kit

Evaluating Expressions

Evaluating expressions is an important skill in algebra. To evaluate an expression, replace the variable by the given value and simplify by using the Order of Operations.

Directions: Evaluate each expression according to the given values. Write your answers in the blank after the expression. Next, find each answer in the Answer Bank and write the letter of the answer in the space before the expression. When you are done, write the letters in order, starting with the first problem, in the blanks to complete the statement at the end of the activity.

$$a = 3 \quad b = -1 \quad c = 0 \quad d = 1$$

1. _____ $3b + 2d =$ _____

2. _____ $c - 7 =$ _____

3. _____ $b^2 =$ _____

4. _____ $\dfrac{12}{a} =$ _____

5. _____ $9 + b =$ _____

6. _____ $7d - a =$ _____

7. _____ $a - 3b =$ _____

8. _____ $a + db =$ _____

9. _____ $4(a + 2b) =$ _____

10. _____ $2(a^2 + 5b) =$ _____

11. _____ $6(ad) - 3b =$ _____

12. _____ $\dfrac{c}{7ab} =$ _____

13. _____ $-(b - a) =$ _____

14. _____ $a(d - b) =$ _____

15. _____ $(a - b)^2 =$ _____

16. _____ $\dfrac{a + d}{b} =$ _____

17. _____ $-2ab + 3d =$ _____

18. _____ $\dfrac{2(a + d)}{d - b} =$ _____

19. _____ $6a + 10b =$ _____

20. _____ $\dfrac{-8}{b - d} =$ _____

21. _____ $-(7b + d) =$ _____

22. _____ $a-b =$ _____

23. _____ $\dfrac{-ab}{abd} =$ _____

Answer Bank

Q. 9	J. 2	L. 6	H. –1
I. –7	B. 8	S. 1	U. –4
R. 21	W. 0	M. 16	A. 4

The word algebra comes from a 9th century text by al-Khwarizmi, entitled

___ ___ ___ ___ ___ ___ ___-___ ___ ___ ___ ___ ' ___ ___ ___

____ ___ ___ ___ ___ ___ ___ ___ ____ , which means "the science of reunion and reduction."

Finding the Absolute Value

The *absolute value* of a number is its distance from zero on the number line. Direction does not matter. For example, $|5| = 5$ and $|-5| = 5$. Imagine that you and a friend each walked one mile on different days. The directions or destinations don't matter. The total distance you each walked is still one mile.

Directions: Simplify each expression. Circle the letter of your answer. Then write the letters in order, starting with the first letter, in the blanks to complete the statement at the end of the activity.

1. $|15| = $ _____	Y. 15	I. −15
2. $|-4| = $ _____	O. 4	H. −4
3. $|-6 + 3| = $ _____	A. −3	U. 3
4. $|7 - 15| = $ _____	A. 8	V. −8
5. $|-4 + 19| = $ _____	R. 15	E. −15
6. $|3 - 3| = $ _____	A. 6	E. 0
7. $-|-18| = $ _____	L. 18	A. −18
8. $-|20| = $ _____	B. −20	G. 20
9. $|-9| = $ _____	P. −9	S. 9
10. $|16| - |-12| = $ _____	O. 4	R. −4
11. $|-8| + |6| = $ _____	L. 14	O. −2
12. $|-3| + 8 = $ _____	U. 11	B. 5
13. $12 + |-13| = $ _____	L. −1	T. 25
14. $-6 + |4| = $ _____	E. −2	M. −10
15. $-|4 - 16| = $ _____	L. −12	E. 12
16. $|7 - (-4)| = $ _____	W. −11	Y. 11
17. $|4| - |10| = $ _____	I. 6	C. −6
18. $-|4| - |15| = $ _____	T. 9	O. −19
19. $6|-4| = $ _____	R. 24	H. 10
20. $|7 - (-5)| = $ _____	R. 12	T. −12
21. $5 + |-6| = $ _____	E. 11	H. −11
22. $|5 - 6| = $ _____	I. −1	C. 1
23. $|5 + 6| - |17| = $ _____	T. −6	S. 28

___ ___ ___   ___ ___ ___

___ ___ ___ ___ ___ ___ ___ ___ ___ ___ ___

___ ___ ___ ___ ___ ___ ___.

Algebra Teacher's Activities Kit

Using Scientific Notation

Scientific notation is a way of expressing a number as a product of a number times a power of 10. It is a type of mathematical shorthand for writing very large or very small numbers.

Directions: Rewrite the underlined numbers in scientific notation.

1. Earth is <u>93,000,000</u> miles from the sun. _____

2. Earth travels around the sun at a speed of about <u>66,000</u> miles per hour.
   _____

3. The sun is a medium-sized star with a diameter of <u>864,000</u> miles.
   _____

4. Mars is a very dry world compared to Earth. It possesses <u>0.0001</u> as much water in its atmosphere as Earth. _____

5. Pluto, the smallest planet, has a mass of <u>0.0017</u> that of Earth.
   _____

6. Pluto is also the farthest planet from the sun at a distance of <u>3,600,000,000</u> miles. _____

7. Your weight on Pluto is <u>0.05</u> times your weight on Earth.
   _____

8. The hottest place in the solar system is the core of the sun with a temperature of about <u>35 million</u> degrees F. _____

9. Most astronomers believe that hydrogen, the simplest element, is the most abundant element throughout the universe. The size of a hydrogen atom is <u>0.00000001</u> cm. _____

10. Distances between the stars are so great that they are measured in light years, the distance a beam of light travels in one year. Since light travels at roughly <u>186,000</u> miles per second, a light year is about 6 trillion miles.
    _____

Reviewing the Concepts and Skills of Integers

The problems in this activity focus on a variety of concepts and skills. Completing the worksheet will show how well you understand integers.

Directions: Each problem below can be simplified so that the answer is an integer. Write your answers in the blanks that follow the problems. Next, find each answer in the Answer Bank, then write the letter of the answer in the blank before each problem. When you are finished with the problems, write the letters in order, starting with the first problem, to complete the statement at the end of the activity.

1. _____ $-|-6 - 14| =$ _____

2. _____ The difference between -6 and $-1 =$ _____

3. _____ 17 decreased by $-19 =$ _____

4. _____ The sum of 19 and $-1 =$ _____

5. _____ $-2(5 - 8) + 18 \div 3 =$ _____

6. _____ $-|12| =$ _____

7. _____ $-8 + 3x - 2x + 5^2 - x =$ _____

8. _____ 12 less than the product of 14 and $-2 =$ _____

9. _____ $1 + 7(1 - 4) =$ _____

10. _____ If $x = 6$, $3x^2 + 4 =$ _____

11. _____ $12 \div (4 + 2) - 7 =$ _____

12. _____ If $x = -1$, $(-5x)^2 =$ _____

13. _____ $6^2 - 5^2 =$ _____

14. _____ $-6^2 - 2^2 =$ _____

15. _____ The sum of -19 and $-1 =$ _____

Algebra Teacher's Activities Kit

Copyright © 2003 John Wiley & Sons, Inc.

Reviewing the Concepts and Skills of Integers

16. _____ If a = 5, $a^2 - 7$ = _____

17. _____ Twice the sum of –3 and 9 = _____

18. _____ 4 more than $\frac{1}{3}$ of 24 = _____

19. _____ 1.8×10^1 = _____

20. _____ If x = –1, $-5x^2$ = _____

21. _____ $3^3 - 2^4$ = _____

22. _____ The difference between 19 and –1 = _____

23. _____ If a = 3 and b = –4, $\frac{4a^2}{b}$ = _____

24. _____ 3 more than half of –30 = _____

25. _____ $-(6^2 + 2^2)$ = _____

26. _____ $-12 + 2 \times 3$ = _____

27. _____ The opposite of 40 = _____

28. _____ One less than the product of 3 and 4 = _____

29. _____ If x = –2, $-5x^2$ = _____

Answer Bank						
T. –12	N. –9	A. 25	E. –40	S. –20	I. 20	U. –5
M. 36	O. 18	G. –6	H. 17	F. 12	R. 11	Q. 112

Joseph Louis Lagrange, an 18th-century Italian mathematician, found that every natural number can be written as the ___ ___ ___ ___ ___ ___ ___ ___

___ ___ ___ ___ ___ ___ ___ ___ ___ ___ ___ ___ ___

___ ___ ___ ___ ___ ___ ___ ___ .

Linear Equations and Inequalities

This section focuses on the skills and concepts needed for writing and solving linear equations and inequalities. The twenty-four activities that follow range from identifying solutions of equations and inequalities to solving systems of equations and using matrices. The section also includes specific equations and formulas that apply to temperature, direct variation, and percents. Examples of how equations and inequalities can be applied to solving real-life problems appear throughout the section.

Teaching Suggestions for the Activities

3-1 Identifying Solutions of Equations and Inequalities

Before students can solve equations and inequalities, they must be able to identify correct solutions. This activity provides your students with examples of equations and inequalities as well as possible solutions.

Begin the activity by discussing equations and inequalities. Note that equations have an equal sign, denoting that both sides of the equation have the same value, while the sides of inequalities might be equal or unequal. Be sure that your students understand the meanings of the inequality symbols, $<$, $>$, $\leq$, and $\geq$.

Review the instructions on the worksheet. Emphasize that your students are to substitute the number in braces for the variable and determine whether or not the number is a solution of the equation or inequality. If the number is not a solution, they are to correct the equation or inequality. Remind them to follow the Order of Operations.

3-2 Writing and Solving One-Step Equations I

In this activity your students are given a statement for which they are to write and solve an equation. The equations involve sums, differences, products, and quotients. Make sure that your students understand that if –n equals a number, then n equals the opposite of the number.

Start the activity by briefly reviewing the process of writing equations. Note that words such as "is," "are," and "equal" are often cues for the equal sign when translating a statement into an equation.

Go over the instructions on the worksheet with your students. Note that Problem 13 asks students to follow a set of directions to determine their score. You may wish to tell them that if they complete the worksheet correctly, their score will equal 100.

3-3 Writing and Solving One-Step Equations II

The problems of this activity relate to situations encountered in daily life. Each equation can be solved by using one transformation. Activity 3-2 is a prerequisite for this activity.

Introduce the activity by explaining that many events and occurrences in life can be described in mathematical terms through equations. In fact, many situations, when described mathematically, can become more clear.

Review the instructions on the worksheet with your students. Note that for each problem they are to identify the variable, write an equation, and solve the problem.

Suggest that they choose letters for variables that remind them of what they are trying to find. For example, if they are trying to find the height of a structure, the letter "h" is a good choice for the variable.

3-4 Creating Word Problems

Students are familiar with having to solve word problems. A different twist when working with word problems is to ask students to create their own. In this case, your students must formulate problems and come up with the answers as well.

Begin the activity by asking your students to think of some situations that may be the basis for word problems that can be solved by writing an equation. Suggest topics such as sports and recreation, finance, health, and sales.

For this activity, instruct your students to create word problems based on the guidelines found on the worksheet. Remind them that they are to write problems, write equations, and also provide solutions to the problems. Upon completion of the activity, you might want to select some of the best problems and make them available to the class as a challenge or extra credit assignment.

3-5 Using Formulas for Finding Temperatures

This activity focuses on application of the formulas for converting temperatures from Fahrenheit to Celsius and from Celsius to Fahrenheit. You might mention that the two scales are quite different. On the Fahrenheit scale, the freezing point and boiling point of water are 32° and 212° respectively, while on the Celsius scale water freezes at 0° and boils at 100°.

Start the activity by reading and discussing the example on the worksheet. Stress the importance of using the correct label when referring to temperature on the Fahrenheit and Celsius scales. Discuss the formulas with your students, noting that there are two formulas for converting temperatures from Fahrenheit to Celsius and two others for converting from Celsius to Fahrenheit.

Go over the instructions on the worksheet and suggest that they use whichever formula they wish to complete the problems. Remind them to round their answers to the nearest degree.

3-6 Solving Multi-step Equations I

This activity requires your students to extend their problem-solving skills to solving equations with variables on one side. Some of the problems require your students to combine similar terms and/or use the Distributive Property.

Introduce this activity by writing the following equation (or a similar equation) on the board or an overhead projector: $2x - 1 = -15$. Encourage your students to isolate the variable or "get 2x all alone" by adding 1 to each side. The result is a one-step equation that your students may then solve. You may wish to extend this line of reasoning to combining similar terms and using the Distributive Property. (The steps are provided on the worksheet.)

Go over the instructions on the worksheet with your students. Remind them that after they solve the equations, they must complete the statement at the end of the sheet.

3-7 Solving Multi-step Equations II

This activity provides practice both in substituting numbers for variables as well as solving multi-step equations. Given a value for x, your students must substitute the value and solve for y. Before assigning this activity, be sure that your students understand how to solve multi-step equations, examples of which are presented in Activity 3-6.

Introduce this activity by discussing multi-step equations. Offer this example on the board or an overhead projector:

$$x = 8 \qquad \begin{aligned} 3x + y &= -15 \\ 24 + y &= -15 \\ y &= -39 \end{aligned}$$

Be sure to discuss the steps so that students understand the procedure.

Review the instructions on the worksheet. Note that students will be given various equations that they are to solve.

3-8 Writing and Solving Multi-step Equations

This activity requires your students to write and solve equations. All of the equations on the worksheet can be written with the variables on one side. The solutions require more than one step.

Start the activity by presenting an example for which your students must write and solve an equation. Offer the following example on the board or an overhead projector:

6 less than the product of a number and 3 is 21.
Let n represent the number, therefore . . .
$$\begin{aligned} 3n - 6 &= 21 \\ n &= 9 \end{aligned}$$

Here is another example you might wish to offer your students:

An initial deposit of $100 and saving a specific amount of money for twenty-two weeks results in a balance of $562. Let n represent the amount of money saved per week, therefore . . .
$$\begin{aligned} 100 + 22n &= 562 \\ n &= 21 \end{aligned}$$

Go over the instructions on the worksheet with your students. Emphasize the importance of identifying the variable, writing and solving the equation, and checking the solution. This activity is self-correcting because all of the answers are required to solve Problem 10.

3-9 Writing and Using Direct Variations

Direct variation is a special type of relationship between two quantities. In a direct variation, two quantities are related by a constant non-zero number.

Begin the activity by providing examples of direct variation such as an hourly wage, the cost of movie tickets, distance traveled, and doubling recipes. Be sure that your students recognize the constant of variation in each case. In the example of the hourly wage, the constant of variation is the pay per hour. To further ensure that your students understand direct variation, discuss the examples on the worksheet.

Go over the instructions for the activity with your students. Note that they are to write an equation and solve the problem for each direct variation.

3-10　Solving Proportions

In this activity your students are to solve proportions. To complete the activity successfully, they must be able to find cross products and solve linear equations.

Introduce the activity by reviewing proportions that your students have used before, such as $\frac{3}{4} = \frac{6}{8}$. Identify the cross products, and make sure they understand that in a proportion the cross products are equal.

Depending on the abilities of your students, you may find it helpful to review the use of the Distributive Property in solving a proportion. Offer the following example on the board or an overhead projector, and note how the use of cross products results in the solution.

$$\frac{x-4}{3} = \frac{5}{2}$$
$$2(x-4) = (3)(5)$$
$$2x - 8 = 15$$
$$2x = 23$$
$$x = 11.5$$

Review the instructions on the worksheet. Remind your students to complete the statement at the end of the activity.

3-11　Solving Simple Percent Problems

This activity requires your students to solve three types of percent problems: finding the percent of a number, finding the number, and finding the percent.

Begin the activity by reviewing the steps for solving proportions. Explain the formula provided on the worksheet, being sure that your students understand how the formula relates to proportions. Note that the base is always the number or phrase to the right of the word "of." Recalling this makes substituting values into the proportion easier.

Review the instructions on the worksheet with your students and emphasize that all of the problems can be solved by using a proportion.

Since each answer is used in the next problem, encourage your students to double-check their answers before moving on. If an answer is expressed as a percent, students should drop the percent symbol and use only the number they recorded.

3-12 Solving Word Problems Involving Percents

This activity requires your students to solve a variety of word problems on topics such as commissions, sales, and discounts. To complete this activity successfully, your students should have a solid understanding of percents. Depending on their abilities, you may find it helpful that they complete Activity 3-11 first.

Start the activity by reviewing percents and the basic types of percent problems. Explain that whenever attempting to solve a problem, it is essential to formulate the correct strategy and follow the proper procedure. Understanding the problem and identifying what one wishes to find is vital to finding the solution.

Review the instructions on the worksheet with your students. Emphasize that, although answers are provided for the problems in this activity, some of the answers are incorrect. Note that the errors are not computational. If an answer is incorrect, your students must identify the error and solve the problem.

3-13 Finding the Percent of Increase or Decrease

This activity requires students to be proficient in solving proportions as well as solving equations with variables on both sides. They will use these skills to complete a table, after which they will be able to complete a statement at the end of the activity.

Start the activity with a brief discussion of percents of increase and decrease. Refer to the formulas on the worksheet and offer the following example to demonstrate how to use the formula for the percent of increase.

Suppose the price of the shares of a stock increase from $3.00 to $3.50 per share. What is the percent of increase? Note that the increase was $0.50 and that the original price of the stock was $3.00. Show the formula on the board or an overhead projector.

$$\text{Percent of Increase} = \frac{\text{increase}}{\text{original}}$$
$$\frac{n}{100} = \frac{0.5}{3}$$
$$n = 16\frac{2}{3}$$

The stock increased by $16\frac{2}{3}\%$.

Go over the instructions on the worksheet with your students. Explain that they must complete the chart by substituting the appropriate numbers in the equations. After they have completed the chart, they are to complete the statement at the end of the activity.

3-14 Writing Equivalent Equations

This activity requires students to write an equation and match it with an equivalent equation. To complete this activity successfully, your students should be able to write equations. Activity 3-2 is a helpful warm-up for this activity.

Introduce the activity by reviewing equivalent equations (two or more equations that have the same solution). Briefly discuss the properties that result in equivalent equations, including adding or subtracting the same number to or from both sides of the equation, multiplying or dividing both sides by a non-zero number, simplifying one or both sides, and interchanging the sides. You might ask your students questions such as: Is $x - 2 = 15$ equivalent to $x = 15 + 2$? Such questions can hone your students' thinking about equivalent equations.

Go over the instructions on the worksheet with your students. Explain that equations may be written in various forms. Note that when your students write equations for the problems on the worksheet, the equations may or may not be in the same form as the equations appearing at the end of the activity. Caution your students that they may need to transform equations to find matches. Remind them that some equations are used more than once and some are not used at all.

3-15 Solving Equations with Variables on Both Sides

This activity focuses on the skills necessary for solving multi-step equations. The equations in this activity have variables on both sides of the equal sign.

Begin the activity by explaining to your students that they can add and subtract variable expressions in the same way they add or subtract numbers. The key to solving equations is to solve for a variable by simplifying each side of the equation, then isolating the variable. Review the example on the worksheet and make sure that your students understand the various steps.

Go over the instructions on the worksheet with your students. Remind them to complete the statement at the end of the activity.

3-16 Writing and Solving Equations with Variables on Both Sides

This activity contains eight word problems. Your students must write and solve equations, most of which can be written with variables on both sides. If the equations are solved correctly, your students will be able to use the solutions to complete a message at the end of the activity.

Introduce the activity by reviewing the basic steps for problem solving: read the problem carefully, identify what you are asked to find, write and solve an equation, and check the result.

Go over the instructions on the worksheet with your students and point out that the variable is identified for them. Note that equations may vary and that most of the equations will have variables on both sides. (Problems 3 and 8, however, cannot be written in that manner.) Remind your students to complete the statement at the end of the activity.

3-17 Solving One-step Inequalities

The inequalities contained in this activity involve only one transformation per problem. All four operations, however, are included. To complete this activity successfully, your students should be able to solve linear equations. They should also understand the meaning of the inequality symbols: <, >, ≤, and ≥.

Begin the activity by explaining that inequalities and equations are solved in the same manner: adding or subtracting the same number to or from both sides of the equation, and multiplying or dividing both sides of the equation by the same nonzero number. Note that the only difference between solving equations and inequalities is that when both sides of an inequality are multiplied or divided by a negative number, the direction of the inequality symbol must be changed.

Go over the instructions on the worksheet with your students. Emphasize that each solution in the Answer Bank will be used only once. Remind them to complete the statement at the end of the activity.

3-18 Solving Multi-step Inequalities

This activity extends the skills necessary to solving single-step inequalities, as in Activity 3-17, to the skills needed for solving inequalities requiring several steps. A few of the inequalities contained on the worksheet have no solution; others include all real numbers as their solution.

Start this activity by reviewing the rules for solving equations and inequalities as noted on the worksheet. Emphasize that if both sides of an inequality are multiplied by a negative number, the direction of the inequality symbol must be changed.

Go over the instructions on the worksheet with your students. Remind them that once they have solved the inequalities, they must complete the statement at the end of the activity.

3-19 Writing and Solving Inequalities

This activity contains word problems that can be solved by writing inequalities. Some of the inequalities contained on the worksheet require multi-steps in finding a solution. The data in the word problems apply to numbers and real-life situations.

Start the activity by reviewing the meanings of the inequality symbols:

< which means is less than
> which means is greater than
≤ which means is less than or equal to
≥ which means is greater than or equal to

Extend these descriptions to include other meanings. For example, ≤ can also mean "at most" or "no more than," and ≥ can also mean "at least" and "no less than."

Review the instructions on the worksheet with your students. Emphasize that they are to write and solve an inequality for each problem, then match their solution with one of the provided solutions. Note that some of the solutions will not be used. When they are finished solving the inequalities, they should complete the statement at the end of the activity.

3-20 Verifying Solutions of Systems of Linear Equations

For this activity your students are given systems of equations and some values for variables. They are then asked to state whether or not the values are solutions to the system. They are not required to solve the system.

Begin the activity by reviewing the definition of a system of equations, as shown on the worksheet. Be sure that your students understand that a solution of the system must be a solution of each equation and not just one.

Review the instructions on the worksheet with your students. Depending on the abilities of your students, you may find it helpful to do the first problem together. Emphasize that they are to circle the letter below "Yes" if the values are a solution, or circle the letter below "No" if the values are not a solution. Remind them to complete the statement at the end of the activity.

3-21 Solving Systems of Linear Equations

This activity is designed to be used after Activity 3-20. It contains problems that can be solved in a variety of ways.

Begin the activity by reviewing steps for solving systems of linear equations. Include these points:

1. Substitution should be used if the coefficient of one variable is 1 or –1.
2. Addition or subtraction should be used if the coefficients of one variable are opposites, or if the coefficients are the same.
3. Multiplication with addition or subtraction should be used if the coefficient of a variable is a factor (other than 1) of the other, or if the coefficients of a variable are relatively prime (have a greatest common factor of 1.)

Go over the instructions on the worksheet with your students. Note that they must solve each system and record the value for x first. Also note that some answers will be used more than once. Remind them to complete the statement at the end of the activity.

3-22   Solving Word Problems by Writing Systems of Equations

This activity includes twelve word problems, which should be solved by writing and solving systems of equations. To be able to complete this activity successfully, your students should be able to solve systems of equations. Depending on the abilities of your students, you may consider Activity 3-21 as a prerequisite for this activity.

Begin the activity by reviewing systems of equations. Note that there must be at least two variables and two equations in each system. Emphasize that, to solve word problems efficiently, students must read the problem with care and identify the variable.

Review the instructions on the worksheet with your students. Mention that they may use various methods to solve these systems of equations. Caution them to read each problem carefully and make certain they understand what is being asked before they attempt to solve the problems.

3-23   Adding and Subtracting Matrices

This activity requires students to add and subtract matrices. Be sure that your students can add and subtract integers before assigning this activity.

Begin this activity by explaining that a matrix is a rectangular array of numbers. Matrices are used to organize numbers so that the numbers are easier to read.

Go over the instructions on the worksheet with your students. Depending on the abilities of your students and their experience with matrices, you may find it helpful to do the first problem together.

3-24 Multiplying Matrices

Unlike the addition and subtraction of matrices, which are relatively simple, multiplying matrices can be a difficult concept for many students. Begin the activity by explaining that a matrix is a rectangular array of numbers, the purpose of which is to make data easier to use.

For the worksheet, your students are to multiply the given matrices. Depending on the abilities of your students, you may find it beneficial to do the first problem together. If necessary, go over each step of the multiplication process.

Answer Key for Section 3

3-1. Corrections may vary; possible corrections include the following: 1. incorrect; $3 - y = 2$ 2. correct   3. incorrect; $a \div 3 = 1$ 4. incorrect; $c \div 5 = 0$ 5. correct   6. incorrect; $3n = 12$ 7. incorrect; $z - 2 > -4$ 8. correct   9. correct   10. incorrect; $x + (-2) = -11$ 11. incorrect; $a + 3 = 15$ 12. correct   13. incorrect; $2x \le -15$ 14. incorrect; $-2 = -15 + n$ 15. incorrect; $-2 + x \le -7$ 16. correct

3-2. 1. $n - 2 = 10; n = 12$ 2. $3n = 12; n = 4$ 3. $10 + n = 4; n = -6$ 4. $-5 - n = -6; n = 1$ 5. $n + -2 = 1; n = 3$ 6. $-12 = 3 - n; 15 = n$ 7. $n + -9 = 15; n = 24$ 8. $-3n = 24; n = -8$ 9. $\frac{n}{-6} = -8; n = 48$ 10. $96 = 48n; n = 2$ 11. $2 - n = -39; n = 41$ 12. $\frac{41}{n} = 1; n = 41$ 13. $2 \times 41 = 82; 82 + 16 = 98; 98 + 2 = 100$

3-3. Equations may vary; possible answers include the following: 1. l = the length in inches; $2.5l = 15; l = 6$ 2. t = the time the train traveled in hours; $73t = 584; t = 8$ 3. w = the number of calories in a half cup of watermelon; $2w = 56; w = 28$ 4. a = Ann's present age; $a + 3 = 18; a = 15$ 5. t = the time in years; $36t = 396; t = 11$ 6. u = Uri's time in seconds; $u - 1.8 = 56.7; u = 58.5$ 7. t = the current temperature in degrees Fahrenheit; $t - 5 = 32; t = 37$ 8. w = the cost of the water; $w + 1.95 = 3.10; w = \$1.15$ 9. c = the cost of one CD; $1.5c = 22.5; c = \$15$ 10. d = Dad's present age; $14 = \frac{1}{3} d; d = 42$ 11. s = the cost of the stereo; $1.06s = 100.7; s = \$95$ 12. p = the original price; $0.8p = 68; p = \$85$

3-4. Answers may vary.

3-5. 1. 7° C   2. 32° C   3. 118° F   4. 28° C   5. 208° F   6. 32° F   7. 37° C   8. 83° F   9. 13° F   10. −11° F   11. 176° F   12. 100° F   13. 104° F   14. 50° F   15. 23° F   16. 190° C   17. 35° C   18. −11° C   19. 60° C   20. 45° C

3-6. T. $y = -6$ O. $x = 11$ L. $n = -175$ H. $c = -105$ S. $w = -5$ G. $u = -1$
M. $q = -16$ A. $s = -12$ I. $b = 1$ R. $d = -7$ The step-by-step methods of problem solving invented by al-Khwarizmi in the 1100s are called <u>algorithms</u>, a Latinized form of his name.

3-7. 1. $y = 10$ 2. $y = -64$ 3. $y = 1$ 4. $y = 7$ 5. $y = 12$ 6. $y = -2$ 7. $y = 1$
8. $y = 13$ 9. $y = 16$ 10. $y = 17$ 11. $y = 10$

3-8. Equations may vary; possible equations and their solutions follow.

1. b = the number of boys
    $b + 5$ = the number of girls
    $b + b + 5 = 35$
    $b = 15$

2. x = the amount saved each week
    $\$177 + 19x = \$500$
    $x = \$17$

3. l = the number of votes for the loser
    $l + 2{,}700$ = the number of votes for the winner
    $l + l + 2{,}700 = 13{,}300$
    $l = 5{,}300$ = loser
    $l + 2{,}700 = 8{,}000$

4. n = the number
    $10n + 24 = 74$
    $n = 5$

5. n = the number
    $\dfrac{n}{4} - 6 = 22$
    $n = 112$

6. n = the smaller number
    $n + 10$ = the larger number
    $n + n + 10 = 30$
    $n = 10$

7. n = the number
    $10(n - 8) = 50$
    $n = 13$

8. n = the number of shirts to be sold
    $(7 - 4.75)n = 1{,}179$
    $n = 524$

9.   r = René's age

      r − 17 = Jennifer's age

      r − 10 = Melissa's age

      r + r − 17 + r − 10 = 60

      r = 29

10.   n = the number

      $15 + 8{,}000 + 112 + 13 + 29 − 10 \times 524 = 17 \times 5 + n$

      $2929 = 85 + n$

      n = 2,844

3-9. 1. E = 6h; E = \$108   2. P = 4s; P = 60   3. C = \$1.29p; C ≈ \$3.23   4. D = 500n; D = 375   5. $e = 2\frac{3}{8}M$; M ≈ 41   6. M = 3.5t; M = 2,184   7. S = 0.8p; S ≈ \$12.79   8. S = 5n; S = 75   9. $S = \frac{2}{3}c$; $S = 4\frac{2}{3}$ 10. n = 220P; P ≈ 1

3-10. F. x = 12   M. x = 7   A. x = 36   S. x = 30   O. x = 2.4   N. x = 20   E. x = 0.25   R. x = −2.5   H. x = 3   G. x = 1.8   I. x = 11   T. x = 9   W. x = −11   The term "proportion" is taken from the Greek term "proportione," <u>meaning "for its own share."</u>

3-11. 1. 20%   2. 50   3. 12.5   4. 80   5. 40%   6. 64   7. 24   8. 7.2   9. 48%   10. 100%

3-12. 1. incorrect—The weekly salary was not added; correct answer is \$462.50.   2. correct   3. incorrect—The student found 8% of \$368,000; correct equation is 92% of n = 368,000 where n represents the selling price of the home, which should be \$400,000.   4. correct   5. incorrect— The student found 2.9 × \$250,000 instead of 0.029 × \$250,000; the correct answer is \$7,250.   6. incorrect—The student found 20% of 15 and subtracted the answer from 15; the correct equation is 0.8n = 15 where n represents the marked price, which is \$18.75.   7. incorrect—The student found 6% of \$14.31 and rounded to the nearest penny; the correct equation is 1.06n × \$14.31 where n is the cost of the bill without the tax. The cost is \$13.50.   8. correct   9. correct   10. incorrect—The student found 3% of \$3,179 but forgot to add this to the salary; the correct solution is 3% of \$3,179 plus \$275. The earnings were \$370.37.

3-13. 1. T, 6; W, 20   2. I, 27; C, 25   3. E, 8; T, 6   4. H, 24; E, 8   5. O, 16; R, 22   6. I, 27; G, 80   7. I, 27; N, 30   8. A, 150; L, 135   9. C, 25; O, 16   10. S, 18; T, 6   If the price increases 100%, then the new price is always <u>twice the original cost.</u>

3-14. 1. R, L = 2W + 1   2. O, W = 2L + 1   3. B, LW = 12   4. E, L = W   5. R, L = 2W + 1   6. T, L + W = 12   7. R, L = 2W + 1   8. E, L = W   9. C, W = L + 2   10. O, W = 2L + 1   11. R, L = 2W + 1   12. D, L = 2 + W   13. E, L = W   In 1557 <u>Robert Recorde</u> first used the "=" in the first algebra book written in English.

3-15. 1. P, –9   2. R, 1.5   3. L, 4   4. O, –0.5   5. B, 9   6. W, ø   7. N, 21   8. K, –1   9. U, –3   10. H, 1   11. A, –4   12. F, 0   13. V, 3   14. T, –5   15. E, –5.5   16. S, –2.6   In 1637 René Descartes used the first letters of the <u>alphabet for known values</u>.

3-16. Equations may vary; possible equations follow. 1. a + 5 = 40 – 4a; a = 7   2. 2(n + –6) = –6(n + 4); n = –1.5   3. 85p + 425 = 6,800; p = 75   4. 3b = b + 12; b = 6   5. 50 + 10w = 25 + 15w; w = 5   6. h = 16 + –h; h = 8   7. 2(10 + y) = 45 + y; y = 25   8. 6s + 10 = 82; s = 12   Two problems cannot be solved by writing equations with variables on both sides. Which ones? Problems 3 and 8.

3-17. 1. P   2. E   3. D   4. F   5. O   6. R   7. N   8. W   9. I   10. S   11. L   12. A   13. H   The first European mathematician to use the horizontal fraction bar as it is used today was <u>Leonard of Pisa who</u> is also known as Fibonacci.

3-18. 1. S   2. Y   3. M   4. B   5. O   6. L   7. H   8. E   9. N   10. O   11. T   12. I   13. C   14. E   15. D   Thomas Harriot (1560–1621) first used the ">" and "<" symbols in a work published posthumously in 1631. It is believed he developed these symbols from a marking he saw on an arm of a Native American. This was the <u>symbol he noticed</u>: ⋊⋉

3-19. 1. 8 + n ≥ 0; n ≥ –8; I   2. n – 7 < –6; n < 1; D   3. n + –4 > 15; n > 19; R   4. $\frac{3}{4}$n > –24; n > –32; L   5. –2n ≥ 12; n ≤ –6; S   6. 6 – 3n < 30; n > –8; U   7. 102 + 75 + 50 + n ≥ 300; n ≥ 73; N   8. 180 + 0.2n ≤ 300; n ≤ 600; K   9. 349 + n ≤ 500; n ≤ 151; Y   10. 30 · 20 < n; n < 600; A   11. (87 + 91 + 86 + n) ÷ 4 ≥ 90; n ≥ 96; E   12. 3 · 2 + 0.3n ≤ 15; n ≤ 30; Q   13. 2 · 50 + 2n ≥ 130; n ≥ 15; O   Your skills are unequalled.

3-20. All values are solutions except Problems 1 and 8. The numbers of the problems that have incorrect solutions begin <u>with a vowel</u>.

3-21. 1. x = 2; y = 4   2. x = 5; y = 1   3. x = –3; y = –1   4. x = –5; y = –2   5. x = 30; y = 6   6. x = 5; y = –6   7. x = –1; y = 7   8. x = –22; y = –33   9. x = –1; y = –5   10. x = 2; y = 10   11. x = 4; y = –1   <u>Diophantus of Alexandria</u> (c. 275) was an outstanding Greek mathematician who catalogued all the algebra the Greeks had achieved.

3-22.   1. l = the larger integer

s = the smaller integer

$s = \frac{2}{3}l$

l − s = 35

l = 105

2. c = the number of children's tickets sold

a = the number of adult tickets sold

c + a = 175

6a + 2c = 750

c = 75

3. l = the larger number

s = the smaller number

l − s = 40

6s − l = 5

l = 49

4. m = the number of miles

c = the total cost

18 + 0.15m = c

20 + 0.1m = c

m = 40

5. l = the length of the longer piece

s = the length of the shorter piece

l + s = 40

l = 9s

l = 36

6. l = the larger positive integer

s = the smaller positive integer

l = s + 18

2l + 3s = 86

l = 28

7. g = the number of girls

b = the number of boys

5g = 3b

3 + g = b − 3

b = 15

8. x = the number of workstations for two students

y = the number of workstations for three students

x + y = 16

2x + 3y = 38

x = 10

9. s = the number of students in the smaller group

l = the number of students in the larger group

2s + 2l = 26

l = s + 1

s = 6

10. y = the number of years

s = the total salary

$30,000 + $2,000y = s

$25,000 + $3,000y = s

y = 5

11. l = the length

w = the width

16 = 2l + 2w

w = l − 2

w = 3

12. h = the cost of a hamburger

s = the cost of a soda

7h + 3s = $19

8h + 2s = $19.50

h = $2.05

s = $1.55

Change is $1.40

<u>The answers are in descending order.</u>

3-23.

1. $\begin{bmatrix} 1 & 13 \\ 11 & 10 \end{bmatrix}$
2. $\begin{bmatrix} -9 & -6 \\ -1 & 0 \end{bmatrix}$
3. $\begin{bmatrix} 0 & 10 & 2 \\ 6 & 16 & 11 \end{bmatrix}$
4. $\begin{bmatrix} 7 & -3 & 1 \\ -10 & -4 & -4 \end{bmatrix}$

5. $\begin{bmatrix} 6 & 1 & 3 \\ 6 & 1 & 1 \\ 5 & 0 & 1 \end{bmatrix} + \begin{bmatrix} 3 & 0 & 0 \\ 4 & 0 & 1 \\ 4 & 0 & 1 \end{bmatrix} + \begin{bmatrix} 4 & 1 & 0 \\ 4 & 1 & 1 \\ 3 & 0 & 0 \end{bmatrix} + \begin{bmatrix} 4 & 1 & 1 \\ 5 & 0 & 1 \\ 3 & 0 & 1 \end{bmatrix} = \begin{bmatrix} 17 & 3 & 4 \\ 19 & 2 & 4 \\ 15 & 0 & 3 \end{bmatrix}$

3-24.

1. $[12]$
2. $\begin{bmatrix} -6 & 19 \\ -18 & 46 \end{bmatrix}$
3. $\begin{bmatrix} 0 & 2 \\ 4 & 5 \end{bmatrix}$
4. $\begin{bmatrix} 9 & 8 & 26 \\ 0 & -42 & 12 \end{bmatrix}$

5. $\begin{bmatrix} 4 & 2 & 4 \end{bmatrix} \times \begin{bmatrix} 6 \\ 3 \\ 1 \end{bmatrix} = [34]$

Identifying Solutions of Equations and Inequalities

A *solution* of an equation or inequality is a number, or numbers, that makes an equation or inequality true.

Directions: A number follows each equation or inequality below. Sometimes the number is a solution, but most often the number is not a solution. Identify the problems for which the number is not a solution by rewriting the equation or inequality so that the number is a solution. If the number is a solution, write "correct." The first one is done for you. Hint: The number of incorrect solutions > the number of correct solutions.

1. $y - 2 = 3$ $\{1\}$ _____ $3 - y = 2$ _____

2. $2k - 4 = -8$ $\{-2\}$ _____

3. $a \div 3 = -1$ $\{3\}$ _____

4. $c \div 0 = 5$ $\{0\}$ _____

5. $-n + 5 = 9$ $\{-4\}$ _____

6. $\frac{n}{12} = 3$ $\{4\}$ _____

7. $z - 2 < -4$ $\{-1\}$ _____

8. $z + 3 \geq -6$ $\{-9\}$ _____

9. $4x - 2 = 48$ $\{12.5\}$ _____

10. $x - (-2) = -11$ $\{-9\}$ _____

11. $-(a + 3) = 15$ $\{12\}$ _____

12. $1 - 3h > 4$ $\{-2\}$ _____

13. $2x < -15$ $\{-7.5\}$ _____

14. $-2 = -15 - n$ $\{13\}$ _____

15. $-2 - x \leq -7$ $\{-5\}$ _____

16. $17 - (-n) = 22$ $\{5\}$ _____

Writing and Solving One-Step Equations I

Accuracy is always important when writing and solving equations. It is particularly important in this activity, because each equation includes the answer to the previous problem.

Directions: Write and solve an equation for each set of clues below. Follow the steps in the last problem to determine your score.

1. 2 less than a number is 10. _____

2. The product of three times a number equals the answer to Problem 1.
   _____

3. The sum of 10 and a number equals the answer of Problem 2.
   _____

4. A number subtracted from negative 5 equals the answer to Problem 3.
   _____

5. The sum of a number and the opposite of 2 equals the answer to Problem 4.
   _____

6. −12 is equal to a number subtracted from the answer to Problem 5.
   _____

7. The sum of a number and −9 is equal to the answer of Problem 6.
   _____

8. −3 times a number equals the answer to Problem 7.
   _____

9. A number divided by −6 equals the answer to Problem 8.
   _____

10. 96 is the same as the answer to Problem 9 multiplied by a number.
    _____

11. If the answer to Problem 10 is decreased by this number, the result is −39.
    _____

12. The quotient of the answer to Problem 11 and a number equals 1.
    _____

13. To determine your score for this activity, double your answer to Problem 12, add 4^2, and add 2.

    Score = _____

Writing and Solving One-Step Equations II

Real-life situations can often be described in terms of mathematics. All of the problems in this activity relate to daily occurrences.

Directions: Identify the variable in each of the descriptions below. Write and solve an equation for each one.

1. The area of a rectangle is 15 square inches. The width is 2.5 inches. Find the length.

2. A train traveled 584 miles at an average rate of 73 miles per hour. How long was the train traveling?

3. A half cup of grapes contains 56 calories. This is twice the number of calories in a half cup of watermelon. How many calories are in a half cup of watermelon?

4. In three years, Ann will be 18 and will be able to vote. How old is Ann now?

5. By installing two storm doors that cost a total of $396, the Smiths estimate that they will save $36 per year on heating bills. In how many years will the savings equal the cost of the doors?

6. Manuel ran the 400-meter race in 56.7 seconds, which was 1.8 seconds faster than Uri. What was Uri's time?

Writing and Solving One-Step Equations II

7. If the temperature drops 5 degrees Fahrenheit, water will freeze. What is the temperature now?

   _____

8. Wayne was charged $3.10 for a school lunch. He ordered a sandwich and a bottle of spring water. The sandwich cost $1.95. Find the cost of the water.

   _____

9. A record store has a sale on CDs: Buy one and get another at half-price. The bill for two CDs came to $22.50. Assuming the original price of the two CDs is the same, find the cost of one CD.

   _____

10. Sue is 14, which is $\frac{1}{3}$ of her father's age. How old is Sue's father?

   _____

11. There is a 6% sales tax in New Jersey. A portable stereo, plus the sales tax, costs $100.70. Find the cost of the stereo.

   _____

12. An item on sale costs $68. This is 20% off the original price. What was the original price?

   _____

Algebra Teacher's Activities Kit

Copyright © 2003 John Wiley & Sons, Inc.

Creating Word Problems

Usually students are asked to solve word problems. For this activity, you are asked to *create and solve* word problems of your own.

Directions: Create four word problems according to the instructions below. Try to write them so that they apply to events or situations that occur in daily life. Then, for each one, write an equation and solve the problem.

1. To solve this equation, you must add a number to each side.

2. To solve this equation, you must subtract a number from both sides.

3. To solve this equation, you must multiply each side by an integer.

4. To solve this equation, you must divide each side of the equation by the same number.

Using Formulas for Finding Temperatures

James has a pen pal, Miguel, who lives in Portugal. Last summer, Miguel came to New York City to visit James. After James and his family picked up Miguel at the airport, Miguel mentioned that the weather was hot, at least 35°. James looked at Miguel with surprise and told him the temperature was at least 90°. Now it was Miguel's turn to look surprised. Suddenly the two boys realized what had happened. Miguel was thinking of temperature on the Celsius scale, while James was thinking of it on the Fahrenheit scale.

Fortunately, formulas make it easy to convert degrees from Celsius to Fahrenheit and Fahrenheit to Celsius, as shown below.

To convert temperatures from Celsius to Fahrenheit use either of these two formulas:

$$F = \frac{9C}{5} + 32 \qquad\qquad F = (C \times 1.8) + 32$$

To convert temperatures from Fahrenheit to Celsius use either of these two formulas:

$$C = \frac{(F - 32)}{9} \times 5 \qquad\qquad C = (F - 32) \div 1.8$$

Directions: Use the formulas above to convert the following degrees. Round your answers to the nearest degree if necessary.

1. 45° F to °C = _____   2. 90° F to °C = _____

3. 48° C to °F = _____   4. 82° F to °C = _____

5. 98° C to °F = _____   6. 0° C to °F = _____

7. 98.6° F to °C = _____   8. 28.5° C to °F = _____

9. –10.5° C to °F = _____   10. –23.8° C to °F = _____

Directions: Convert these Celsius readings to the Fahrenheit scale. Round your answers to the nearest degree if necessary.

11. 80° C (hot soup) = _____   12. 38° C (a warm bath) = _____

13. 40° C (a high fever) = _____   14. 10° C (a cool day) = _____

15. –5° C (a snowy day) = _____

Directions: Convert these Fahrenheit readings to the Celsius scale. Round your answers to the nearest degree if necessary.

16. 374° F (a hot oven) = _____   17. 95° F (a hot summer day) = _____

18. 12° F (frozen yogurt) = _____   19. 140° F (broiled steak) = _____

20. 113° F (a hot bath) = _____

Solving Multi-step Equations I

To solve multi-step equations, do the following:

1. Simplify first.
2. Add or subtract the same number to or from each side of the equation.
3. Multiply or divide both sides of the equation by the same non-zero number.

Directions: Solve each equation. Then write the letter of the problem above the solution at the end of the activity to complete the statement.

Work Space

T. $4y + 43 = 19$

O. $2x - 9 = 13$

L. $\frac{n}{5} + 25 = -10$

H. $\frac{3}{7}c + 45 = 0$

S. $5w - w = -20$

G. $u - 4u + 4 = 7$

M. $8(q + 7) = -72$

A. $-\frac{3}{2}(s - 2) = 21$

I. $2(b + 8) - 9 = 9$

R. $d + 4(d + 6) = -11$

The step-by-step methods of problem solving invented by al-Khwarizmi in the 1100s are

called ___ ___ ___ ___ ___ ___ ___ ___ ___ ___, a Latinized form of his name.
       −12 −175 −1   11   −7   1   −6 −105 −16 −5

Solving Multi-step Equations II

Solving multi-step equations requires concentration and accuracy.

Directions: A value for x is given for each equation. Solve for y so that the equation and solution are correct. Write the answers for y on the space after the problem.

1. $x = -5$ $\dfrac{x}{-5} + y = 11$ _____

2. $x = -4$ $9x + 7x = y$ _____

3. $x = -3$ $4(x - y) - 3x = -7$ _____

4. $x = -2$ $11 = y - 2x$ _____

5. $x = -1$ $x - 4x + y = 15$ _____

6. $x = 0$ $3x - 2 = y$ _____

7. $x = 1$ $5x + y = 6$ _____

8. $x = 2$ $y - 3x = 7$ _____

9. $x = 3$ $3x + 7 = y$ _____

10. $x = 4$ $7(x - 1) - x = y$ _____

11. $x = 5$ $0 = x + y - 3x$ _____

Algebra Teacher's Activities Kit

Copyright © 2003 John Wiley & Sons, Inc.

Writing and Solving Multi-step Equations

An important problem-solving skill is the ability to write and solve an equation that represents a problem or real-life situation. Part of any problem-solving strategy is to check your solutions.

Directions: Write and solve equations based on the information below. Be sure to check each solution.

1. How many boys are in a class of thirty-five students if the girls outnumber boys by five?

   _____

2. Manuel opened a savings account with an initial deposit of $177. If he wants to save $500 (not counting interest) during the next nineteen weeks, how much must he save each week?

   _____

3. In a recent election, the winning candidate had 2,700 more votes than the loser. If the total number of votes was 13,300, how many votes did the winner receive?

   _____

4. The sum of ten times a number and 24 is 74. What is the number?

   _____

5. The quotient of a number and 4 decreased by 6 is 22. Find the number.

   _____

6. One number is 10 more than another. If the sum of the two numbers is 30, what is the smaller of the two numbers?

   _____

Writing and Solving Multi-step Equations

7. If a number is decreased by 8 and the difference is multiplied by 10, this product is 50. Find the number.

   _____

8. The Valley View High School has decided to print their own T-shirts for various teams and clubs. The equipment necessary to print the shirts costs $1,179. The shirts cost $4.75 and will be sold for $7.00. How many shirts must be sold to cover the initial investment?

   _____

9. At a family reunion three cousins were comparing their ages. Jennifer is 17 years younger than René and René is 10 years older than Melissa. Their ages total 60 years. How old is René?

   _____

10. The sum of the answers to the odd-numbered problems decreased by the products of the answers to Problems 6 and 8 exceeds the product of the answers to Problems 2 and 4 by this amount. Find the amount.

    _____

Algebra Teacher's Activities Kit

Writing and Using Direct Variations

Direct variations are used every day. Buying notebooks for school is an example. One notebook costs $1.50, two cost $3.00, and three cost $4.50. The total cost varies directly with the cost of the notebooks. The equation that models this relationship is $C = 1.5n$ where C is the total cost and n is the number of notebooks.

> $y = kx$ is the general formula for expressing a direct variation between two quantities x and y. k is the constant, a non-zero number.

Directions: Write the equation that models each direct variation below. Then solve the equation. The first problem is done for you.

1. The earnings, E, are $6.00 per hour, h. Find the earnings if a student works 18 hours.

$$E = 6h$$
$$E = 6 \times 18$$
$$E = \$108$$

2. The perimeter, P, of a square is four times the length of a side, s. Find the perimeter if the sides are 15 inches long.

3. The cost, C, of apples is $1.29 per pound, p. Find the cost of 2.5 pounds of apples. Round your answer to the nearest cent.

4. A map scale shows that 1 inch on the map represents an actual distance of 500 miles. Let n equal the number of inches on a map. Find the actual distance, D, represented by $\frac{3}{4}$ inch.

Writing and Using Direct Variations

5. A person's weight on Earth would be about $2\frac{3}{8}$ times what he or she would weigh on Mars. Let e represent the weight of the person on Earth. Let M represent the weight of the same person on Mars. Find how much a 98-pound student on Earth would weigh on Mars. Round your answer to the nearest pound.

6. The total amount of money, M, collected at the door of a school play is the cost of a ticket times the number of tickets, t, that were sold. Each ticket sells for $3.50. Find the amount of money collected if 624 tickets were sold.

7. A record store has a special sale. All CDs are discounted 20%. The sale price, S, is 80% of the original price, p. Find the sale price of a CD that originally sold for $15.99. Round your answer to the nearest cent.

8. The total score, S, on a twenty-problem multiple-choice quiz is five times the number of correct answers, n. Find the score if fifteen problems are correct.

9. A recipe for three dozen cookies requires two cups of sugar. Let c equal the number of dozens of cookies and S equal the number of cups of sugar. Find the amount of sugar required to make seven dozen cookies.

10. One gallon of paint covers 220 square feet. Let P equal the number of gallon paint cans and let n equal the number of square feet. Find the number of paint cans needed to paint the ceiling of a 12×18 foot room.

Algebra Teacher's Activities Kit

Solving Proportions

A *proportion* is a statement that two ratios are equal. To solve a proportion write an equation stating that the cross products are equal, then solve the proportion.

Directions: Solve each proportion. Write the letter of the proportion above its solution at the end of the activity to complete the statement.

F. $\dfrac{1}{4} = \dfrac{x}{48}$ x = _____

M. $\dfrac{x}{4} = \dfrac{28}{16}$ x = _____

A. $\dfrac{8}{6} = \dfrac{x}{27}$ x = _____

S. $\dfrac{57}{95} = \dfrac{18}{x}$ x = _____

O. $\dfrac{3}{x} = \dfrac{5}{4}$ x = _____

N. $\dfrac{x}{4} = 5$ x = _____

E. $\dfrac{5}{2x} = 10$ x = _____

R. $-2 = \dfrac{4x}{5}$ x = _____

H. $\dfrac{9}{2x} = \dfrac{3}{2}$ x = _____

G. $\dfrac{4}{3} = \dfrac{12}{5x}$ x = _____

I. $\dfrac{x-5}{4} = \dfrac{3}{2}$ x = _____

T. $\dfrac{x-3}{8} = \dfrac{3}{4}$ x = _____

W. $\dfrac{1-4x}{5} = 9$ x = _____

The term "proportion" is taken from the Greek term "proportione,"

___ ___ ___ ___ ___ ___ ___   " ___ ___ ___   ___ ___ ___
7 0.25 36 20 11 20 1.8   12 2.4 −2.5   11   9   30

                    ___ ___ ___   ___ ___ ___ ___ ___."
                    2.4 −11 20   30   3   36 −2.5 0.25

Solving Simple Percent Problems

Proportions can be used to solve percent problems. Use the following formula:

$$\frac{percent}{100} = \frac{part}{base}$$

Directions: Solve each problem for the missing number. Check each answer before going on to the next problem.

1. What percent of 50 is 10? _____%

2. The answer to Problem 1 is 40% of what number? _____

3. What number is 25% of the answer to Problem 2? _____

4. Use the answer to Problem 3 as the percent. This percent of what number is 10? _____

5. The answer to Problem 4 is what percent of 200? _____%

6. 62.5% of what number is the answer to Problem 5? _____

7. What is 37.5% of the answer to Problem 6? _____

8. Use the answer to Problem 7 as the percent. Find this percent of 30. _____

9. The answer to Problem 8 is what percent of 15? _____%

10. The answer to Problem 9 is what percent of 48? _____%

Note: The answer to Problem 10 is your final score.

Solving Word Problems Involving Percents

Percents are used in countless everyday situations. Understanding percents and being able to solve problems are important skills in mathematics.

Directions: Ten problems and answers are provided. Some of the answers are incorrect. Solve each problem and compare your answer to the one provided. If the answer is correct, write "correct" on the line. If the answer is wrong, write "incorrect," explain why the original answer is wrong, and write the correct answer. Hint: 40% of the answers are correct.

1. Juan works in a sporting goods store for a salary of $450 per week, plus a 6% commission on his sales. One week his sales were $210. What was his income that week?

   $12.60 _____

   _____

2. How much money is saved by purchasing a mountain bike priced $320 at a 20% discount rather than one marked $320 with discounts of 10% and 10%?

   $3.20 _____

   _____

3. The Joneses wish to sell their home. They agree to pay the real estate agent 8% of the selling price. After they pay the commission, they need to have $368,000 left to be able to buy their new home. What must the selling price of their home be?

   $29,440 _____

   _____

4. Kara recently lost interest in tennis. She sold her $58 tennis racket to a friend at a 20% loss from the amount she originally paid for the racket. How much did Kara charge her friend for the tennis racket?

   $46.40 _____

   _____

Solving Word Problems Involving Percents

5. School taxes are 2.9% of the assessed value of property in the town of Centerville. Find the school tax on a home whose value is assessed at $250,000.

   $725,000 _____

   _____

6. John purchased a CD for $15 after receiving a discount of 20%. Find the original price of the CD.

   $12.00 _____

   _____

7. The sales tax in New Jersey is 6%. If the bill, including the tax, on a meal at a fast-food restaurant is $14.31, what is the cost of the meal without the tax?

   $0.86 _____

   _____

8. The population of Pleasant Lake is 51,736. This is 145% of what it was ten years ago. What was the population of Pleasant Lake ten years ago?

   35,680 _____

   _____

9. In a recent city election, 27,720 people out of 70,000 registered voters voted. What percent of the voters cast a ballot?

   39.6% _____

   _____

10. Mr. Wallace sells appliances and receives a salary of $275 per week, plus a 3% commission on all of his sales. Last week business was slow and his sales totaled $3,179. What were his total earnings for the week?

    $95.37 _____

    _____

Algebra Teacher's Activities Kit

Copyright © 2003 John Wiley & Sons, Inc.

Finding the Percent of Increase or Decrease

People refer to percents of increase and decrease every day. Some examples are raises in pay, increases in the cost of living, or increases or decreases in the prices of stocks.

When you must find the percent of increase or decrease, use the following formulas:

$$\text{Percent of Increase} = \frac{\text{increase}}{\text{original number}}$$
$$\text{Percent of Decrease} = \frac{\text{decrease}}{\text{original number}}$$

Directions: Complete the table below. Find your answers in the Answer Bank, then write your answers in the appropriate row. Round your answers to the nearest dollar or nearest percent. Read across each row and write each letter, in order, in the blanks at the end of the activity to complete the statement.

Original Price	New Price	Change	Percent of Change
1. $30	$24	$_____ decrease	_____% decrease
2. $36	$_____	$9 decrease	_____% decrease
3. $_____	$14	$_____ increase	75% increase
4. $_____	$16	$_____ decrease	33.$\overline{3}$% decrease
5. $72	$88	$_____ increase	_____% increase
6. $15	$_____	$12 increase	_____% increase
7. $90	$63	$_____ decrease	_____% decrease
8. $_____	$_____	$15 decrease	10% decrease
9. $_____	$9	$_____ decrease	64% decrease
10. $_____	$12	$_____ decrease	33.$\overline{3}$% decrease

Answer Bank

C. 25	O. 16	I. 27	G. 80	S. 18	E. 8	A. 150
R. 22	T. 6	N. 30	W. 20	L. 135	H. 24	

If the price increases 100%, then the new price is always ___ ___ ___ ___ ___

___ ___ ___   ___ ___ ___ ___ ___ ___ ___   ___ ___ ___ ___.

Writing Equivalent Equations

Equivalent equations are two or more equations that have the same solution. Since equivalent equations may be written in various forms, it is important to be able to identify which equations are, in fact, equivalent.

Directions: Write an equation for each statement. Find the equation in the Equation Bank on the next page. If you can't find the equation, try to write an equivalent equation and find this one in the Equation Bank. Then write the letters of the equations in the Equation Bank on the lines before the corresponding problems. When you are done, write the letters in order, starting with the first one, to complete the statement at the end of the activity. Some equations are used more than once; others are not used at all.

For Problems 1 through 5, let L stand for the length and W stand for the width of a rectangle.

1. _____ The length is one more than twice the width. _____

2. _____ The width is one more than twice the length. _____

3. _____ The area of a rectangle is twelve square units. _____

4. _____ A rectangle is a square. _____

5. _____ The length exceeds twice the width by one unit. _____

For Problems 6 through 10, let L stand for the number of games lost and W stand for the number of games won.

6. _____ The team played twelve games with no ties. _____

7. _____ The team lost one more than twice the number of games they won.

_____

8. _____ The team won half of the games they played. _____

9. _____ The wins exceeded the losses by two. _____

10. _____ The number of games won is one more than twice the number of losses.

_____

Algebra Teacher's Activities Kit

Copyright © 2003 John Wiley & Sons, Inc.

Writing Equivalent Equations

For Problems 11 through 13, let L stand for the number of "Lims" and W stand for the number of "Wams."

11. _____ One less than the number of Lims is twice the number of Wams.

_____

12. _____ There are two more Lims than Wams. _____

13. _____ The number of Lims and Wams are the same. _____

Equation Bank		
T. $L + W = 12$	D. $L = 2 + W$	A. $L = 2W - 1$
O. $W = 2L + 1$	E. $L = W$	B. $LW = 12$
I. $12 = 2L + 2W$	C. $W = L + 2$	R. $L = 2W + 1$

In 1557, ____ ____ ____ ____ ____ ____   ____ ____ ____ ____ ____ ____ ____ first used the "=" in the first algebra book written in English.

Solving Equations with Variables on Both Sides

Sometimes equations are written with variables on both sides of the equal symbol. In order to solve these types of equations, you must rewrite the equations so that the variables are on the same side of the equation.

Directions: Solve each equation below. Write the letter of the problem above its solution to complete the statement at the end of the activity.

P. $7x = x - 54$ U. $-8x - x = 24 - x$

R. $4x - 9 = 3 - 4x$ H. $-8 + 5x = 3x - 11 + 5x$

L. $x - 10 = -2x + 2$ A. $-13 + x = 4x + 23 + 6x$

O. $-1 + x = 7x + 2$ F. $3(2x - 1) + x = x - 3$

B. $3x - 7 = x + 11$ V. $4(3x - 5) - x = -x + 16$

W. $4x - 9 = 3 + 4x$ T. $2(1 - x) = 3(x + 9)$

N. $3(x - 7) = 2x$ E. $2(3 - 4x) = 4 + 4(6 - x)$

K. $9x = 3(x - 2)$ S. $9(2x + 3) = -36 - 27(x + 2)$

In 1637, René Descartes used the first letters of the

$\overline{}\ \overline{}\ \overline{}\ \overline{}\ \overline{}\ \overline{}\ \overline{}\ \overline{}\quad \overline{}\ \overline{}\ \overline{}$
$\ \ -4\ \ \ \ 4\ \ \ -9\ \ \ \ 1\ \ \ -4\ \ \ \ 9\ \ -5.5\ \ -5\ \ \ \ \ \ \ \ 0\ \ -0.5\ \ 1.5$

$\overline{}\ \overline{}\ \overline{}\ \overline{}\ \overline{}\quad \overline{}\ \overline{}\ \overline{}\ \overline{}\ \overline{}\ \overline{}.$
$\ \ -1\ \ \ 21\ \ -0.5\ \ \ \text{ø}\ \ \ 21\ \ \ \ \ \ \ \ 3\ \ \ -4\ \ \ \ 4\ \ \ -3\ \ -5.5\ -2.6$

Writing and Solving Equations with Variables on Both Sides

Writing and solving equations are important skills, not only in algebra but in other branches of mathematics. Some equations have variables only on one side of the equal symbol, while others have variables on both sides.

Directions: Write and solve an equation for each problem below. Use the given variable. Write the variable above its numerical value to complete the statement at the end of the activity. Be sure to answer the final question.

1. The area of a rectangle increased by 5 is equal to 40 decreased by 4 times the area. Let a stand for the area. Solve for a.

$$a = \text{_____}$$

2. Twice the sum of a number and –6 equals –6 times the sum of the number and 4. Let n stand for the number. Solve for n.

$$n = \text{_____}$$

3. The class officers sold bids for the prom for $85 per couple. At the end of the day the officers had collected $6,800, which included $425 they had started with. Let p stand for the number of prom bids that day. Solve for p.

$$p = \text{_____}$$

4. The Rams won three times the number of games as the Bears. The Lions won twelve more games than the Bears. The Rams and the Lions are both in first place, having won the same number of games. Let b equal the number of games the Bears won. Solve for b.

$$b = \text{_____}$$

Linear Equations and Inequalities

Writing and Solving Equations with Variables on Both Sides

5. Joe opens a savings account with $50 and then saves $10 each week. Jean opens a savings account with $25 and then saves $15 each week. Without including any interest the accounts earn, after how many weeks will the balances be equal? Let w stand for the number of weeks. Solve for w.

$$w = \underline{\hspace{2cm}}$$

6. What number is 16 more than its opposite? Let h stand for the number. Solve for h.

$$h = \underline{\hspace{2cm}}$$

7. Sunil is ten years old and his mother is forty-five. How long will it be before she is twice as old as he is? Let y stand for the number of years. Solve for y.

$$y = \underline{\hspace{2cm}}$$

8. Suzanne received 6 points for each question she answered correctly on a test. The 10-point extra-credit problem was also correct. Her total score was 82. Let s stand for the number of problems Suzanne answered correctly, not counting the bonus problem. Solve for s.

$$s = \underline{\hspace{2cm}}$$

T $\underline{\hspace{0.5cm}}$ o $\underline{\hspace{0.5cm}}$ ro $\underline{\hspace{0.5cm}}$ lem $\underline{\hspace{0.5cm}}$ c $\underline{\hspace{0.5cm}}$ $\underline{\hspace{0.5cm}}$ $\underline{\hspace{0.5cm}}$ ot $\underline{\hspace{0.5cm}}$ e $\underline{\hspace{0.5cm}}$ olved $\underline{\hspace{0.5cm}}$ $\underline{\hspace{0.5cm}}$
   5   75   6   12   7   −1.5 −1.5   6   12   6   25

$\underline{\hspace{0.5cm}}$ riti $\underline{\hspace{0.5cm}}$ g   equ $\underline{\hspace{0.5cm}}$ tio $\underline{\hspace{0.5cm}}$ $\underline{\hspace{0.5cm}}$ $\underline{\hspace{0.5cm}}$ it $\underline{\hspace{0.5cm}}$ v $\underline{\hspace{0.5cm}}$ ri $\underline{\hspace{0.5cm}}$ $\underline{\hspace{0.5cm}}$ le $\underline{\hspace{0.5cm}}$
  5   −1.5   7   −1.5   12   5   8   7   7   6   12

on $\underline{\hspace{0.5cm}}$ ot $\underline{\hspace{0.5cm}}$ $\underline{\hspace{0.5cm}}$ ide $\underline{\hspace{0.5cm}}$. $\underline{\hspace{0.5cm}}$ $\underline{\hspace{0.5cm}}$ ic $\underline{\hspace{0.5cm}}$ o $\underline{\hspace{0.5cm}}$ e $\underline{\hspace{0.5cm}}$?
     6   8   12   12   5   8   8   −1.5   12

Algebra Teacher's Activities Kit

Copyright © 2003 John Wiley & Sons, Inc.

Solving One-step Inequalities

The steps for solving an inequality are the same as the steps for solving an equation but *with one important difference*. When you multiply or divide both sides of an inequality by a negative number, you must change the direction of the inequality symbol.

Directions: Solve each inequality below. Find the solution in the Answer Bank and write the letter of the solution in the space before the inequality. When you are finished, write each letter above its problem number to complete the statement at the end of the activity.

1. _____ $n - 4 \geq 6$

2. _____ $n + 1 < 5$

3. _____ $n + 5 \leq -5$

4. _____ $2 + n < -13$

5. _____ $n - 3 > 5$

6. _____ $n + 1 \geq 7$

7. _____ $n - 4 > -2$

8. _____ $15n > 1,200$

9. _____ $-7n > 21$

10. _____ $2n \geq -30$

11. _____ $-5n > -40$

12. _____ $-\frac{5}{8}n > -50$

13. _____ $\frac{n}{2} \leq 3$

Answer Bank

O. $n > 8$

S. $n \geq -15$

H. $n \leq 6$

E. $n < 4$

W. $n > 80$

D. $n \leq -10$

F. $n < -15$

A. $n < 80$

N. $n > 2$

I. $n < -3$

P. $n \geq 10$

R. $n \geq 6$

L. $n < 8$

The first European mathematician to use the horizontal fraction bar as it is used today

was ___ ___ ___ ___ ___ ___ ___   ___ ___   ___ ___ ___ ___
     11 2   5   7 12   6   3   5   4   1   9 10 12

___ ___ ___ is also known as Fibonacci.
 8 13   5

Solving Multi-step Inequalities

The rules that apply to solving equations apply to solving inequalities as well. Follow these steps:

1. Simplify each side of the inequality.
2. Add or subtract.
3. Multiply or divide by any nonzero number.

If you multiply or divide both sides of the inequality by a negative number, you must change the direction of the inequality sign.

Directions: Solve each inequality. Find the solution in the Answer Bank and write the letter of the solution in the blank before the problem number. Then write the letters in order, starting with the first problem, in the blanks to complete the statement at the end of the activity. Some letters will be used more than once.

1. _____ $5x - 7x > 40$
2. _____ $6x - 5 > 11 - 2x$
3. _____ $-5x + 6 < 16$
4. _____ $5x - 4 - 6x \geq -10$
5. _____ $7 - 2x \geq 19$
6. _____ $\frac{-x}{3} + 5 < -2$
7. _____ $8x - 7x \geq 0$
8. _____ $2(4 - x) - 2 \leq -2x + 6$
9. _____ $3 - \frac{2}{5}x > 5$
10. _____ $4x + 6 \leq 2x - 6$
11. _____ $3x - 2(x - 4) > 7$
12. _____ $4(3x - 1) \geq 2(x + 3)$
13. _____ $2(x - 6) > 2x - 2$
14. _____ $3(5 - x) - 7 \geq -3x + 8$
15. _____ $7x - (9x + 1) > -5$

Answer Bank
H. $x \geq 0$
E. all real numbers
Y. $x > 2$
C. $\emptyset$
B. $x \leq 6$
L. $x > 21$
I. $x \geq 1$
S. $x < -20$
O. $x \leq -6$
M. $x > -2$
D. $x < 2$
N. $x < -5$
T. $x > -1$

Thomas Harriot (1560–1621) first used the ">" and "<" symbols in a work published posthumously in 1631. It is believed he developed these symbols from a marking he saw on an arm of a Native American. This was the

___ ___ ___ ___ ___ ___   ___ ___

___ ___ ___ ___ ___ ___ ___:

Algebra Teacher's Activities Kit

Writing and Solving Inequalities

Writing and solving an inequality often involves problem-solving skills. It also requires clear thinking and accurate work.

Directions: Let n represent the missing number or quantity in each of the problems that follow. Write and solve an inequality for each one. Find your solution in the Answer Bank on the next page and write the letter of the answer in the space beɪore the pɪ ɔb-lem. Then write the letters above their problem numbers in the blanks to complete the statement at the end of the activity. Some of the solutions will not be used.

1. _____ 8 more than a number is greater than or equal to 0. Find the number.

2. _____ A number decreased by 7 is less than –6. Find the number.

3. _____ The sum of a number and –4 is greater than 15. Find the number.

4. _____ $\frac{3}{4}$ of a number is greater than –24. Find the number.

5. _____ –2 times a number is greater than or equal to 12. Find the number.

6. _____ 6 minus 3 times a number is less than 30. Find the number.

7. _____ Prior to making deposits of $75 and $50, Marian had a balance of $102 in her checking account. How much must she deposit so that her balance will be at least $300 and she can avoid a service fee?

8. _____ A local car rental agency charges $180 per week plus $0.20 per mile. How far can a person drive with the weekly fee remaining less than or equal to $300?

Writing and Solving Inequalities

9. _____ A plumber estimates that the parts and labor needed to install a new hot water heater will be no more than $500. Find the cost of the labor if the hot water heater costs $349.

10. _____ The Simones are planning to build a deck running thirty feet along the length of their house. The width must be less than twenty feet. What is the area of the deck?

11. _____ Alicia needs a test average of at least 90 to get an "A" this marking period in math. Her three test grades are 87, 91, and 86. What score must she get on her fourth test to receive at least a 90 for the marking period?

12. _____ The Student Council of Rivermont High is advertising its annual garage sale in a local newspaper. The first three lines of the ad cost $2 per line. After that the fee is $0.30 per word. The council members know that they will need more than three lines. How many additional words can they use if they are to stay within their budget of $15 for the ad?

13. _____ A rectangular dog run is being constructed so that Dexter, the family pooch, will have an enclosed area in which to romp. The length of the dog run is 50 feet. Find the width so that the perimeter is at least 130 feet.

Answer Bank				
D. $n < 1$	B. $n \geq -6$	I. $n \geq -8$	N. $n \geq 73$	U. $n > -8$
Y. $n \leq 151$	S. $n \leq -6$	K. $n \leq 600$	A. $n < 600$	L. $n > -32$
Q. $n \leq 30$	R. $n > 19$	E. $n \geq 96$	O. $n \geq 15$	

$\overline{}\ \overline{}\ \overline{}\ \overline{}\quad \overline{}\ \overline{}\ \overline{}\ \overline{}\ \overline{}\ \overline{}\quad \overline{}\ \overline{}\ \overline{}$
  9 13   6   3   5   8   1   4   4   5   10   3   11

$\overline{}\ \overline{}\ \overline{}\ \overline{}\ \overline{}\ \overline{}\ \overline{}\ \overline{}\ \overline{}\ \overline{}$.
  6   7   11 12   6   10   4   4   11   2

Verifying Solutions of Systems of Linear Equations

A *system of linear equations* is a group of two or more equations, each containing a variable. A *solution of a system of equations* refers to the values of the variables that make each equation of the system a true statement.

Directions: Determine whether the values of the variables are solutions to the system of equations. If they are solutions, circle the letter in the "Yes" column. If the values are not solutions, circle the letter in the "No" column. Then write the letters you have circled in order, starting with the first one, in the blanks to complete the statement at the end of the activity.

Are the values a solution?

	Yes	No
1. $4x + 3y = 8$ $3x + y = 0$ $x = -1, y = 4$	S	W
2. $7x = 12 - 3y$ $y = 2x - 9$ $x = 3, y = -3$	I	O
3. $y = 4x$ $x + y = 20$ $x = 4, y = 16$	T	O
4. $x - 2y = 0$ $x + 2y = 12$ $x = 6, y = 3$	H	N
5. $3x - 8y = 7$ $x + 2y = -7$ $x = -3, y = -2$	A	W
6. $2x + 3y = 12$ $3x + 2y = 13$ $x = 3, y = 2$	V	I

Linear Equations and Inequalities

Verifying Solutions of Systems of Linear Equations

7. $2x + 5y = 9$
   $3x - 2y = 4$ O   L
   $x = 2, y = 1$

8. $2x + y = 6$
   $3x - 2y = 2$ L   W
   $x = 3, y = 0$

9. $4x - z = 7$
   $8x + 5y - z = 0$
   $-x - y + 5z = 6$ E   N
   $x = 2, y = -3, z = 1$

10. $x - 2y + 3z = 7$
    $2x + y + z = 4$
    $-3x + 2y - 2z = -10$ L   E
    $x = 2, y = -1, z = 1$

The numbers of the problems that have incorrect solutions begin

___ ___ ___ ___   ___   ___ ___ ___ ___ ___.

Algebra Teacher's Activities Kit

Solving Systems of Linear Equations

A *system of linear equations* is a group of two or more equations, each containing a variable. There are several ways to solve systems of linear equations, including: substitution, the addition-or-subtraction method, and multiplication with the addition-or-subtraction method.

Directions: Solve each system of equations. Write your answer in the space provided. Find the answer in the Answer Bank, then write the letter of the answer before the problem. Be sure to write the letter that corresponds to the x value first. Some answers will be used more than once. When you are finished, write the letters in order, starting with the first one, on the blanks to complete the statement at the end of the activity.

1. _____ $y = x + 2$ $x =$ _____
   _____ $y = 3x - 2$ $y =$ _____
2. _____ $x + y = 6$ $x =$ _____
   _____ $x - 4 = y$ $y =$ _____
3. _____ $8x + 3y = -27$ $x =$ _____
   _____ $2x - 3y = -3$ $y =$ _____
4. _____ $2x = 5y$ $x =$ _____
   _____ $3y + x = -11$ $y =$ _____
5. _____ $x - 4y = 6$ $x =$ _____
   _____ $x - 2y = 18$ $y =$ _____
6. _____ $3x - y = 21$ $x =$ _____
   _____ $2x + y = 4$ $y =$ _____
7. _____ $8x + 3y = 13$ $x =$ _____
   _____ $3x + 2y = 11$ $y =$ _____
8. _____ $8x - 5y = -11$ $x =$ _____
   _____ $3y = 4x - 11$ $y =$ _____
9. _____ $y = 3x - 2$ $x =$ _____
   _____ $x - y = 4$ $y =$ _____
10. _____ $x - y = -8$ $x =$ _____
    _____ $x + y = 12$ $y =$ _____
11. _____ $5x + 3y = 17$ $x =$ _____
    _____ $2x - 3y = 11$ $y =$ _____

Answer Bank
H. –3
E. –22
P. 1
F. –6
D. 2
A. –1
O. 5
R. 10
I. 4
T. –2
X. –33
S. 6
L. 7
N. –5
U. 30

___ ___ ___ ___ ___ ___ ___ ___ ___ ___ ___ ___   ___ ___

___ ___ ___ ___ ___ ___ ___ ___ ___ ___ (c. 275) was an outstanding Greek mathematician who catalogued all of the algebra the Greeks had achieved.

Solving Word Problems by Writing Systems of Equations

Practical applications for solving systems of equations range from making decisions about selecting jobs to renting cars to completing number puzzles. The problems that follow offer some examples.

Directions: Each problem can be solved by writing a system of equations. Identify the variables, write the equations, and solve them. If you follow the directions closely, you will notice a pattern in your answers.

1. Find the larger of two positive integers if one is $\frac{2}{3}$ of the other and their difference is 35.

2. Movie tickets at a local theater cost $6 for adults and $2 for children under twelve. If 175 tickets were sold, with cash receipts of $750, how many children's tickets were sold?

3. The difference of two numbers is 40. Six times the smaller one minus the larger one is 5. Find the larger number.

4. Car-4-Hire charges $18 per day plus 15¢ per mile for the rental of a standard car. The same type of car at U-Rent-It costs $20 per day plus 10¢ per mile. What mileage results in equal rental charges for both cars?

5. A forty-foot rope was cut into two pieces. The length of one piece is 9 times the length of the other. What is the length of the longer piece?

6. One positive integer is 18 more than a second positive integer. If the sum of twice the greater and three times the smaller is 86, find the larger integer.

Solving Word Problems by Writing Systems of Equations

7. The ratio of boys to girls at a school dance was 5:3. There would have been an equal number of boys and girls if there had been three more girls and three fewer boys. How many boys were at the dance?

8. A chemistry lab can be used by 38 students at one time. The lab has 16 workstations, some set up for two students each and the others set up for three students each. How many workstations accommodate two students?

9. For a mathematics project, 26 students were divided into four groups. Two groups had the same number of students. The other two groups each had one more student than the smaller groups. How many students were in the smaller group?

10. When she graduated from college, Regina was offered two jobs. One paid a starting salary of $30,000 annually, plus guaranteed increases of $2,000 per year. The other paid a starting salary of $25,000 annually, plus guaranteed increases of $3,000 per year. After how many years would the salaries be equal?

11. The perimeter of a rectangle is 16 feet. The width is 2 feet less than the length. Find the width.

12. If you buy 7 hamburgers and 3 sodas at a local fast-food restaurant, you receive $1 in change from a $20 bill. If you buy 8 hamburgers and 2 sodas, you receive $0.50 in change from a $20 bill. How much change will you receive from a $5 bill if you buy 1 hamburger and 1 soda?

What is the pattern? _____

_____

Adding and Subtracting Matrices

A *matrix* is a rectangular array of numbers. A matrix that has m rows and n columns is an m × n matrix. This is called the order of the matrix. Matrices may only be added or subtracted if the order is the same.

To add matrices, add corresponding entries.

To subtract matrices, subtract corresponding entries.

Directions: Add or subtract the matrices below.

1. $\begin{bmatrix} 2 & 4 \\ 3 & 6 \end{bmatrix} + \begin{bmatrix} -1 & 9 \\ 8 & 4 \end{bmatrix} =$

2. $\begin{bmatrix} -6 & -5 \\ 1 & 4 \end{bmatrix} - \begin{bmatrix} 3 & 1 \\ 2 & 4 \end{bmatrix} =$

3. $\begin{bmatrix} 3 & 2 & 1 \\ 4 & 6 & 0 \end{bmatrix} + \begin{bmatrix} -3 & 8 & 1 \\ 2 & 10 & 11 \end{bmatrix} =$

4. $\begin{bmatrix} 4 & 1 & 3 \\ -2 & -8 & 6 \end{bmatrix} - \begin{bmatrix} -3 & 4 & 2 \\ 8 & -4 & 10 \end{bmatrix} =$

5. The top of the order of a baseball team had the following statistics for the four games they played this week:

	At Bats	Runs	Hits	At Bats	Runs	Hits
		Game 1			Game 2	
Batter 1	6	1	3	3	0	0
Batter 2	6	1	1	4	0	1
Batter 3	5	0	1	4	0	1
		Game 3			Game 4	
Batter 1	4	1	0	4	1	1
Batter 2	4	1	1	5	0	1
Batter 3	3	0	0	3	0	1

Express the statistics for each game as a matrix. Then find the sum. Use the space below or the back of this sheet for your answers.

Algebra Teacher's Activities Kit

Multiplying Matrices

A *matrix* is a rectangular array of numbers. The purpose of a matrix is to organize information so that the data is easier to use. Matrices can be multiplied only if the number of columns in the first matrix is the same as the number of rows in the second matrix.

To multiply two matrices, multiply the numbers in each row in the first matrix by the corresponding numbers in the column of the second matrix and add the products. Multiplication is not commutative.

Directions: Multiply each matrix.

1. $[3 \quad 6] \times \begin{bmatrix} 2 \\ 1 \end{bmatrix} =$

2. $\begin{bmatrix} 1 & 3 \\ 4 & 6 \end{bmatrix} \times \begin{bmatrix} -3 & 4 \\ -1 & 5 \end{bmatrix} =$

3. $\begin{bmatrix} 2 & 0 \\ 1 & 4 \end{bmatrix} \times \begin{bmatrix} 0 & 1 \\ 1 & 1 \end{bmatrix} =$

4. $\begin{bmatrix} 2 & 5 \\ 3 & -6 \end{bmatrix} \times \begin{bmatrix} 2 & -6 & 8 \\ 1 & 4 & 2 \end{bmatrix} =$

5. Organize the following into two matrices. Then find the product. Hint: Let one matrix be the number of each type of score and the other be the number of points for each type of score.

   At a recent football game a running back scored 2 touchdowns, the place kicker kicked 2 field goals and 4 extra points, a wide receiver scored 1 touchdown, and a defensive cornerback scored 1 touchdown on an intercepted pass. All points were scored for the home team. (A touchdown is worth 6 points, a field goal is worth 3 points, and an extra point is worth 1 point.)

Linear Equations and Inequalities

Graphing Linear Equations and Inequalities

Recognizing the connections between equations and their graphs is an important skill not only in algebra but in more advanced mathematics as well. It is also useful in understanding and solving real-life problems, a common example being the interpretation of graphs in newspapers and magazines.

This section covers graphing linear equations and inequalities. Starting with the number line and graphing solutions of equations and inequalities with one variable, the fifteen activities of the section include graphing solutions of combined equations and inequalities, graphing the equation of a line on the coordinate plane, graphing inequalities with two variables, and systems of equations and inequalities.

Teaching Suggestions for the Activities

4-1 Graphing the Solutions of Equations and Inequalities on a Number Line

Graphing is a vital skill for students. An understanding of the basic concepts of graphing enables them to visualize numbers and interpret relationships.

Begin the activity by discussing the number line. Note that number lines do not end; they continue in both directions infinitely. Also note that each point on a number line is paired with one number, called the coordinate.

Go over the guidelines for graphing equations and inequalities that are included on the worksheet. Emphasize that inequalities such as –3 < x can be rewritten as x > –3, resulting in a form that is consistent with direction. Depending on the abilities of your students, you may feel it is necessary to provide some examples. You may ask students to complete simple graphs on the board or an overhead projector.

Review the instructions on the worksheet with your students. Note that each graph will be used once, and remind them that they must answer the question.

4-2 Graphing the Solutions of Combined Inequalities on the Number Line

For this activity your students are required to graph the solutions of conjunctions and disjunctions and solve combined inequalities. Before attempting this activity, your students should be able to solve inequalities and graph the solutions on a number line.

Begin the activity by discussing the two types of combined inequalities: conjunctions and disjunctions. Review the definitions of these terms on the worksheet. If necessary, offer examples of solutions showing the empty set, such as x > 2 and x < 0, and examples showing the solution as all real numbers, such as x > 2 or x < 3.

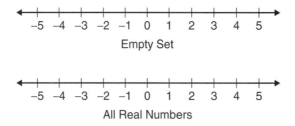

Next discuss solving combined inequalities, being sure to note how to form two inequalities by rewriting the combined inequalities. For example, –2 < x – 8 < 10 can be rewritten as –2 < x – 8 and x – 8 < 10. Also, review the process for solving inequalities, reminding your students to change the direction of the inequality symbol when they divide both sides by a negative number.

Finally, review the instructions on the worksheet with your students. Note that each graph is used only once.

4-3 Graphing Points on the Coordinate Plane

For this activity your students will graph and connect points on a coordinate plane to create an optical illusion. Students will need graph paper and rulers to complete the activity. Be sure to have extra graph paper on hand.

Begin the activity by discussing the coordinate plane with your students. Depending on the abilities of your students, you may wish to review the procedures for plotting points and then graph some points as examples on the board or an overhead projector.

Go over the directions on the worksheet, noting there are two parts to the activity. For the first part, students are to graph the points and use a ruler to connect the points, starting with A and returning to A. For the second part, they are to follow the steps. The result, if plotted correctly, will be an optical illusion.

4-4 Finding the Slope and Y-intercept from a Graph

In this activity eight lines are graphed on a coordinate plane. Your students must identify the slope and y-intercept of each line.

Begin the activity by defining the slope and y-intercept of a line, which are noted on the worksheet. Explain that the slope of a line may be determined in various ways, one of which is to choose any two points. Suggest that students choose the y-intercept, then select another point where the line intersects the points where the grids cross.

Discuss the example on the worksheet. Note that "up" is positive, "down" is negative, "right" is positive, and "left" is negative. Remind your students to move up or down first, then right to left. Also note that any fractions should be simplified but should not be expressed as mixed numbers.

Go over the instructions on the worksheet with your students. Make sure that they find the slope first, then find the y-intercept.

4-5 Using the Slope and Y-intercept to Graph a Line

This activity requires your students to graph lines, given the slope and y-intercept. Students will need graphing paper and rulers to complete this activity.

Start the activity by reviewing the concept of the slope of a line and the y-intercept. Note that when discussing slope and y-intercept, "m" stands for slope and "b" represents the y-intercept. Students should always start from the y-intercept, then move up or down, then right or left, depending on the slope. Mention that the slope should be expressed as a fraction to help them move up or down. For example, if the slope equals 2, it should be written as $\frac{2}{1}$.

Go over the instructions on the worksheet with your students. Caution them to carefully connect each pair of points with a straight line that extends to the end of the grid. Remind your students to write the letters of the points in the space after the problem numbers. Ten abbreviations will be revealed, although the letters of some abbreviations may need to be switched.

4-6 Finding the Slope of a Line

This activity requires your students to determine the slope of a line when given two points on a line and the equation of a line in slope-intercept and standard form. To complete this activity successfully, your students should be familiar with these forms and be able to transform equations.

Begin the activity by explaining that students can determine the slope of a line without graphing, provided they are given two points. Discuss the formulas and equations included on the worksheet. Emphasize that 0 divided by any number is 0, and that any number divided by 0 is undefined. This is represented by the ø symbol.

Review the instructions on the worksheet with your students. Note that while some numbers are not used, others are used more than once.

4-7 Finding the X- and Y-intercepts

The focus of this activity is to find the x- and y-intercepts, given the equation of a line expressed in various forms. To complete this activity successfully, your students should have a basic understanding of graphing linear equations.

Introduce the activity by discussing the x- and y-axes. Note that the "y value" of any point on the x-axis is 0, and that the "x value" of any point on the y-axis is 0. Offer the following examples on the board or an overhead projector.

$$y = 2x + 10$$

To find where the graph of this line crosses the x-axis, let y = 0 and solve for x.

$$0 = 2x + 10$$
$$x = -5$$

The x-intercept is –5.

To find where the graph of the line crosses the y-axis, let x = 0 and solve for y.

$$y = 2 \times 0 + 10$$
$$y = 10$$

The y-intercept is 10.

Explain that the graph of x = a constant value is a vertical line and has no y-intercept (unless x = 0). The graph of y = a constant value is a horizontal line and has no x-intercept (unless y = 0).

Review the instructions on the worksheet with your students. Note that some numbers will be used more than once, but others will not be used at all.

4-8 Using the X- and Y-intercepts to Graph a Line

For this activity your students are to graph the equation of a line given the x- and y-intercepts. Your students will need a ruler and a sheet of graph paper, although it is prudent to have extra graph paper available.

Start the activity by reviewing the procedure to graph the equation of a line, given two points. Discuss the examples on the worksheet, emphasizing that the value of the y-coordinate on the x-axis is 0, and the value of the x-coordinate on the y-axis is 0.

Go over the instructions on the worksheet. Remind your students to extend the lines to the end of the graph paper, then identify the shapes they see. Encourage them to find as many as they can and justify their responses.

4-9 Writing the Equation of a Line When Given Two Points

Your students will write equations in slope-intercept form or standard form for this activity. To complete the activity successfully, your students should be able to find the slope and transform equations.

Introduce the activity by asking your students to find the slope of a line that includes the points (3,8) and (5,2). Write this example on the board or an overhead projector: $m = \frac{6}{-2} = -3$. Instruct your students to choose one of the two points (it doesn't matter which one) and substitute the values for x, y, and m into the equation $y = mx + b$ and solve for b. $b = 17$. Now substitute for m and b and get $y = -3x + 17$. This can also be expressed in standard form as $3x + y = 17$.

Also note that if the slope is 0, the line is horizontal and the form is $y = $ a number. If there is no slope, the line is vertical and the form is $x = $ a number.

Go over the instructions on the worksheet with your students. Explain that the equations may be written in slope-intercept form or standard form. All equations will be used once.

4-10 Writing About Graphs of Lines

This activity requires your students to compare and contrast the lines on a grid. It serves as a fine review for the study of graphing linear equations.

Begin the activity by discussing the meaning of comparing and contrasting. Comparing, in the case of lines and graphs, means to identify the ways lines and graphs are the same. Contrasting means to state the differences.

Review the directions on the worksheet with your students. You might offer some suggestions for comparison and contrast, including slopes, x-intercepts, y-intercepts, points of intersection, parallelism, and perpendicularity.

4-11 Determining Whether Data Suggests a Line

In this activity your students are required to graph data and decide whether the points resemble a line. Graph paper and rulers are needed for the activity.

Begin the activity by explaining that graphs may take many forms. You may find it helpful to refer to various examples in your students' math texts, magazines, or newspapers. Note that among line graphs there is much variation. Some line graphs show an increase in data; others show a decrease. Some may be used for comparison of data, while the purpose of still others is to identify trends. Also discuss scale and mention that the scales of graphs vary.

Go over the directions on the worksheet with your students. Remind them to graph each set of data on a separate graph. Stress the importance of selecting the appropriate scale for their graphs.

4-12 Finding the Equation of the Line of Best Fit

This activity requires your students to make a scattergram by plotting sets of data, draw the line of best fit, and find the equation of the line they have drawn. They will need a ruler and enough graph paper to draw three graphs. Extra graph paper should be available. To complete this activity successfully, your students should have completed Activity 4-11, because the first problem of that activity is used as the introduction to this activity.

Begin this activity by reviewing the first problem of Activity 4-11. Students were to have determined whether the data suggested a line. You may find it helpful to list the points of the problem on the board or an overhead projector and have your students plot them on graph paper. Instruct your students to use rulers to draw a line of best fit. (This is the line that is suggested by the data.) Next, ask them to select any two points on the line they have drawn to find the equation of the line. Answers may vary, depending on how accurately they have drawn their lines. One answer is $y = 50x$.

Review the directions on the worksheet with your students. Note that all sets of data will suggest a line. Encourage your students to be accurate in plotting points, drawing lines, and writing the equations. Note that the third problem also requires students to analyze the data and find the exact equation of the line.

4-13 Graphing Inequalities on the Coordinate Plane

For this activity your students will graph four inequalities on the coordinate plane and then answer questions about the graphs. Each student will need one sheet of graph paper and a ruler, although you should have extra graph paper available. To complete this activity successfully, your students should be able to graph lines on the coordinate plane.

Begin the activity by explaining the similarities and differences between the graphs of inequalities and the graphs of equations. They all have a slope and y-intercept, but the graphs of inequalities are sometimes dotted and their solutions include a half-plane, whereas the solutions of equations are always solid lines. Offer these examples.

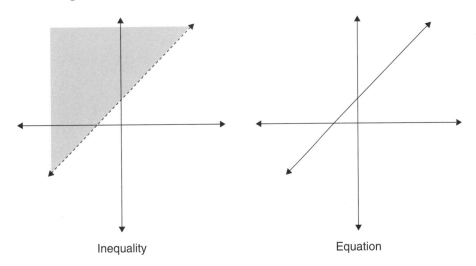

Inequality   Equation

Discuss the procedure for graphing inequalities, which is included on the worksheet. Depending on the abilities of your students, you may want to offer some examples on the board or an overhead projector.

Review the instructions on the worksheet with your students. Note that they are to graph each of the four inequalities listed on the sheet on its own graph. Emphasize that they will refer to the finished graphs as they answer the questions.

4-14 Solving Systems of Equations by Graphing

In this activity your students are required to graph systems of equations to find solutions. Students will need enough graph paper to draw nine small graphs; they will, of course, also need rulers. To complete this activity successfully, your students should be able to graph the equation of a line.

Start the activity by writing the following equations on the board or an overhead projector:

$$y = 3x + 1 \qquad 3x + y = 1$$

Graph the equations of each line on the same axes. Note that both lines intersect at (0,1). Explain that this is a solution to the system of equations. Instruct your students to verify this by substituting the values in each equation. Note that some systems have no solution, for example, those whose graphs are parallel lines. Other systems have a solution set of all real numbers, an example being those whose graphs are the same line.

Go over the instructions on the worksheet with your students. Remind them to draw accurate graphs.

4-15 Solving Systems of Inequalities by Graphing

Visualization is an important ability in recognizing spatial relationships. In this activity your students will be asked to match the solutions of systems of inequalities with a tan or combination of tans (pieces of a tangram) pictured on the worksheet. When your students find the solution of the systems of inequalities, the solution will match one of the shapes or a combination of shapes.

To complete this activity successfully, your students should be able to graph the solution of a linear inequality and the solution of systems of equations. They will need graph paper and a ruler.

Introduce the activity by graphing the solution of a linear inequality such as $x + y > 5$ on the board or an overhead projector. First graph the line $y = -x + 5$. Then graph $y > -x + 5$ by making the line dashed or broken. Choose any point not on the line and shade that portion of the plane that makes the inequality true. Extend this concept to graphing the solution of a system of inequalities by graphing the inequalities on the same axes. The overlap of the regions is the solution.

Review the instructions on the worksheet with your students. Note that they must draw the graphs and then match their solutions with a geometric shape or shapes.

Answer Key for Section 4

4-1. 1. E   2. P   3. F   4. G   5. A   6. N   7. H   8. O   9. R   10. T   11. L   The graph of one type of inequality has exactly one solution less <u>than the graph of all</u> real numbers. <u>The inequality is x ≠ a number.</u>

4-2. 1. E   2. R   3. L   4. I   5. S   6. C   7. X   8. N   9. Y   10. P   11. T   12. A   Thomas Harriot (1560-1621) first used the ">" and "<" symbols in <u>Artis Analyticae Praxis</u>, published in 1631.

4-3.

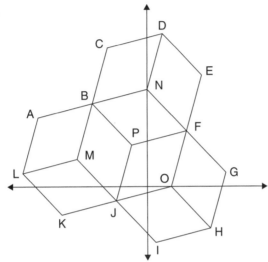

4-4.   Line 1, slope = –1; y-intercept = 5   Line 2, slope = $\frac{1}{2}$; y-intercept = 0
Line 3, slope = 2; y-intercept = –3   Line 4, slope = –1; y-intercept = –5
Line 5, slope = 2; y-intercept = 7   Line 6, slope = –3; y-intercept = 4
Line 7, slope = 2; y-intercept = –5   Line 8, slope = $-\frac{1}{2}$; y-intercept = –1
<u>Slope is defined</u> as rise over run.

4-5. 1. DE, Delaware   2. PA, Pennsylvania   3. NJ, New Jersey   4. GA, Georgia   5. CT, Connecticut   6. MA, Massachusetts   7. MD, Maryland   8. SC, South Carolina   9. NH, New Hampshire   10. VA, Virginia   These states, in order, are the first ten states to enter the Union. (The names of each state are not required for the students' answers; they are included for your information.)

4-6. 1. O, 0   2. U, $-\frac{3}{5}$ 3. G, 3   4. H, –1   5. T, $-\frac{1}{3}$ 6. R, –2   7. E, 6   8. D, ø
9. H, –1   10. E, 6   11. R, –2   12. I, $\frac{1}{4}$ 13. G, 3   14. O, 0   15. N, $\frac{3}{2}$
16. E, 6   William <u>Oughtred</u> first used the symbol for parallel and Pierre <u>Herigone</u> first used the symbol for perpendicular.

4-7. 1. S, $x = -2$; A, $y = 4$ 2. M, $x = -\frac{1}{3}$; E, $y = 1$ 3. S, $x = -2$; L, $y = 6$
4. O, $x = 24$; P, $y = -6$ 5. E, $x = 1$; B, $y = -5$ 6. U, $x = 7$; T, $y = \emptyset$
7. D, $x = -36$; I, $y = 12$ 8. F, $x = 0$; F, $y = 0$ 9. E, $x = 1$; R, $y = -\frac{1}{2}$
10. E, $x = 1$; N, $y = -3$ 11. T, $x = \emptyset$; Y, $y = 15$ Parallel lines have the
<u>same slope but different y-intercepts</u>.

4-8.

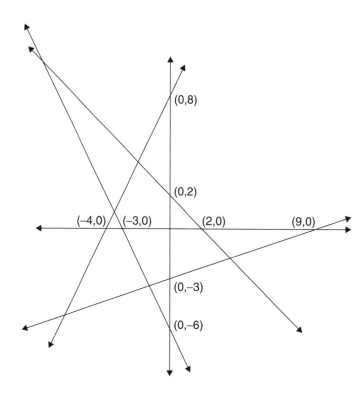

Answers may vary, but will likely include triangles, quadrilaterals, pentagons, and five-pointed stars.

4-9. 1. A, $y = -2x$ 2. O, $y = 2x - 8$ 3. E, $y = x - 9$ 4. G, $y = -3x + 8$ 5. F,
$y = 3x - 9$ 6. R, $y = \frac{4}{5}x$ 7. U, $y = \frac{1}{2}x$ 8. Q, $y = x - 1$ 9. D, $x - 2y = 4$
10. N, $3x - 2y = 6$ 11. T, $x - 4y = -6$ 12. I, $x = -3$ 13. S, $y = 2$ René
Descartes (1596–1650) studied geometry by analyzing coordinates of
points <u>and equations of figures</u>.

4-10. Accept any valid similarities and differences.

4-11. The data in Problem 1 suggest a line.

4-12. Answers may vary; possible answers include the following.   1. $y =$
$2x - 0.35$ 2. $y = \frac{1}{4}x + 40$ 3. $y = -\frac{9}{10}x + 88$ <u>Complementary angles</u>.
$y = -x + 90$

4-13. 1. (–14,1) 2. (20,10) 3. (1,10) 4. (–20,–20) 5. (0,0)

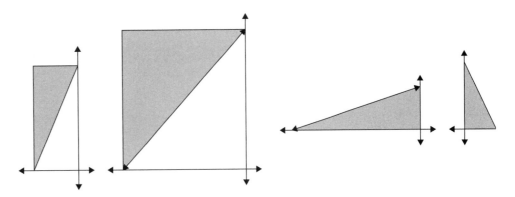

4-14. E. (4,–3) D. (–1,2) I. (–3.5,2.5) C. (–2.5,5.5) S. (2,–5) T. (–1,6)
N. (1,–2) O. ø P. R A system of equations of two or more parallel lines
is called an <u>inconsistent</u> system. A system of equations of the same lines
is called a <u>dependent</u> system.

4-15. 2. IV 3. VI, VII 4. I 5. II 6. VII 7. II, III

Graphing the Solutions of Equations and Inequalities on a Number Line

Solutions to equations and inequalities can be graphed on a number line, provided there is only one variable in the equation or inequality.

To graph the solution to an equation, locate the coordinate (number) on the number line and place a dot on the number line above the coordinate.

To graph the solution of an inequality, locate the coordinate on the number line and follow these steps:

- If $x >$ a number, circle the point above that number and shade the number line to the right.
- If $x \geq$ a number, place a darkened circle on the point above that number and shade the number line to the right.
- If $x <$ a number, circle the point above that number and shade the number line to the left.
- If $x \leq$ a number, place a darkened circle on the point above that number and shade the number line to the left.
- If $x \neq$ a number, circle the point above that number and shade to the left and right.

Directions: Match each equation or inequality with its graph on the next page. Write the letter of the graph in the blank in front of the equation or inequality it matches. Then write the letter above the problem number to complete the statement at the end of the activity.

1. _____ $x \geq -3$ 2. _____ $x > -1$

3. _____ $x = -2$ 4. _____ $x \geq 0$

5. _____ $x < 5$ 6. _____ $x < -4$

7. _____ $x < 1$ 8. _____ $x = -4$

9. _____ $x \neq -2$ 10. _____ $2 < x$

11. _____ $-1 > x$

Algebra Teacher's Activities Kit

Graphing the Solutions of Equations and Inequalities on a Number Line

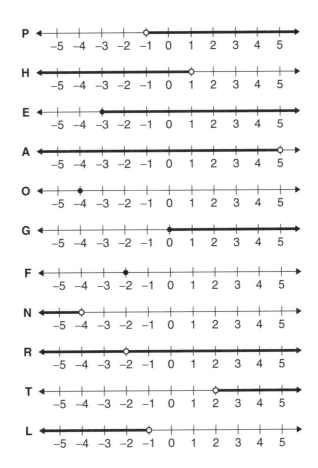

The graph of one type of inequality has exactly one solution less ___ ___ ___ ___
                                                                10 7 5 6

___ ___ ___ ___ ___ ___ ___ ___ ___ ___ ___ ___ ___ real numbers.
10 7 1   4 9 5 2 7   8 3   5 11 11

What is this inequality? _____

Graphing the Solutions of Combined Inequalities on the Number Line

A *combined inequality* is an inequality composed of two inequalities. Combined inequalities may be *conjunctions* (inequalities joined by "and") or *disjunctions* (inequalities joined by "or").

A conjunction is true if both of its sentences are true. The graph of a conjunction is the intersection of the graph of the inequalities.

A disjunction is true if either sentence is true, or if both sentences are true. The graph of a disjunction is the union of the graphs of the inequalities.

Combined inequalities can be solved by writing a conjunction or disjunction and following the steps for solving inequalities.

Directions: Match the solution of each combined inequality with its graph on the next page. Write the letter of the graph in the blank before the inequality. Then write the letters above each problem number to complete the statement at the end of the activity.

1. _____ x > 3 or x < –1

2. _____ x < 3 and x > –1

3. _____ x ≥ 2 or x ≤ –1

4. _____ x ≤ –2 or x ≥ –1

5. _____ x > 3 and x ≤ 1

6. _____ x > 3 or x ≤ 1

7. _____ x ≤ 4 or x > –3

8. _____ x ≤ 4 and x > –3

9. _____ 4 < x < 5

10. _____ 3 < x + 1 < 5

11. _____ x – 1 < –3 or x – 1 ≥ 4

12. _____ 3 < 5 – 2x < 7

Algebra Teacher's Activities Kit

Graphing the Solutions of Combined Inequalities on the Number Line

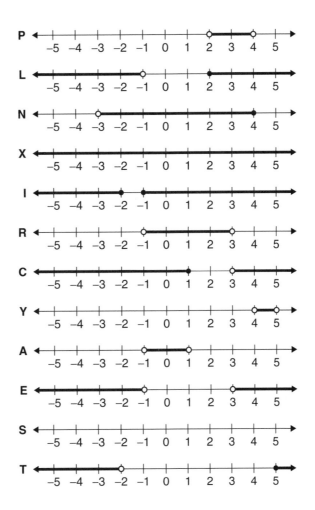

Thomas Harriot (1560–1621) first used the ">" and "<" symbols in ___ ___ ___ ___ ___
                                                                               12 2 11 4 5

___ ___ ___ ___ ___ ___ ___ ___ ___ ___   ___ ___ ___ ___ ___ ___, published in 1631.
12 8 12 3 9 11 4 6 12 1   10 2 12 7 4 5

Graphing Points on the Coordinate Plane

In this activity you will graph points on the coordinate plane. If you complete the graph correctly, you will create an optical illusion.

Directions: *Part 1.* Use graph paper to graph each point. Label each point with the given letter. Connect each point in alphabetical order from A to L, and return to A.

A (–8,5)	E (4,8)	I (1,–4)
B (–4,6)	F (3,4)	J (–2,–1)
C (–3,10)	G (6,1)	K (–6,–2)
D (1,11)	H (5,–3)	L (–9,1)

Directions: *Part 2.* Follow the instructions for each point.

- Graph M (–5,2) and connect it to B.
- Graph N (0,7) and connect it to B.
- Connect N to F.
- Graph O (2,0) and connect it to F.
- Connect O to J.
- Connect J to M.
- Graph P (–1,3).
- Connect these points: L and M; N and D; O and H; B and P; P and J; and P and F.

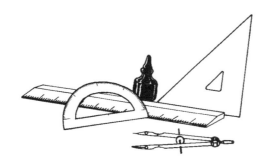

Algebra Teacher's Activities Kit

Finding the Slope and Y-intercept from a Graph

The graph of a linear equation consists of all of the points that are solutions to the equation. By examining the graph, you can determine the slope of the line and the y-intercept.

The *slope* of a line is the ratio of the change in y to the change in x. The slope is always constant. It can be found by choosing any two points on a line.

The y-*intercept* is the point where the line crosses the y-axis. It is located at only one point.

Directions: Find each line on the grid on the next page. Starting with l_1, find the letter in the Answer Bank that corresponds to the slope of l_1 and write the letter in the first space in the blanks below. Then find the letter in the Answer Bank that corresponds to the y-intercept of l_1 and write that in the blank next to the slope of l_1. Follow the same procedure with the other seven lines. (For each line, the letter that corresponds to the slope should be written in the first blank, and the letter that corresponds to the y-intercept should be written in the second blank.) Break the letters into words to reveal a statement. The first one is done for you.

Answer Bank				
N. 4	S. −1	E. 2	A. $-\frac{1}{2}$	F. 7
O. $\frac{1}{2}$	I. −3	L. 5	D. −5	P. 0

$\underset{l_1}{\underline{\text{S}\ \ \text{L}}}$ $\underset{l_2}{\underline{\ \ \ \ }}$ $\underset{l_3}{\underline{\ \ \ \ }}$ $\underset{l_4}{\underline{\ \ \ \ }}$ $\underset{l_5}{\underline{\ \ \ \ }}$ $\underset{l_6}{\underline{\ \ \ \ }}$ $\underset{l_7}{\underline{\ \ \ \ }}$ $\underset{l_8}{\underline{\ \ \ \ }}$ rise over run.

Finding the Slope and Y-intercept from a Graph

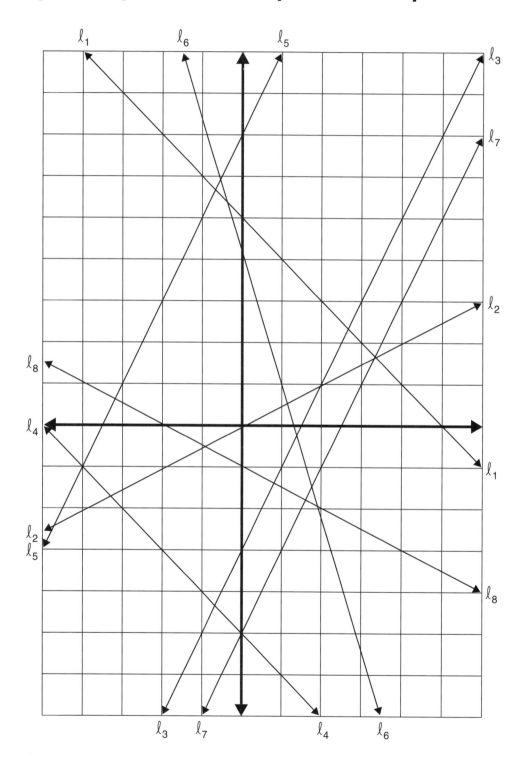

Algebra Teacher's Activities Kit

Using the Slope and Y-intercept to Graph a Line

The slope and y-intercept enable you to draw the graph of a linear equation. If the graph is drawn correctly, it contains all of the points that are solutions to the equation.

Directions: Use a ruler to graph the equation of each line described below. The graph is given on the next page. If you are accurate, each line should pass through two labeled points. Write the letters of these points on the lines before each problem. Hint: Some letters might need to be reversed.

1. _____ $m = 2, b = 4$

2. _____ $m = -\frac{1}{2}, b = -1$

3. _____ $m = 2, b = -6$

4. _____ $m = -\frac{1}{4}, b = -2$

5. _____ $m = 2, b = 0$

6. _____ $m = -\frac{3}{2}, b = 3$

7. _____ $m = \frac{7}{4}, b = 3$

8. _____ $m = \frac{5}{2}, b = -1$

9. _____ $m = -1, b = -6$

10. _____ $m = 1, b = -7$

What do these letters represent? _____

_____

_____

Using the Slope and Y-intercept to Graph a Line

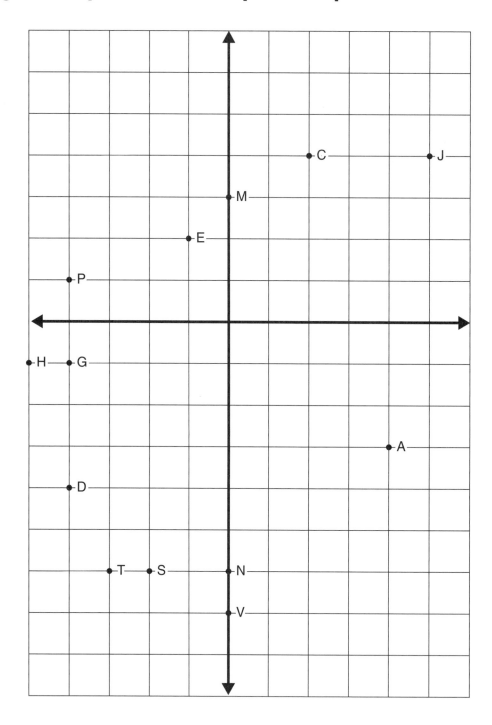

Finding the Slope of a Line

If you know two points on a line, or the equation of a line, you can find the slope of a line.

To find the slope of a line, do one of the following:

- If you are given two points, use the formula $m = \frac{y_2 - y_1}{x_2 - x_1}$ where m stands for the slope and (x_1, y_1) and (x_2, y_2) are two points on the line.
- If you are given an equation in slope-intercept form, use the formula $y = mx + b$ where m stands for the slope.
- If you are given an equation in standard form, use the formula $Ax + By = C$. Write the formula in slope-intercept form. The slope is $\frac{-A}{B}$.

Directions: Each line is described by two points or an equation. Find the slope, then locate the slope in the Answer Bank. Write the letter of each answer in the blank before its problem. Then write the letters in order, starting with the first one, to complete the statement at the end of the activity. Some letters are used more than once; others are not used at all.

1. _____ (0,2) and (5,2)
2. _____ (−3,1) and (2,−2)
3. _____ y = 3x + 4
4. _____ (6,−3) and (1,2)
5. _____ (−1,0) and (−4,1)
6. _____ 2x + y = −1
7. _____ y = 6x − 1
8. _____ (−3,8) and (−3,4)
9. _____ y = −x − 7
10. _____ (0,1) and (1,7)
11. _____ (1,−2) and (−2,4)
12. _____ x − 4y = 7
13. _____ 3x − y = 10
14. _____ (−3,−4) and (2,−4)
15. _____ −3x + 2y = 6
16. _____ 18x − 3y = −20

Answer Bank
O.   0
R.   −2
N. $\frac{3}{2}$
Y.   2
D.   ø
T. $-\frac{1}{3}$
G.   3
H.   −1
I. $\frac{1}{4}$
U. $-\frac{3}{5}$
A.   −3
E.   6

William __ __ __ __ __ __ __ __ first used the symbol for parallel and Pierre

__ __ __ __ __ __ __ __ first used the symbol for perpendicular.

Finding the X- and Y-intercepts

Since two points determine a line, using the x-intercept and the y-intercept is one way to graph the equation of a line. The point where a graph intersects the x axis is (x,0). x is called the x-intercept of the graph. The point where a graph intersects the y axis is (0,y). y is called the y-intercept of the graph.

To find the x-intercept, substitute 0 for y and solve for x.
To find the y-intercept, substitute 0 for x and solve for y.

Directions: Find the x- and y-intercepts of the graph of each equation. Write your answer in the space provided after the intercepts. Then find the letter of your answer in the Answer Bank and write the letter in the blank before the intercepts. Finally, write the letters in order, starting with the first one, in the blanks to complete the statement at the end of the activity on the next page. Some letters will be used more than once; others will not be used at all.

1. $y = 2x + 4$

   _____ x-intercept = _____

   _____ y-intercept = _____

2. $y = 3x + 1$

   _____ x-intercept = _____

   _____ y-intercept = _____

3. $-3x + y = 6$

   _____ x-intercept = _____

   _____ y-intercept = _____

4. $y = \frac{1}{4}x - 6$

   _____ x-intercept = _____

   _____ y-intercept = _____

5. $y = 5x - 5$

   _____ x-intercept = _____

   _____ y-intercept = _____

Answer Bank
F. 0
S. −2
V. $\frac{1}{3}$
E. 1
X. 10
Y. 15
O. 24
U. 7
M. $-\frac{1}{3}$
B. −5
L. 6
I. 12
T. ø
D. −36
R. $-\frac{1}{2}$
A. 4
C. 2
P. −6
N. −3

Finding the X- and Y-intercepts

6. x = 7

_____ x-intercept = _____

_____ y-intercept = _____

7. $y = \frac{1}{3}x + 12$

_____ x-intercept = _____

_____ y-intercept = _____

8. y = 3x

_____ x-intercept = _____

_____ y-intercept = _____

9. 2y = x − 1

_____ x-intercept = _____

_____ y-intercept = _____

10. $x = \frac{1}{3}y + 1$

_____ x-intercept = _____

_____ y-intercept = _____

11. y = 15

_____ x-intercept = _____

_____ y-intercept = _____

Parallel lines have the __ __ __ __   __ __ __ __ __   __ __ __

__ __ __ __ __ __ __ __ __   ___-intercepts.

Using the X- and Y-intercepts to Graph a Line

Intersecting lines can create unusual geometric figures. In this activity, if you complete the graphs correctly, you will create several recognizable shapes.

- The x-intercept is the point at which a line crosses the x-axis. The x-intercept of a line that passes through the point (5,0) has an x-intercept of 5.

- The y-intercept is the point at which the line crosses the y-axis. The y-intercept of a line that passes through the point (0,3) has a y-intercept of 3.

Directions: Graph the lines that pass through each pair of points. The intersecting lines and axes will form a design of various figures. Identify these shapes and write their names on the lines below.

1. (−4,0), (0,8)

2. (−3,0), (0,−6)

3. (2,0), (0,2)

4. (9,0), (0,−3)

_____

_____

_____

_____

Writing the Equation of a Line When Given Two Points

Since two points determine a line, these two points can be used to write the equation of a line in both slope-intercept form and standard form. Follow these steps.

- Use the formula m $= \frac{y_2 - y_1}{x_2 - x_1}$ to find the slope.
- Choose one point and substitute the values for x, y, and m into the equation y = mx + b.
- Solve for b.
- Substitute values for m and b into the slope-intercept form: y = mx + b. Then write the equation in standard form (if necessary): Ax + By = C, where A is a positive integer, B and C are integers, and A and B are not both equal to 0.

Directions: Find the equation of each line, then find the equation in the Answer Bank. Some equations are written in slope-intercept form, and others are written in standard form. After you find the equation in the Answer Bank, write its corresponding letter in the blank before the problem. Then write each letter above its problem number to complete the statement at the end of the activity.

1. _____ (1,–2), (4,–8)
2. _____ (–2,–12), (5,2)
3. _____ (2,–7), (–1,–10)
4. _____ (1,5), (–1,11)
5. _____ (5,6), (6,9)
6. _____ (0,0), (5,4)
7. _____ (2,1), (4,2)
8. _____ (3,2), (5,4)
9. _____ (0,–2), (4,0)
10. _____ (0,–3), (2,0)
11. _____ (–2,1), (2,2)
12. _____ (–3,4), (–3,2)
13. _____ (0,2), (5,2)

Answer Bank	
U.	$y = \frac{1}{2}x$
S.	y = 2
Q.	y = x – 1
T.	x – 4y = –6
R.	$y = \frac{4}{5}x$
A.	y = –2x
F.	y = 3x – 9
D.	x – 2y = 4
O.	y = 2x – 8
N.	3x – 2y = 6
G.	y = –3x + 8
I.	x = –3
E.	y = x – 9

René Descartes (1596–1650) studied geometry by analyzing coordinates of points

___ ___ ___   ___ ___ ___ ___ ___ ___ ___ ___ ___   ___ ___
1 10   9   3   8   7   1 11 12   2 10 13   2   5

___ ___ ___ ___ ___ ___ ___.
5 12   4   7   6   3 13

Graphing Linear Equations and Inequalities

Writing About Graphs of Lines

Not only must mathematicians excel in problem solving, but they must also be able to communicate in the language of mathematics. A person must first understand a concept fully before he or she can hope to explain it to someone else.

Directions: Study the diagram below. Write an explanation comparing and contrasting the seven lines that are shown.

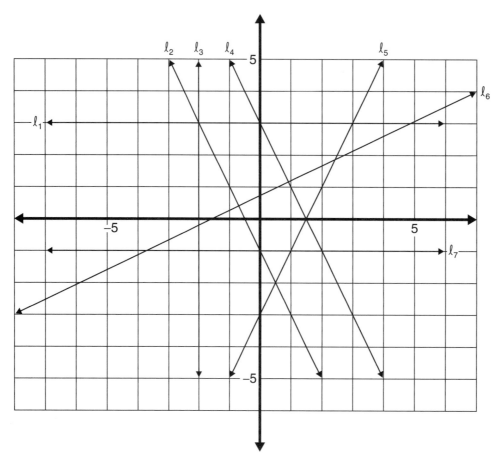

_____

_____

_____

_____

Algebra Teacher's Activities Kit

Determining Whether Data Suggests a Line

Data may or may not be presented on a graph as a straight line, especially in real-life situations. In this activity you will examine data for various situations and determine whether or not the data will result in a straight line when graphed.

Directions: Graph each set of data on a separate graph to determine if a line results.

1. On a car trip to Florida, Ms. Wilson checked and recorded the mileage on the odometer every hour. She was then able to record her travel time and distance. The data below describe her trip.

   (1, 55), (2, 100), (3, 150), (4, 180), (5, 240), (6, 300), (7, 350), (8, 400)

   The first number in each pair of numbers represents the time in hours, and the second number represents the miles. For example, (4, 180) means that after traveling four hours, she had traveled a total of 180 miles.

2. The cost of renting a cottage by a lake in upstate New York for the summer is $6,000. A family, including grandparents, aunts, uncles, and cousins, decides they would like to rent the cottage, but not everyone is able to make a firm commitment. The data below describe the cost per family, depending on the number of families that may rent and assuming that every family that rents pays an equal share of the costs.

   (1, $6,000),   (2, $3,000), (3, $2,000), (4, $1,500), (5, $1,200), (6, $1,000), (8, $750), (10, $600), (12, $500)

3. Based on data adopted from various sources on nutrition, an average one-year-old boy needs 1,100 calories per day, a five-year-old boy needs 1,800 calories, and so on. The data below describe the amount of calories an average male would require at various ages throughout his life.

   (1, 1,100), (5, 1,800), (10, 2,500), (15, 2,800), (20, 3,000), (25, 2,700), (30, 2,700), (35, 2,700), (40, 2,700), (45, 2,700), (50, 2,300), (55, 2,300), (60, 2,300), (65, 2,300), (70, 2,300), (75, 2,000), (80, 2,000)

   Which of the above three examples and data suggest a line?

   _____

Finding the Equation of the Line of Best Fit

Sometimes a straight line does not pass through all of the points of a set of data that have been plotted, even though the points may suggest a line. A line can be drawn that "fits" through most of the points. This line is called the *line of best fit,* and it is drawn as close as possible to the plotted points.

To approximate the line of best fit, do the following:

- Plot the points.
- Use a ruler to sketch the line that fits the data.
- Locate two points on the line you have drawn.
- Use these two points to find the equation of the line of best fit.

Directions: For each set of data, plot the given points on graph paper, draw the line of best fit, and find the equation of the line of best fit.

1. Sandra is saving money for a trip. She read in a magazine that one way to save is to make purchases with paper money and not coins. Any change she would then receive could be saved in a cookie jar. Sandra followed this procedure and recorded the total amount of change she saved each week. After the first week, she had accumulated $2.00 in change, after the second she had accumulated $3.50, and so on as shown in the data below.

   (1, $2.00), (2, $3.50), (3, $7.00), (4, $8.00), (5, $9.75), (6, $10.99), (7, $15.00), (8, $17.25)

   The equation of the line of best fit is _____.

Algebra Teacher's Activities Kit

Finding the Equation of the Line of Best Fit

2. Some people believe that a cricket's chirp can indicate the temperature. On several summer nights, Joe recorded the number of times a cricket chirped in a minute and then checked the outdoor thermometer. He recorded the temperature in degrees Fahrenheit. For example, when the cricket chirped two hundred times in a minute, the temperature was 90°. Here are the rest of his results.

   (200, 90°), (188, 87°), (160, 80°), (216, 94°), (140, 75°), (168, 82°), (120, 70°), (200, 90°), (108, 67°)

   The equation of the line of best fit is _____.

3. The students in Mrs. Valendi's geometry class are measuring special pairs of angles. For example, the pair of numbers (5°, 86°) means that one angle of the pair measures 5° and the other measures 86°. Since measurements are not always exact, their results vary. Following are the results of the measurements taken by Mrs. Valendi's students.

   (5°, 86°), (15°, 75°), (29°, 60°), (45°, 50°), (55°, 39°), (10°, 78°), (20°, 68°), (8°, 80°), (38°, 46°)

   The equation of the line of best fit is _____.

   What type of angles do you think the students are measuring? _____

   Use this fact to write the exact equation of the line. _____

Graphing Inequalities on the Coordinate Plane

Follow these steps to graph inequalities.

- Graph the inequality as if it were an equation, finding the slope and y-intercept. This will enable you to find the boundary, which is a line that divides the coordinate plane into two parts.
- If the inequality symbol is ≥ or ≤, draw a solid line, because the points on the line are solutions of the inequality.
- If the inequality symbol is > or <, draw a dotted line, because the points on the line are not solutions of the inequality.
- Choose any point that is not on the line and substitute this point in the inequality. If this point satisfies the inequality, shade the half-plane that includes the point. If the point does not satisfy the inequality, shade the other half-plane.

Directions: Graph each inequality below on its own graph. Then refer to the graphs and select the appropriate point from the Answer Bank to complete each statement below. Each answer is used once.

$y > 3x + 13$

$y \geq x$

$y \leq \frac{1}{4}x + 4$

$y < -2x + 6$

Answer Bank		
(0,0)	(−14,1)	
(1,10)	(−20,−20)	(20,10)

1. _____ is a solution of every inequality except $y \leq \frac{1}{4}x + 4$.

2. _____ is not a solution of any inequality.

3. _____ is only a solution of $y \geq x$.

4. _____ is a solution of every inequality.

5. _____ is a solution of every inequality except $y > 3x + 13$.

Algebra Teacher's Activities Kit

Copyright © 2003 John Wiley & Sons, Inc.

Solving Systems of Equations by Graphing

Graphing is a powerful tool that can be used to solve systems of equations. Follow these steps:

- Graph the equations of two or more lines on the same axes.
- Find the point where the lines intersect.

The ordered pair at the point of intersection is a solution of all the equations in the system. If the graphs of the equations do not intersect, then the system has no solution and is denoted by ø. If the graphs of the equations are the same line, the solution is all real numbers and is denoted by "R."

Directions: Solve each system of equations by using the graphical method outlined above. Locate the solution in the message at the end of the activity. Write the letter of the system above the solution.

E. $x + 4y = -8$
    $3x + 2y = 6$

I. $y = x + 6$
    $y = -x - 1$

S. $3x + y = 1$
    $2x + 3y = -11$

N. $y = -2$
    $x = 1$

P. $x + y = 2$
    $3x + 3y = 6$

D. $2x + 3y = 4$
    $3x - y = -5$

C. $3x + y = -2$
    $x - y = -8$

T. $2x + y = 4$
    $3x + 2y = 9$

O. $2x + y = 5$
    $y = -2x + 1$

A system of equations of two or more parallel lines is called an

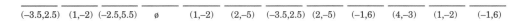

$\overline{\quad}$ $\overline{\quad}$ $\overline{\quad}$ $\overline{\quad}$ $\overline{\quad}$ $\overline{\quad}$ $\overline{\quad}$ $\overline{\quad}$ $\overline{\quad}$ $\overline{\quad}$ $\overline{\quad}$
(–3.5,2.5) (1,–2) (–2.5,5.5)   ø   (1,–2)   (2,–5) (–3.5,2.5) (2,–5)   (–1,6)   (4,–3)   (1,–2)   (–1,6)

system. A system of equations of the same lines is called a

$\overline{\quad}$ $\overline{\quad}$ $\overline{\quad}$ $\overline{\quad}$ $\overline{\quad}$ $\overline{\quad}$ $\overline{\quad}$ $\overline{\quad}$ system.
(–1,2)   (4,–3)   R   (4,–3)   (1,–2)   (–1,2)   (4,–3)   (1,–2)   (–1,6)

Graphing Linear Equations and Inequalities   145

Solving Systems of Inequalities by Graphing

To solve systems of inequalities by graphing, follow these steps:

- Graph each inequality on the same axes.
- Find the overlap of the regions of the graphs, including portions of the boundary lines. This is the solution.

Directions: Pictured below are the seven pieces of a tangram. Each piece is called a tan. Graph the solutions of the systems of equations, then match your solution with a shape or shapes identified by a Roman numeral. Write the Roman numerals in the spaces provided. The first one is done for you.

1. __VI__ $y \geq -2$

          $y < x + 3$

          $y \leq -x + 1$

2. _____ $y < 4$

          $y \geq -x + 1$

          $y > x + 3$

3. _____ $y < x + 3$

          $y \geq -2$

          $x \leq 3$

4. _____ $x > -5$

          $y \geq x + 7$

          $y \leq 6$

5. _____ $y > x + 3$

          $x > -5$

          $y \leq -x - 3$

6. _____ $y \geq -x + 1$

          $y < x + 3$

          $x \leq 3$

7. _____ $x > -5$

          $y > x + 3$

          $y \leq x + 7$

          $y \leq -x + 1$

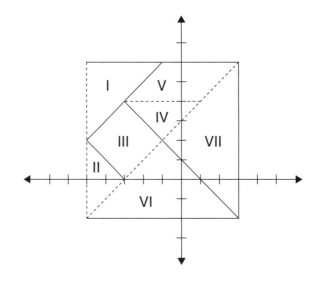

Basic Operations with Monomials and Polynomials

The twelve activities in this section cover monomials and polynomials. The section begins with basic operations with monomials, advances to operations with monomials and polynomials, and then progresses to activities that focus on polynomials. The skills addressed in this section are essential for building a solid foundation in factoring.

Teaching Suggestions for the Activities

5-1 Writing Expressions in Exponential Form

This activity requires your students to write expressions in factored form. Some examples require the use of parentheses as well as exponents.

Start the activity by reviewing the concept of exponents, for example, $4 \times 4 = 4^2$ or 16. Explain that 4×4 is in factored form while 4^2 is in exponential form. Note that the number 4 is called the base and 2 is the exponent. Also mention the rule for a zero exponent: $n^0 = 1$, if n is a real number and not equal to zero.

Review the directions on the worksheet with your students. Remind them to describe the pattern once they have completed the exercises. Note that the small lines to the top right of some variables (see the first problem) are included so that students can write in the exponents.

5-2 Using the Terms of Polynomials

This activity provides your students with an opportunity to define and use various terms that apply to polynomials. The activity will reinforce the vocabulary related to polynomials.

Begin the activity by explaining that a polynomial is "a sum of monomials." Monomials are terms that are either numerals, variables, or products of a numeral and one or more variables. Like other topics in algebra, polynomials have special words and terms that apply to them. Many of these words and terms are listed on the worksheet. Also discuss palindromes, which are mentioned in Problem 15. (Palindromes are numbers or words that are the same whether they are read left to right or right to left. For example, the word "Mom" is a palindrome, as is the number "1221.")

Go over the instructions on the worksheet with your students. Make sure that they understand they are to write one letter per blank and then record the boxed letters in order, starting with the first letter, to complete the statement at the end of the activity.

5-3 Adding and Subtracting Polynomials

Although adding and subtracting polynomials is much the same as adding real numbers, some prerequisite skills are necessary. For example, to complete this activity successfully, your students should be able to identify similar terms.

Begin the activity by discussing similar terms, referring to the definition on the worksheet. You might wish to offer these additional examples: $3x$ and $-3x$, $4x^2$ and $2x^2$, and $3xy$ and $-7xy$. Note, however, that $3x$ and $3x^2$ are not similar. Provide other examples if necessary.

Go over the instructions on the worksheet with your students. Remind them that to subtract a polynomial they must add the opposite of each term.

5-4 Multiplying Monomials

This activity focuses on multiplying two or more monomials. To complete this activity successfully, your students should be familiar with both the Commutative and Associative Properties for Multiplication.

Introduce the activity by reviewing the concept of bases, exponents, and their meanings. Offer these examples on the board or an overhead projector:

$$5^4 \text{ means } 5 \cdot 5 \cdot 5 \cdot 5 = 625$$
$$x^4 \text{ means } x \cdot x \cdot x \cdot x$$
$$x^3 \cdot x^2 = x \cdot x \cdot x \cdot x \cdot x = x^5$$

Discuss the example on the worksheet. Depending on the abilities of your students, you may wish to offer additional examples.

Review the instructions. Emphasize that some answers will be used more than once.

5-5   Finding Powers of Monomials

This activity requires your students to find the powers of monomials, using the definition of a power. Successfully completing Activity 5-4 or similar material is necessary before students attempt this activity.

Begin the activity by reviewing the procedures for multiplying monomials. On the board or an overhead projector, offer the following examples:

$$(3x^2)(4x) = 12x^3$$
$$(x^2y^2)(xy^5) = x^3y^7$$

Extend the concept of multiplying monomials to using the definition of a power and discuss the examples on the worksheet. Depending on the abilities of your students, you may find it helpful to offer some additional examples. Note that to find the power of a product, your students must first find the power of each factor.

Review the directions on the worksheet with your students. Note that they are to fill in all the blanks and write the explanation on the lines provided. You might also mention that the small lines after the parentheses for numbers 11 to 14 are for exponents.

5-6   Dividing Monomials

This activity requires your students to divide monomials. To complete this activity successfully, your students should be able to find the powers of monomials.

Start the activity by discussing the rule to simplify fractions. Offer this example on the board or an overhead projector, noting that students can divide the numerator and denominator by the same non-zero number.

$$\frac{3x}{4x} = \frac{3}{4} \qquad x \neq 0$$

Discuss the rule of exponents for division, which is included on the worksheet. If necessary, offer additional examples.

Review the directions on the worksheet with your students, making sure that they understand each base in the quotient appears only once. Note that there are no powers of powers and that all fractions are simplified.

5-7 Simplifying and Evaluating Expressions

For this activity your students must simplify and evaluate expressions, given numerical values for variables. This activity can be used as a review of adding and subtracting polynomials, multiplying monomials, finding the powers of monomials, and dividing monomials.

Begin the activity by reviewing the operations listed above. You might include the following, and similar, examples on the board or an overhead projector.

$$3a + 4 - (2a + 6) = a - 2$$
$$2a^2 \cdot 3a^5 = 6a^7$$
$$(3a^2)^3 = 27a^6$$
$$\frac{6a^4}{a^3} = 6a$$

Ask your students to evaluate each expression if $a = 2$ and discuss the procedures they followed. (The answers to the examples are 0, 768, 1,728, and 12.)

Review the directions on the worksheet with your students. Note that they should write each expression in simplest form and then evaluate the expression.

5-8 Multiplying a Polynomial by a Monomial

In this activity your students must use the Distributive Property to multiply a polynomial by a monomial. To complete this activity successfully, your students should be able to apply the Distributive Property, multiply monomials, and combine similar terms.

Start the activity by reviewing the Distributive Property: $a(b + c) = ab + ac$ for all real numbers, a, b, and c. Discuss the examples on the worksheet. Depending on the abilities of your students, you may find it helpful to provide additional examples with negative integers such as $-3(x - 7) - 4(x + 8) = -3x + 21 - 4x - 32 = -7x - 11$.

Go over the instructions on the worksheet with your students, emphasizing that a monomial is missing somewhere in each problem. Also note that some monomials in the Answer Bank are used more than once.

5-9 Multiplying Binomials

Being able to multiply binomials is an essential algebraic skill. It provides the foundation for factoring, which enables students to solve problems involving quadratic equations.

Begin the activity by asking your students to generate two-digit multiplication problems. You can either use the FOIL method (First,

Outer, Inner, Last) and multiply mentally, or show students the process and challenge them to multiply the numbers. Extend the process to include variables.

Review the instructions on the worksheet with your students, making sure they realize that similar terms can be added. Also note that the Commutative Property applies when multiplying binomials, for example, xy + yx can be written as 2xy.

5-10 Multiplying Two Polynomials

This activity requires your students to multiply a trinomial by a binomial. To complete this work successfully, your students should be familiar with the Distributive Property and also be able to write expressions in descending order with respect to a variable.

Begin the activity by reviewing the Distributive Property and the concept of writing expressions in descending order. Discuss the example on the worksheet, providing some additional examples if your students seem uncertain about the process.

In the activity, your students will decode a message related to Pascal's Triangle. Although this triangle was named for Blaise Pascal (1623–1662) because he was the first to write about many of its unique properties, it was known to the Chinese as early as 1300.

Discuss Pascal's Triangle and explain that each interior number of the triangle is found by adding the pair of numbers to its left and right in the row above. The first four rows are pictured below.

$$
\begin{array}{ccccccc}
 & & & 1 & & & \\
 & & 1 & & 1 & & \\
 & 1 & & 2 & & 1 & \\
 1 & & 3 & & 3 & & 1 \\
1 & & 4 & & 6 & & 4 & 1 \\
\end{array}
$$

Review the directions on the worksheet with your students. Note that the polynomials and answers must be written in descending order with respect to x. After your students complete the assignment, explain how Pascal's Triangle relates to the coefficient of the expansion of a + b: $(a + b)^0 = 1$, $(a + b)^1 = 1a + 1b$, $(a + b)^2 = 1a^2 + 2ab + 1b^2$, and so on.

5-11 Dividing a Polynomial by a Binomial

This activity requires your students to use the division algorithm to divide a polynomial by a binomial. Students are required to complete division problems in which steps are missing.

Begin the activity by discussing the division algorithm shown on the worksheet. Provide an example on the board or an overhead projector comparing the dividing of whole numbers with the dividing of polynomials. You may wish to use the following:

$$\begin{array}{r} 20\frac{16}{29} \\ 29\overline{)596} \\ \underline{58} \\ 16 \\ \underline{0} \\ 16 \end{array} \qquad \begin{array}{r} x+1+\frac{8}{x-3} \\ x-3\overline{)x^2-2x+5} \\ \underline{x^2-3x} \\ x+5 \\ \underline{x-3} \\ 8 \end{array}$$

Explain each step of the process. Note that in the first example, the remainder must be less than 29. In the second example, the remainder must be 0 or of a lesser degree than the degree of the divisor. Also note that the polynomial must be in order of decreasing degree. It is sometimes necessary (for example, in Problems 8 and 9 on the worksheet) to include terms with coefficients of zero.

Go over the instructions on the worksheet with your students. Emphasize that the answers for the blanks appear in the Answer Bank. Each answer in the Answer Bank will be used only once.

5-12 Finding Cubes of Binomials

Cubes of binomials lend themselves well to applications of the Distributive Property, various multiplication principles, and the combining of similar terms. Students who master the concept of cubes of binomials often gain insight to other concepts of algebra.

Start the activity by reviewing the example on the activity sheet. Be sure that your students understand the steps involved. Point out that the shortcut eliminates much of the work. Depending on the abilities of your students, you may find it helpful to work out the general form of $(a - b)^3$, again making certain that your students understand the steps.

Go over the directions with your students. Mention that in the first seven problems, the answer is missing. In the last three problems, a binomial is missing, and your students must work backward to solve the problem.

Answer Key for Section 5

5-1. 1. 3 2. 1 3. 7 4. 9 5. 6 6. 4 7. 2 8. 0 9. 5 10. 8 Explanations may vary. Each line is filled with a digit from 0 to 9.

5-2. 1. exponent 2. five 3. coefficient 4. fourth 5. binomial 6. polynomial 7. cubed 8. zero 9. squared 10. four 11. trinomial 12. simplest

13. variables   14. second   15. eleven   Although known as a poet, Persian-born Omar Khayyam (1048–1131) contributed significantly to mathematics. He was the first to solve every type <u>of cubic equation</u> that has a positive solution.

5-3.   1. 7x + 8   2. 15x + 4y   3. 3x – 5   4. 2x + 2y   5. 9x – y + 3   6. 2x – 7
7. 11x + 1   8. –2y + 8   9. 2x – 8   10. 8x – 2   11. 3x – 5   12. 9x – y + 3
13. 2x – 7   14. –2y + 8   15. 15x + 4y   16. 8x – 2   17. 2x + 2y   18. 2x – 8
19. 7x + 8   20. 11x + 1   The following problems have the same answers: 1 and 19, 2 and 15, 3 and 11, 4 and 17, 5 and 12, 6 and 13, 7 and 20, 8 and 14, 9 and 18, 10 and 16.

5-4.   1. F, x^7 2. O, x^4 3. R, $12x^2$ 4. A, $–12x^2$ 5. L, $18x^4$ 6. L, $18x^4$
7. P, $36x^3y^2$ 8. O, x^4 9. S, $6x^2y^2$ 10. I, $–9x^2y$ 11. T, $36x^2y^2$ 12. I, $–9x^2y$
13. V, x^2y^2 14. E, $18x^2y^6$ 15. I, $–9x^2y$ 16. N, $–2x^4y^2$ 17. T, $36x^2y^2$ 18. E, $18x^2y^6$ 19. G, x^2y^3 20. E, $18x^2y^6$ 21. R, $12x^2$ 22. S, $6x^2y^2$ The Rule of Exponents for Multiplication states that $a^m \cdot a^n = a^{m+n}$ <u>for all positive integers</u> m and n.

5-5.   1. x^8 2. x^2 3. $8x^9$ 4. $–32x^5$ 5. $–27x^6$ 6. $16x^4$ 7. $5x^3$ or $–5x^3$ 8. $8x^4$ or $–8x^4$ 9. $2x^2y$ 10. $–2x$ 11. 3   12. 4   13. 4   14. 2   Explanations may vary but should note that a positive number squared is positive and a negative number squared is also positive.

5-6.   1. S, $4a^2$ 2. I, a^2 3. M, 4   4. P, 3   5. L, $\frac{1}{2a}$ 6. I, a^2 7. F, 1   8. I, a^2
9. E, $\frac{5a}{4}$ 10. D, $\frac{3b}{5}$ 11. P, 3   12. R, $–\frac{5}{a}$ 13. O, a   14. V, 4a   15. I, a^2
16. D, $\frac{3b}{5}$ 17. E, $\frac{5a}{4}$ 18. D, $\frac{3b}{5}$ 19. T, 9   20. H, –1   21. E, $\frac{5a}{4}$ All monomials in this activity can be <u>simplified, provided the</u> denominator does not equal zero.

5-7.   1. J, 6a; A, –12   2. M, 2a – 4; E, 6   3. S, $6a^4$; H, 486   4. U, $9a^2$; M, 9
5. E, 7b + 2; A, –12   6. N, 2b; D, –2   7. P, 4b; I, 24   8. E, 7b + 2; R, 23
9. R, $6a^2$; E, 6   10. H, –6a; E, 6   11. R, $6a^2$; I, 24   12. G, b^2, O, 100
13. N, 2b; E, 6   In 1637, René Descartes used a raised number to represent an exponent. This was an improvement on the notation suggested by <u>James Hume and Pierre Herigone</u>. The former suggested a raised Roman numeral to represent an exponent. The latter suggested writing a number to the right of the variable to represent an exponent.

5-8.   1. G, 24   2. R, 5x   3. E, $4x^2$ 4. E, $4x^2$ 5. K, 77x   6. W, $3x^2$ 7. O, $–2x^2$
8. R, 5x   9. D, $2x^2y^2$ 10. A, $11x^2y^2$ 11. X, $–4x^2$ 12. I, $11x^2$ 13. O, $–2x^2$
14. M, 3x   15. A, $11x^2y^2$ The Distributive Property is sometimes called the Distributive Axiom. Axiom is taken from the <u>Greek word axioma</u>, meaning "that which is thought fitting."

5-9. 1. $x^2 - 4x - 5$ 2. $a^2 - a - 12$ 3. $x^2 + 7x + 12$ 4. $x^2 + 2x - 8$ 5. $6c^2 - 5c - 25$ 6. $3x^2 - 8x - 35$ 7. $p^2 - 8p + 12$ 8. $12x^2 - 64x + 45$ 9. $a^2 - b^2$ 10. $a^2 + 2ab + b^2$ 11. $9x^2 - 16$ 12. $9x^2 - 12x + 4$ 13. $16y^2 - z^2$ 14. $x^2 + 10x + 21$ 15. $3a^2 - 5ab - 2b^2$ 16. $8x^2 - 14x + 3$ 17. $ax + ay + bx + by$ 18. $y^2 + 10y + 24$ 19. $8x^2 + 6x - 27$ 20. $2a^2 + 3ab + b^2$

5-10. 1. L, $5x^2$ 2. I, $5x$ 3. T, 12 4. M, $17x$ 5. O, $7x^2$; B, $7x$ 6. F, $9x^2$ 7. N, $13x$; X, 4 8. H, $10x^2$ 9. S, $3x^2$; A, 10 10. P, x^3; E, 2 Pascal's Triangle relates the coefficient to the <u>expansion of the binomial</u> $a + b$.

5-11. If two terms are missing from the same problem, the missing terms are listed in order, from the quotient to the work. 1. 6 2. $14x$ 3. $-6x$ 4. $2, -5x$ 5. $2x, -2x$ 6. $x, -4x$ 7. $4x^2, 3$ 8. $1, x^2$ 9. $4x$ 10. $5x, 24x$

5-12. 1. F, $x^3 - 6x^2 + 12x - 8$ 2. T, $x^3 + 6x^2 + 12x + 8$ 3. S, $x^3 - 9x^2 + 27x - 27$ 4. U, $x^3 + 9x^2 + 27x + 27$ 5. R, $x^3 + 6x^2y + 12xy^2 + 8y^3$ 6. E, $x^3 - 6x^2y + 12xy^2 - 8y^3$ 7. A, $8x^3 + 12x^2y + 6xy^2 + y^3$ 8. O, $2x + 3$ 9. M, $x - 4$ 10. H, $3x - 1$ The cube of a binomial always <u>has four terms</u>.

Writing Expressions in Exponential Form

Powers of a number can be written in factored form or in exponential form. For example, n squared can be written in factored form as $n \cdot n$ or in exponential form as n^2.

Directions: Write each expression in exponential form by filling in the empty blank with either an exponent or base. Then look at the numbers you have used to fill in the blanks. Describe any pattern you find on the lines at the end of the worksheet.

1. $a \cdot a \cdot a = a—$

2. $a = a—$

3. $7 \cdot 7 = \underline{\hspace{0.8cm}}^2$ or 49

4. $3a \cdot a \cdot 3 \cdot a = 3^2 a^3$ or $\underline{\hspace{0.8cm}} a^3$

5. $1 + 6 \cdot 6 = 1 + \underline{\hspace{0.8cm}}^2$ or 37

6. $-2 \cdot -2 \cdot -2 \cdot -2 = (-2)—$ or 16

7. $-2 \cdot 2 \cdot 2 \cdot 2 = -\underline{\hspace{0.8cm}}^4 = -16$

8. $1 = a—$

9. $25 = \underline{\hspace{0.8cm}}^2$

10. $2 \cdot 2 \cdot 2 = 2^3 = \underline{\hspace{0.8cm}}$

_____

_____

Using the Terms of Polynomials

Like most concepts of algebra, polynomials have special names and words that apply to them. Some of these include the following:

monomial	binomial	trinomial
base	exponent	squared
coefficient	simplified or simplest form	polynomial
degree of a monomial	degree of a non-zero constant	cubed

Directions: Use your text, dictionary, or a math reference source to define each of the terms above. Apply the definitions to complete the statements that follow by filling in each blank with the correct word. Then write the "boxed" letters in order, starting with the first problem, to complete the statement at the end of the activity.

1. It describes the three in 5^3. ___ ___ ___ □ ___ ___ ___ ___

2. It is the base in 5^2. □ ___ ___ ___

3. It is –3 in the term $-3x^2y$. ___ ___ ___ ___ ___ ___ □ ___ ___ ___ ___

4. 7^4 is read seven to this power. ___ ___ □ ___ ___ ___

5. It is a polynomial that has two terms. □ ___ ___ ___ ___ ___ ___ ___

6. It is the sum of monomials. ___ ___ ___ ___ ___ ___ ___ □ ___ ___

7. 7^3 can be read as 7 _____. □ ___ ___ ___ ___

8. It is the degree of any non-zero constant. ___ □ ___ ___

9. 3^2 is nine or three _____. ___ □ ___ ___ ___ ___

10. It equals two squared. ___ ___ □ ___

11. It is a polynomial that has three terms. ___ ___ ___ ___ ___ ___ ___ □ ___

12. $3x^2 + 2x + 5$ is in this form because no two of its terms are similar.
    ___ ___ ___ ___ ___ ___ ___ □ ___ ___ ___ ___ ___ ___ ___ ___

13. The degree of a monomial is the total number of times these occur as factors.
    ___ ___ ___ □ ___ ___ ___ ___ ___

14. Five squared means the same as five to this power. ___ ___ ___ □ ___ ___

15. It is the smallest two-digit palindrome whose square is also a palindrome.
    ___ ___ ___ ___ ___ □

Although known as a poet, Persian-born Omar Khayyam (1048–1131) contributed significantly to mathematics. He was the first to solve every type ___ ___ ___ ___ ___ ___ ___ ___ ___ ___ ___ ___ ___ ___ ___ ___ ___ that has a positive solution.

Algebra Teacher's Activities Kit

Adding and Subtracting Polynomials

Adding and subtracting polynomials is easy if you remember to combine similar terms. (Similar terms are terms that are the same except for their numerical coefficients.)

- To add polynomials, simplify by adding similar terms.
- To subtract, add the opposite of each term. Then simplify by adding similar terms.

Examples: $3x + 7 + 5x - 2 = 8x + 5$

$3x + 7 - (5x - 2) = 3x + 7 - 5x + 2 = -2x + 9$

Directions: Add or subtract the polynomials that follow. Write your answers in the spaces provided. Hint: Each correct answer you find will appear twice.

1. $3x + 2 + 4x + 6 =$ _____

2. $7x + 3y + 8x + y =$ _____

3. $4x - 3 - (x + 2) =$ _____

4. $3x - 2y - x + 4y =$ _____

5. $2x + 3 + 7x - y =$ _____

6. $3x - 2 - (x + 5) =$ _____

7. $8x + 2 + 3x - 1 =$ _____

8. $3x - 2y + 8 - 3x =$ _____

9. $3x - 7 - (x + 1) =$ _____

10. $9x - 1 - (x + 1) =$ _____

11. $2x + 8 + x - 13 =$ _____

12. $12x - y - (3x - 3) =$ _____

13. $8x - 1 - (6x + 6) =$ _____

14. $3x - 1 - (3x + 2y - 9) =$ _____

15. $3x - y - (-12x - 5y) =$ _____

16. $6x + 3 + 2x - 5 =$ _____

17. $x - y + x + 3y =$ _____

18. $8x + 4 - (6x + 12) =$ _____

19. $10x + 9 - (3x + 1) =$ _____

20. $20x - 5 - (9x - 6) =$ _____

Multiplying Monomials

Multiplying monomials involves the use of several different properties. Use the Commutative and Associative Properties of Multiplication to change the order and the grouping of the coefficients and variables. Then add the exponents if the powers have the same base. For example:

$$(3xy^2)(-6xy^3) = (3)(-6)(x)(x)(y^2)(y^3) = -18x^2y^5$$

Directions: Multiply the monomials and write the answer in the blank following the problem. Then match your answer with an answer in the Answer Bank and write the letter of the answer in the space before the problem. Finally, write the letters in order, starting with the first problem, in the blanks to complete the statement at the end of the activity. Some answers will be used more than once.

1. _____ $x \cdot x^2 \cdot x^4 =$ _____
2. _____ $x \cdot x \cdot x^2 =$ _____
3. _____ $(3x)(4x) =$ _____
4. _____ $(3x)(-4x) =$ _____
5. _____ $(3x^2)(6x^2) =$ _____
6. _____ $(-2x)(-9x^3) =$ _____
7. _____ $(12x)(3x^2y^2) =$ _____
8. _____ $(6x)(\frac{1}{6}x^3) =$ _____
9. _____ $(3xy)(2xy) =$ _____
10. _____ $(-\frac{3}{5}x)(15xy) =$ _____
11. _____ $(2x)(-3x)(-6y^2) =$ _____

12. _____ $(-3x^2)(3y) =$ _____
13. _____ $(-xy)(-xy) =$ _____
14. _____ $(-3xy)(-6xy^5) =$ _____
15. _____ $(9)(-x^2y) =$ _____
16. _____ $(-\frac{1}{3}x^2y)(3x^2y)(2) =$ _____
17. _____ $(-3x^2)(-3)(4y^2) =$ _____
18. _____ $(-2x)(-9)(xy^6) =$ _____
19. _____ $(-xy)(-xy^2) =$ _____
20. _____ $(\frac{2}{3})(9x^2)(3y^6) =$ _____
21. _____ $(2x)(2x)(3) =$ _____
22. _____ $(\frac{1}{2}x)(6x)(2y^2) =$ _____

Answer Bank				
L. $18x^4$	N. $-2x^4y^2$	E. $18x^2y^6$	T. $36x^2y^2$	V. x^2y^2
A. $-12x^2$	G. x^2y^3	P. $36x^3y^2$	R. $12x^2$	
F. x^7	O. x^4	S. $6x^2y^2$	I. $-9x^2y$	

The Rule of Exponents for Multiplication states $a^m \cdot a^n = a^{m+n}$ ____ ____ ____

____ ____ ____   ____ ____ ____ ____ ____ ____ ____ ____

____ ____ ____ ____ ____ ____ ____ ____ m and n.

Algebra Teacher's Activities Kit

Copyright © 2003 John Wiley & Sons, Inc.

Finding Powers of Monomials

There are two things to consider when finding the powers of monomials: Is the monomial itself a power, which is raised to a power, or is the monomial a product that is raised to a power?

For example, in the first case $(x^6)^2$ means $x^6 \cdot x^6$, the product of which is x^{12}.

An example of the second case is $(3x^4)^2$, which means $(3x^4)(3x^4)$, the product of which is $9x^8$.

Directions: A monomial, an exponent, or a product is missing in each problem. Find what is missing in each. Problems 7 and 8 have two answers. Find both answers and use the lines at the end of the worksheet to write an explanation of why two answers are applicable.

1. $(x^2)^4 =$ _____

2. $(x)^2 =$ _____

3. $(2x^3)^3 =$ _____

4. $(-2x)^5 =$ _____

5. $(-3x^2)^3 =$ _____

6. $(-4x^2)^2 =$ _____

7. $(\rule{1.5cm}{0.4pt})^2 = 25x^6$

8. $(\rule{1.5cm}{0.4pt})^2 = 64x^8$

9. $(\rule{1.5cm}{0.4pt})^3 = 8x^6y^3$

10. $(\rule{1.5cm}{0.4pt})^3 = -8x^3$

11. $(x^2y)^{\rule{0.5cm}{0.4pt}} = x^6y^3$

12. $(3x^2y^3)^{\rule{0.5cm}{0.4pt}} = 81x^8y^{12}$

13. $(-2xy)^{\rule{0.5cm}{0.4pt}} = 16x^4y^4$

14. $(6x^3y^4)^{\rule{0.5cm}{0.4pt}} = 36x^6y^8$

_____

_____

Dividing Monomials

Dividing monomials involves applying the Rule of Exponents for Division. This rule has three separate cases.

The Rule of Exponents for Division states m and n are positive integers and $a \neq 0$.

- If $m > n$, then $\dfrac{a^m}{a^n} = a^{m-n}$

- If $m < n$, then $\dfrac{a^m}{a^n} = \dfrac{1}{a^{n-m}}$

- If $m = n$, then $\dfrac{a^m}{a^n} = 1$

Examples of each case (in order as above) include:

$$\frac{a^3}{a^2} = a^{3-2} = a \qquad \frac{a^7}{a^{10}} = \frac{1}{a^{10-7}} = \frac{1}{a^3} \qquad \frac{a^2}{a^2} = 1$$

Remember to simplify the numerator and denominator if possible before applying the above rules. For example:

$$\frac{\left(3a^4\right)^2}{a^5} = \frac{9a^8}{a^5} = 9a^3$$

Directions: Simplify each monomial and write your answer in the blank after the problem. Match your answer with the correct answer in the Answer Bank, and then write the letter of the answer in the space before the problem. When you are done, write the letters in order, starting with the first one, to complete the statement at the end of the activity. Some answers will be used more than once.

1. _____ $\dfrac{12a^2}{3} =$ _____

2. _____ $\dfrac{a^3}{a} =$ _____

3. _____ $\dfrac{8a}{2a} =$ _____

4. _____ $\dfrac{9a^2}{3a^2} =$ _____

5. _____ $\dfrac{13a}{26a^2} =$ _____

6. _____ $\dfrac{3a^2b}{3b} =$ _____

7. _____ $\dfrac{2a}{2a} =$ _____

8. _____ $\dfrac{(4a)^2}{4^2} =$ _____

9. _____ $\dfrac{15a}{12} =$ _____

10. _____ $\dfrac{3a^2b^2}{5a^2b} =$ _____

Algebra Teacher's Activities Kit

Dividing Monomials

11. _____ $\dfrac{30a^2}{10a^2}$ = _____

12. _____ $\dfrac{-10a^2}{2a^3}$ = _____

13. _____ $\dfrac{-15a^2}{-15a}$ = _____

14. _____ $\dfrac{(-2a)^2}{a}$ = _____

15. _____ $\dfrac{3a^3}{3a}$ = _____

16. _____ $\dfrac{(3b)^2}{15b}$ = _____

17. _____ $\dfrac{5a}{2^2}$ = _____

18. _____ $\dfrac{15b^2}{5^2 b}$ = _____

19. _____ $\dfrac{(3a)^3}{3a^3}$ = _____

20. _____ $\dfrac{(-3a)^3}{(3a)^3}$ = _____

21. _____ $\dfrac{5^3 a}{10^2}$ = _____

Answer Bank			
F. 1	R. $\dfrac{-5}{a}$	P. 3	D. $\dfrac{3b}{5}$
E. $\dfrac{5a}{4}$	I. a^2	O. a	
S. $4a^2$	M. 4	H. -1	
V. 4a	L. $\dfrac{1}{2a}$	T. 9	

All monomials in this activity can be ___ ___ ___ ___ ___ ___ ___ ___ ___ ___,

___ ___ ___ ___ ___ ___ ___ ___   ___ ___ ___ denominator does not equal

zero.

Simplifying and Evaluating Expressions

Working with expressions requires several important skills. Two of the most important are simplifying and evaluating.

Directions: Simplify each expression and match your answer with the correct answer in the Expression Bank. Write the letter of that answer in the first space before the problem, beneath "Simplify." Then evaluate the expression. Find this answer in the Answer Bank and write the letter of the answer in the second space before the problem, beneath "Evaluate." When you have finished, write the letters in order, starting with the first problem and moving *across and down,* to complete the statement at the end of the activity. The first one is done for you. Some answers will be used more than once.

	Simplify	Evaluate		To Evaluate Use:
1.	**J**	**A**	$2a + 8a - 4a$	$a = -2$
2.	___	___	$3a - (a + 4)$	$a = 5$
3.	___	___	$(2a)(3a^3)$	$a = 3$
4.	___	___	$(3a)^2$	$a = -1$
5.	___	___	$4b - 1 + 3b + 3$	$b = -2$
6.	___	___	$\dfrac{6b}{3}$	$b = -1$
7.	___	___	$\dfrac{(4b)^2}{4b}$	$b = 6$
8.	___	___	$\dfrac{14b}{2} + 2$	$b = 3$
9.	___	___	$(3a)(2a)$	$a = -1$
10.	___	___	$\dfrac{36a}{-6}$	$a = -1$
11.	___	___	$2a^2 + 4a^2$	$a = 2$
12.	___	___	$\left(\dfrac{2}{3}b\right)\left(\dfrac{3}{2}b\right)$	$b = 10$
13.	___	___	$3b - b$	$b = 3$

Algebra Teacher's Activities Kit

Copyright © 2003 John Wiley & Sons, Inc.

Simplifying and Evaluating Expressions

```
┌─────────────────────────────────────────────────────────────────────┐
│                         Expression Bank                               │
│                                                                       │
│   H.  −6a        M.  2a − 4     G.  b²          S.  6a⁴      P.  4b    │
│                                                                       │
│   E.  7b + 2     N.  2b         R.  6a²         J.  6a       U.  9a²   │
└─────────────────────────────────────────────────────────────────────┘
```

```
┌─────────────────────────────────────────────────────────────────────┐
│                          Answer Bank                                  │
│                                                                       │
│   A.  −12        E.  6          D.  −2          H.  486               │
│                                                                       │
│   I.  24         M.  9          R.  23          O.  100               │
└─────────────────────────────────────────────────────────────────────┘
```

In 1637, René Descartes used a raised number to represent an exponent. This was

an improvement on the notation suggested by J A __ __ __   __ __ __ __

__ __ __   __ __ __ __ __ __   __ __ __ __ __ __ __ __ __. The former

suggested a raised Roman numeral to represent an exponent. The latter suggested

writing a number to the right of the variable to represent an exponent.

Multiplying a Polynomial by a Monomial

Multiplying a polynomial by a monomial involves using the Distributive Property and the rules for multiplying monomials. For example:

$$3x(2x^2 - 4x + 7) = 6x^3 - 12x^2 + 21x$$

Some problems are more complicated and the Distributive Property is applied more than once. It may be necessary to simplify by combining similar terms. For example:

$$3x(2x^2 - 4x + 7) + 2x^2(4x - 5) =$$
$$6x^3 - 12x^2 + 21x + 8x^3 - 10x^2 =$$
$$14x^3 - 22x^2 + 21x$$

Directions: One monomial is missing from each problem. Find the missing monomial, write it in its proper space, then match your answer with the answers in the Answer Bank. Write the letter of the monomial in the blank before the problem. When you have finished, write the letters in order, starting with the first one, to complete the statement at the end of the activity. Some answers will be used more than once.

1. _____ $-8(x - 3) = -8x +$ _____

2. _____ $5x(2x^2 - 3x - 1) = 10x^3 - 15x^2 -$ _____

3. _____ $4x(x + 3) =$ _____ $+ 12x$

4. _____ $\frac{1}{2}x(8x - 12) =$ _____ $- 6x$

5. _____ $7x(3x - 11) = 21x^2 -$ _____

6. _____ $3x(3x^2 - x - 1) = 9x^3 -$ _____ $- 3x$

7. _____ $-x(2x - 8) =$ _____ $+ 8x$

8. _____ _____ $(3x^2 - 2) = 15x^3 - 10x$

9. _____ $\frac{1}{3}xy(6xy - 3) =$ _____ $- xy$

10. _____ $xy(11xy - 8) =$ _____ $- 8xy$

11. _____ _____ $(x^2 - 3x - 1) = -4x^4 + 12x^3 + 4x^2$

12. _____ $3x(x - 1) + 2x(4x - 1) =$ _____ $- 5x$

13. _____ $x(x - 7) - 3x(x + 8) =$ _____ $- 31x$

14. _____ $8 -$ _____ $(x - 10) = -3x^2 + 30x + 8$

15. _____ $4xy(xy - 1) + 7xy(xy - 3) =$ _____ $- 25xy$

Multiplying a Polynomial by a Monomial

Answer Bank

D. $2x^2y^2$	E. $4x^2$	X. $-4x^2$	W. $3x^2$	A. $11x^2y^2$	I. $11x^2$
O. $-2x^2$	K. $77x$	M. $3x$	R. $5x$	G. 24	

The Distributive Property is sometimes called the Distributive Axiom. "Axiom" is

taken from the ___ ___ ___ ___ ___   ___ ___ ___ ___   ___ ___ ___ ___ ___ ___,

meaning "that which is thought fitting."

Multiplying Binomials

Tricks that enable people to mentally perform what seems to be complicated mathematics are often based on algebraic principles. For example, to multiply 25×15 in his or her head, a mathematician might think $(20 + 5)(10 + 5)$ and then use FOIL, which is an acronym meaning: first, outer, inner, last. It works like this:

First terms:	$20 \times 10 = 200$
Outer terms:	$20 \times 5 = 100$
Inner terms:	$5 \times 10 = 50$
Last terms:	$5 \times 5 = \underline{25}$
Simple addition	$= 375$

People may think that a mathematical trickster is a genius, but in fact he or she is only using simple algebraic procedures.

Directions: Use FOIL to multiply the following binomials.

1. $(x + 1)(x - 5) =$ _____

2. $(a + 3)(a - 4) =$ _____

3. $(x + 4)(x + 3) =$ _____

4. $(x + 4)(x - 2) =$ _____

5. $(3c + 5)(2c - 5) =$ _____

6. $(x - 5)(3x + 7) =$ _____

7. $(p - 6)(p - 2) =$ _____

8. $(2x - 9)(6x - 5) =$ _____

9. $(a + b)(a - b) =$ _____

10. $(a + b)(a + b) =$ _____

11. $(3x - 4)(3x + 4) =$ _____

12. $(3x - 2)(3x - 2) =$ _____

13. $(4y - z)(4y + z) =$ _____

14. $(x + 3)(x + 7) =$ _____

15. $(3a + b)(a - 2b) =$ _____

16. $(4x - 1)(2x - 3) =$ _____

17. $(x + y)(a + b) =$ _____

18. $(y + 6)(y + 4) =$ _____

19. $(2x - 3)(4x + 9) =$ _____

20. $(2a + b)(a + b) =$ _____

Multiplying Two Polynomials

Multiplying two polynomials can be accomplished by applying the Distributive Property twice and combining similar terms as in the example that follows.

$$(2x + 3)(8x^2 + x + 4) = 2x(8x^2 + x + 4) + 3(8x^2 + x + 4) =$$
$$16x^3 + 2x^2 + 8x + 24x^2 + 3x + 12 =$$
$$16x^3 + 26x^2 + 11x + 12$$

In the example, the terms of each polynomial were already arranged in decreasing order. If this is not done in the problem, rearrange the terms of each polynomial in descending order. This makes it easier to combine similar terms.

Directions: Multiply each polynomial and write the product in descending order. Fill in the missing monomial in the blank(s) in each problem. Then write the letter of each answer above its monomial to complete the statement at the end of the activity.

1. $(x + 3)(x^2 + 2x + 1) = x^3 + \underline{} + 7x + 3$
   $$\text{L}$$

2. $(x - 1)(x^2 + 4x - 1) = x^3 + 3x^2 - \underline{} + 1$
   $$\text{I}$$

3. $(x - 4)(x^2 - x - 3) = x^3 - 5x^2 + x + \underline{}$
   $$\text{T}$$

4. $(x + 5)(x^2 - 3x - 2) = x^3 + 2x^2 - \underline{} - 10$
   $$\text{M}$$

5. $(x - 3)(2x^2 - x + 4) = 2x^3 - \underline{} + \underline{} - 12$
   $$\quad\quad\text{O}\quad\quad\text{B}$$

6. $(2x - 1)(x^2 - 4x + 5) = 2x^3 - \underline{} + 14x - 5$
   $$\text{F}$$

7. $(3x + 1)(2x^2 - x - 4) = 6x^3 - x^2 - \underline{} - \underline{}$
   $$\quad\quad\text{N}\quad\quad\text{X}$$

8. $(2x - 3)(-1 + x + 4x^2) = 8x^3 - \underline{} - 5x + 3$
   $$\text{H}$$

9. $(2x + 5)(2 - x + x^2) = 2x^3 + \underline{} - x + \underline{}$
   $$\quad\quad\text{S}\quad\quad\text{A}$$

10. $(2 - x)(1 - x - x^2) = \underline{} - x^2 - 3x + \underline{}$
    $$\quad\text{P}\quad\quad\quad\text{E}$$

Pascal's Triangle relates the coefficients to the

$\underline{}\ \underline{}\ \underline{}\ \underline{}\ \underline{}\ \underline{}\ \underline{}\ \underline{}\ \underline{}\quad\underline{}\ \underline{}\quad\underline{}\ \underline{}\ \underline{}$
 2   4 x^3 10   13x $3x^2$ 5x $7x^2$ 13x $7x^2$ $9x^2$ 12 $10x^2$ 2

$\underline{}\ \underline{}\ \underline{}\ \underline{}\ \underline{}\ \underline{}\ \underline{}\ \underline{}$ $a + b$.
 7x   5x   13x $7x^2$ 17x   5x   10 $5x^2$

Basic Operations with Monomials and Polynomials   167

Dividing a Polynomial by a Binomial

Dividing a polynomial by a binomial is similar to dividing whole numbers. The steps include:

- Estimating
- Dividing
- Multiplying
- Subtracting
- "Bringing down" the next digit or term

To divide whole numbers, continue the above process until the remainder is zero or less than the divisor. When dividing polynomials by binomials, continue the process until the remainder is 0 or a lesser degree than the divisor.

Directions: Complete the problems that follow by filling in the empty boxes with a term from the Answer Bank. Each term in the Answer Bank will be used once.

1.
$$\begin{array}{r} x+2 \\ x-3 \overline{\smash)x^2-\ x-6} \\ \underline{x^2-3x} \\ 2x-\square \\ 2x-6 \end{array}$$

2.
$$\begin{array}{r} 2x-5 \\ x+7 \overline{\smash)2x^2+9x-35} \\ \underline{2x^2+\square} \\ -5x-35 \\ -5x-35 \end{array}$$

3.
$$\begin{array}{r} x-6 \\ x+4 \overline{\smash)x^2-2x-24} \\ \underline{x^2+4x} \\ \square-24 \\ -6x-24 \end{array}$$

4.
$$\begin{array}{r} x+\square \\ x-5 \overline{\smash)x^2-3x-10} \\ \underline{x^2+\square} \\ 2x-10 \\ 2x-10 \end{array}$$

5.
$$\begin{array}{r} \square-1+\frac{4}{2x-1} \\ 2x-1 \overline{\smash)4x^2-4x+5} \\ \underline{4x^2-2x} \\ \square+5 \\ -2x+1 \\ 4 \end{array}$$

6.
$$\begin{array}{r} \square-2+\frac{6}{2x+1} \\ 2x+1 \overline{\smash)2x^2-3x+4} \\ \underline{2x^2+\ x} \\ \square+4 \\ -4x-2 \\ 6 \end{array}$$

Dividing a Polynomial by a Binomial

7.
$$
x+3 \overline{\smash{\big)}\,4x^2+11x-8} \;\; {}^{\displaystyle 4x-1-\frac{5}{x+3}}
$$
$$\square + 12x$$
$$-x-8$$
$$-x-\square$$
$$-5$$

8.
$$
x-1 \overline{\smash{\big)}\,x^3+0x^2+0x-1} \;\; {}^{\displaystyle x^2+\;x+\;\square}
$$
$$x^3-\square$$
$$x^2$$
$$x^2-x$$
$$x-1$$
$$x-1$$

9.
$$
x+2 \overline{\smash{\big)}\,x^3+0x^2+0x+8} \;\; {}^{\displaystyle x^2-2x+4}
$$
$$x^3+2x^2$$
$$-2x^2$$
$$-2x^2-\square$$
$$4x+8$$
$$4x+8$$

10.
$$
4x+3 \overline{\smash{\big)}\,12x^3-11x^2+9x+18} \;\; {}^{\displaystyle 3x^2-\square+6}
$$
$$12x^3+\;9x^2$$
$$-20x^2+\;9x$$
$$-20x^2-15x$$
$$\square + 18$$
$$24x+18$$

			Answer Bank				
–6x	–5x	–2x	1	$4x^2$	3	2x	4x
5x	2	x^2	x	6	–4x	24x	14x

Finding Cubes of Binomials

To find the cube of a binomial such as $(a + b)^3$, you could express the term as $(a + b)(a + b)(a + b)$ and multiply two binomials: $(a^2 + 2ab + b^2)(a + b)$. Then you could use the Distributive Property three times:

$$a^3 + a^2b + 2a^2b + 2ab^2 + ab^2 + b^3$$

When the expression is simplified, it equals $a^3 + 3a^2b + 3ab^2 + b^3$. Using the same procedure, $(a - b)^3 = a^3 - 3a^2b + 3ab^2 - b^3$.

Directions: A polynomial is missing from each problem below. Find the polynomial in the Answer Bank, and write it in the space provided. Then write the letter of the polynomial in the blank before the problem. When you have finished, write the letters over the problem numbers at the end of the activity to complete the statement.

1. _____ $(x - 2)^3 =$ _____

2. _____ $(x + 2)^3 =$ _____

3. _____ $(x - 3)^3 =$ _____

4. _____ $(x + 3)^3 =$ _____

5. _____ $(x + 2y)^3 =$ _____

6. _____ $(x - 2y)^3 =$ _____

7. _____ $(2x + y)^3 =$ _____

8. _____ _____ $= 8x^3 + 36x^2 + 54x + 27$

9. _____ _____ $= x^3 - 12x^2 + 48x - 64$

10. _____ _____ $= 27x^3 - 27x^2 + 9x - 1$

Answer Bank

R. $x^3 + 6x^2y + 12xy^2 + 8y^3$ H. $(3x - 1)^3$

O. $(2x + 3)^3$ M. $(x - 4)^3$

F. $x^3 - 6x^2 + 12x - 8$ T. $x^3 + 6x^2 + 12x + 8$

S. $x^3 - 9x^2 + 27x - 27$ U. $x^3 + 9x^2 + 27x + 27$

E. $x^3 - 6x^2y + 12xy^2 - 8y^3$ A. $8x^3 + 12x^2y + 6xy^2 + y^3$

The cube of a binomial always ___ ___ ___   ___ ___ ___ ___
                               10 7   3   1   8   4   5

___ ___ ___ ___ ___ .
 2   6   5   9   3

Algebra Teacher's Activities Kit

Factors of Monomials and Polynomials

The twelve activities in this section cover the topic of factoring, which is a prerequisite skill for solving quadratic and cubic equations. The activities range from finding the common factor to factoring binomials and trinomials. Specific types of polynomials such as the sum and difference of squares and cubes and factoring by grouping are also included. The last two activities are designed to reinforce the skills covered in the section.

Teaching Suggestions for the Activities

6-1 Finding the GCF of Whole Numbers

This activity requires students to find the greatest common factor, GCF, of whole numbers. This is an important prerequisite skill for factoring polynomials.

Begin the activity by explaining that the greatest common factor of two numbers is the largest factor that is common to both. Note that there are two ways to find the GCF.

The first is to list the factors of each number and circle the largest factor that appears in each list. For example, to find the GCF of 24 and 36, list the factors of each. Show the factors on the board or an overhead projector:

Factors of 24: 1, 2, 3, 4, 6, 8, 12, and 24
Factors of 36: 1, 2, 3, 4, 6, 9, 12, 18, and 36

Note that these two numbers share several factors: 1, 2, 3, 4, 6, and 12. The greatest common factor is 12.

Explain that the second method for finding the GCF is to express each number as the product of prime numbers and identify those pairs of factors common to each. The GCF is the product of the common factors. Again, offer the example of 24 and 36 on the board or an overhead projector:

$$24 = \underline{2} \cdot \underline{2} \cdot 2 \cdot \underline{3}$$
$$36 = \underline{2} \cdot \underline{2} \cdot 3 \cdot \underline{3}$$

Note that $2 \cdot 2$ and 3 (as underlined) are factors common to both numbers. Multiplying $2 \cdot 2 \cdot 3 = 12$, which is the GCF of 24 and 36.

Review the directions on the worksheet. Note that the same procedures apply to three or more numbers.

6-2 Finding the GMF

This activity requires your students to find the greatest monomial factor, GMF, of a group of terms. In order to complete this activity successfully, your students should have completed Activity 6-1 or be familiar with finding the greatest common factor of whole numbers.

Start this activity by reviewing how to find the greatest common factor of whole numbers, and extend this concept to finding the greatest monomial factor of monomials. Discuss the examples on the worksheet. Depending on the abilities of your students, you may find it beneficial to explain the specific steps necessary to finding the GMF. Stress that the variables of the greatest monomial factor must also be a factor of each term.

Go over the instructions on the worksheet with your students. Note that each group of terms will have a GMF.

6-3 Finding the Missing Factor

This activity requires your students to determine the missing factor of a monomial or a polynomial. To complete this activity successfully, your students should be able to divide monomials.

Start the activity by explaining that multiplication and division are inverse operations. Division "undoes" multiplication, and multiplication "undoes" division. Discuss the examples on the worksheet and note that variables in the denominator cannot equal zero, because division by zero is undefined.

Go over the instructions on the worksheet with your students. Remind them that some answers will be used more than once, and encourage them to always check their work.

6-4 Factoring the Difference of Squares

For this activity your students are given a binomial, and they must state whether or not it is the difference of two squares. If it is, they must factor the binomial. To complete this activity successfully, your students should be able to identify perfect squares and multiply binomials.

Begin the activity by reviewing the procedure for multiplying binomials. Offer examples such as $(x + 3)(x - 3) = x^2 - 9$ and $(7x + 5)(7x - 5) = 49x^2 - 25$ on the board or an overhead projector.

Explain the formula $(a + b)(a - b) = a^2 - b^2$ and apply it to the concept of factoring. Offer the following examples: $(x^2 - 25) = (x + 5)(x - 5)$ and $(4x^2 - 81) = (2x - 9)(2x + 9)$. Stress that in order to use this formula, both terms must be perfect squares. Note that a monomial is a perfect square if its exponent is even and the coefficient is the square of an integer. For example, $x^6 = x^3 \cdot x^3$. Thus, x^6 is a perfect square.

Review the directions on the worksheet with your students. Note that they must factor the binomials that can be factored, but also mention that some binomials cannot be factored.

6-5 Finding Factors, Sums, and Differences

This activity prepares your students for factoring trinomials. By factoring a number and then finding a specific sum or difference of the factors, your students are utilizing the prerequisite skills of factoring polynomials of the form $x^2 + bx + c$ where b and c are integers.

Start the activity by asking your students to list the factors of a number such as 12. You should receive responses including 1×12, 2×6, and 3×4. Next ask your students to select one pair of these factors whose sum is 7. The answer, of course, is $(3 + 4)$. Now ask them to find a pair of factors for which the difference is 11. The answer is $(12 - 1)$. Depending on the abilities of your students, you may wish to provide more examples.

Go over the directions on the worksheet with your students. Emphasize that they are to list the letter of the factor in the spaces provided for each problem. Also note that it may be necessary to switch the order of the letters to decode the message, depending on the order in which they write the factors.

6-6 Factoring Trinomials I

This activity requires your students to factor trinomials when the leading coefficient is 1 and the last term is either positive or negative. To complete this activity successfully, your students should have completed Activity 6-5 and also be able to multiply binomials.

Introduce the activity by writing a polynomial such as $x^2 - 8x + 15$ on the board or an overhead projector. Ask what factors of 15 add up to −8. The answer is (−5 and −3). Express this in factored form as $(x - 5)(x - 3)$. Instruct your students to check this product, which equals $x^2 - 8x + 15$. Now offer this example: $x^2 - 2x - 8$. Ask which factors of −8 add up to −2. The answer is (−4 and 2). Express this in factored form as $(x - 4)(x + 2)$. This product is $x^2 - 2x - 8$. If necessary, provide similar examples to ensure that your students understand the process. You might also find it helpful to remind your students that multiplication is commutative. For example, $(x - 4)(x + 2)$ is the same as $(x + 2)(x - 4)$.

Review the directions on the worksheet with your students. Encourage them to always check their work when factoring trinomials.

6-7 Factoring Trinomials II

This activity provides your students with more practice in factoring trinomials. It builds upon the skills covered in Activity 6-6 and requires students to factor a variety of trinomials, including some in which the leading coefficient is not equal to 1.

Begin the activity by reviewing factoring. Write the following polynomials on the board or an overhead projector and instruct your students to factor them.

$$x^2 - 9x - 10 = \quad \text{Answer: } (x - 10)(x + 1)$$
$$x^2 + 7x + 10 = \quad \text{Answer: } (x + 5)(x + 2)$$
$$x^2 + 3x - 10 = \quad \text{Answer: } (x + 5)(x - 2)$$
$$x^2 - 7x + 10 = \quad \text{Answer: } (x - 5)(x - 2)$$

Now ask your students to factor $2x^2 - x - 10$. They should find the factors of −10 so that 2 times a factor plus the other factor equals −1. Listing the factors of 2, which are (2×1) and (-2×-1), and the factors of −10, which are (-10×1), (10×-1), (-5×2), and (5×-2), makes the selection easier. The factors that satisfy the requirements are −5 and 2. $(2 \times 2 + -5 \times 1) = -1$. To express the factors of the polynomial in factored form write $(2x - 5)(x + 2)$. Check by multiplying the binomials.

Offer this example: $6x^2 + 7x - 5$. Instruct your students to list the factors of −5, which are (5×-1) and (-5×1), then list the factors of 6, which are (6×1), (-6×-1), (3×2), and (-3×-2). Explain that they should now look for a combination of products and sums that equal 7. These are $(5 \times 2) + (3 \times -1)$. The factors of the polynomial are $(2x - 1)(3x + 5)$.

Review the directions on the worksheet with your students. Note that one factor of each polynomial will be a factor of the polynomial in the next problem. Remind your students to check their work.

6-8 Factoring Binomials and Trinomials

This activity presents your students with a variety of problems involving factoring binomials and trinomials. The activity focuses on greatest monomial factors and works well as a review of the topic.

Start the activity by reviewing the steps necessary for factoring binomials and trinomials on the worksheet. Offer these examples on the board or an overhead projector.

$$3x^2 - 9x = 3x(x - 3)$$
$$x^2 + 12x + 20 = (x + 10)(x + 2)$$
$$x^2 - 7x + 12 = (x - 4)(x - 3)$$
$$x^2 - 3x - 10 = (x - 5)(x + 2)$$
$$x^2 + 4x - 21 = (x + 7)(x - 3)$$
$$2x^2 - 5x - 3 = (2x + 1)(x - 3)$$

Go over the instructions on the worksheet with your students. Note that only some of the polynomials have a greatest monomial factor. Also point out that once a polynomial is factored, it may be necessary to switch the order of the letters in each problem to complete the statement. Remind your students to check their work by multiplying the binomials.

6-9 Factoring by Grouping

For this activity your students must factor polynomials by grouping terms. Some of the problems require students to group terms and then factor each group. Rulers will be needed to complete the diagram on the worksheet.

Begin the activity by writing the following trinomials on the board or an overhead projector.

$$x^2 - 3x - 10 \qquad x^2 + 7x + 12 \qquad 2x^2 - 9x - 5$$

Instruct your students to factor $3(x - 5) + x(x - 5)$. Now ask them to explain how this polynomial is different from the others. Although their answers may vary somewhat, they should realize that the last polynomial is grouped so that $x - 5$ is multiplied by both x and 3. The polynomial can be written in factored form as $(3 + x)(x - 5)$.

Explain that some factors are opposites. For example, $x - y$ is the opposite of $-x + y$. Offer this example on the board or an overhead projector: $3(x - y) + x(y - x)$ can be factored as $(3 - x)(x - y)$.

Discuss the examples on the worksheet with your students. If necessary, go through the steps of factoring by completing the examples.

Review the instructions on the worksheet with your students. Note that all factors appear on the diagram.

6-10 Factoring the Sum and Difference of Cubes

This activity presents the formulas for finding the sum and difference of cubes. To complete this activity successfully, your students must be able to recognize perfect cubes.

Begin the activity by discussing perfect cubes as shown on the worksheet. Extend the concept to cubes of monomials such as x^6. Note that all variables with an exponent that is a multiple of 3 will be a perfect cube, provided that the coefficient is also a perfect cube.

Review the directions on the worksheet. Mention that all of the polynomials are factored completely and that some steps have been omitted when the polynomial is written in factored form.

6-11 Factoring Polynomials Completely

This activity serves as a solid review of factoring. As they factor the polynomials on the worksheet, your students will need to use various factoring techniques.

Start the activity by discussing the guidelines on the worksheet. Depending on the abilities of your students, you may wish to provide examples as you proceed through the guidelines. Explain that the guidelines are a checklist. If a step does not apply, students should go on to the next step.

Review the instructions on the worksheet with your students. Note that all polynomials can be factored and that each will have three factors. Remind your students that some factors will be used more than once.

6-12 Reviewing Factoring Skills

This activity offers a review of the skills and concepts presented in this section. After having worked on the other activities of this section, most of your students should be able to complete this activity successfully.

Begin the activity by explaining that it is a review exercise. If necessary, explain any concepts or skills your students still may not have fully mastered.

Go over the directions on the worksheet with your students. Emphasize that they are to rewrite the false statements with examples or explanations to make them true.

Answer Key for Section 6

6-1. 1. O, 5 2. F, 7 3. T, 4 4. H, 1 5. E, 2 6. F, 7 7. A, 9 8. C, 8 9. T, 4 10. O, 5 11. R, 11 12. S, 3 13. T, 4 14. H, 1 15. I, 6 16. S, 3 Any positive integer greater than 1 is a prime number or can be expressed as a product of prime numbers. Except for the order <u>of the factors, this</u> expression is unique.

6-2. 1. E, 3 2. G, 7x 3. P, 2x 4. L, 5x 5. S, 3x 6. H, 4 7. O, x 8. M, 5 9. R, 2 10. Y, y 11. N, 5xy 12. F, y^2 13. A, 4x 14. I, 25 15. T, 10 One is the GMF of a prime polynomial.

6-3. 1. F, 14 2. A, 3a 3. C, 2a 4. T, 3ab 5. O, 2b 6. R, 9ab 7. S, 6 8. I, 7 9. S, 6 10. A, 3a 11. P, 3 12. O, 2b 13. L, 6a 14. Y, $3ab^2$ 15. N, ab 16. O, 2b 17. M, a^2b^3 18. I, 7 19. A, 3a 20. L, 6a You can check your answer for this activity by multiplying each factor. If one of the <u>factors is a polynomial</u>, you must use the Distributive Property.

6-4. A total of 9 − 4 or 5 problems *cannot* be factored. They are problems numbered 4, 6, 10, 12, and 15. The problems that *can* be factored follow. 1. (x + 6)(x − 6) 2. (x − 8)(x + 8) 3. (x − 1)(x + 1) 5. (2x − 11)(2x + 11) 7. $(x^2 − 2)(x^2 + 2)$ 8. (4x − 7)(4x + 7) 9. (xy − 3)(xy + 3) 11. (5xy − 6)(5xy + 6) 13. $(x^3y^2 − 13)(x^3y^2 + 13)$ 14. $(x^3y^4 − 10)(x^3y^4 + 10)$

6-5. 1. M, 5; U, 7 2. L, 12; T, 6 3. I, 8; P, 1 4. L, 12; I, 8 5. C, 9; A, 2 6. T, 6; I, 8 7. O, 14; N, 3 8. F, 13; A, 2 9. C, 9; T, 6 10. S, 4; I, 8 11. S, 4; A, 2 12. N, 3; I, 8 13. M, 5; P, 1 14. O, 14; R, 10 15. T, 6; A, 2 16. N, 3; T, 6 Knowing your <u>multiplication facts is an important</u> factor in this activity.

6-6. 1. (x + 2)(x + 3) 2. (x − 7)(x + 1) 3. (x − 8)(x − 4) 4. (x − 2)(x − 2) 5. (x − 8)(x − 1) 6. (x − 4)(x + 5) 7. (x + 5)(x − 6) 8. (x − 10)(x − 6) 9. (x − 7)(x + 4) 10. (x + 3)(x − 5) 11. (x + 1)(x + 2) 12. (x − 3)(x − 12) 13. (x − 1)(x − 5) 14. (x − 9)(x − 3) 15. (x − 10)(x + 4) 16. (x − 12)(x − 9)

6-7. 1. (3x + 1)(x − 4) 2. (3x + 1)(2x − 1) 3. (2x − 1)(x + 7) 4. (x + 7)(x − 8) 5. (x − 8)(x + 3) 6. (4x − 1)(x + 3) 7. (x + 3)(2x + 5) 8. (2x + 5)(3x − 2) 9. (3x − 2)(4x + 3) 10. (4x + 3)(x + 3) 11. (x + 3)(x + 9) 12. (x + 9)(5x + 7) 13. (5x + 7)(2x − 3) 14. (2x − 3)(6x − 5) 15. (6x − 5)(3x + 2)

6-8. 1. (x + 2)(x − 3) 2. (x − 4)(x − 5) 3. (x + 7)(x + 2) 4. (x − 8)(x − 1) 5. (3x + 4)(x + 4) 6. (x − 8)(x − 5) 7. (x − 4)(x − 2) 8. (x − 1)(x + 3) 9. (x + 1)(x − 2) 10. (x + 4)(x + 4) 11. $2x^2$(x − 8) 12. 4(x + 7) 13. (x −2)(2x + 3) 14. $2x^2$(x + 1) 15. (x − 8)(x − 3) 16. 6x(x + 7) Prime polynomials cannot be factored.

6-9. 1. $(5 + c)(a + b)$ 2. $(3 + a)(a + 2b)$ 3. $(c - 1)(a - 2b)$ 4. $(3a + 4)(a - 4)$
5. $(a - 2b)(a - b)$ 6. $(5 + c)(a + 3)$ 7. $(c - 1)(a + 2b)$ 8. $(a - 4)(a - 2b)$
9. $(a - 2b)(3a + 4)$ 10. $(5 + c)(a - 4)$ 11. $(a - b)(c - 1)$ 12. $(3a - b)(a - 4)$
13. $(3 + a)(a + b)$ 14. $(3 + a)(c - 1)$ 15. $(3a - b)(5 + c)$

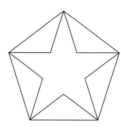

6-10. 1. O, $2xy$ 2. C, 3   3. F, $5x$ 4. R, y^2 5. B, x 6. Y, x^2y 7. E, $6xy$
8. N, 2   9. L, 1   10. U, 9   11. S, $9x$ There are <u>only four cubes</u> less
than one hundred. Name them: <u>1, 8, 27, and 64</u>.

6-11. 1. $2(x - 1)(x - 2)$ 2. $x(x + 4)(x - 1)$ 3. $3(x - 6)(x + 2)$ 4. $4(2x + 1)$
$(2x + 1)$ 5. $3(x - 3)(x + 3)$ 6. $x(2x + 1)(2x - 1)$ 7. $25x^2(x + 2)(x - 2)$
8. $(x - 1)(x + 1)(x^2 + 1)$ 9. $3(5x + 2)(x - 1)$ 10. $2(2x + 1)(3x + 8)$
11. $3x(5x + 1)(2x + 1)$ 12. $2(x^3 - 2)(x^3 + 2)$ 13. $(x^2 + y^2)(x - y)(x + y)$
14. $(y + 3)(x + 3)(x - 3)$

6-12. Explanations may vary.   1. false; 20 is the GCF of 20 and 40.   2. true
3. true   4. false; $x^2 - 16 = (x + 4)(x - 4)$.   5. false; 2 is the GMF of $10x^4$
$+ 12x^2 + 2$.   6. false; $x^2 + x - 12 = (x + 4)(x - 3)$.   7. true   8. false; $x^2 +$
1 is a prime polynomial.   9. false; $(x + 2)(x - 2) = x^2 - 4$ is a binomial.
10. false; the factors of 51 are 1×51 and 3×17.   11. true   12. false;
$16x^2$, $16x^4$, and $16x^6$ are some examples of perfect squares.   13. true
14. true   15. false; $(2x + 3)(x - 4) = 2x^2 - 5x - 12$.   16. false; $2x^3 + 4x^2$
$- 16x = 2x(x + 4)(x - 2)$.   17. true   18. true   19. false; $x^3 - 8 = (x - 2)$
$(x^2 + 2x + 4)$.   20. false   There are 11 false statements (or 12 false
statements if this statement is included). Neither is a factor of 20

Algebra Teacher's Activities Kit

Finding the GCF of Whole Numbers

A *factor* is a number that divides into a larger number evenly. *The greatest common factor, GCF,* is the largest number that divides into two or more numbers evenly. Being able to find the GCF of two or more numbers is not only an important skill for reducing fractions, it is also used to factor polynomials.

Directions: Find the GCF of each set of numbers. Match your answers with the answers in the Answer Bank, and write the corresponding letters in the blanks before the problems. Then write the letters in order, starting with the first problem, to complete the statement at the end of the activity. Some answers will be used more than once.

1. _____ 5, 10
2. _____ 28, 35
3. _____ 28, 24
4. _____ 3, 8
5. _____ 6, 10, 12
6. _____ 14, 35, 42
7. _____ 27, 18, 54
8. _____ 24, 40
9. _____ 8, 12
10. _____ 30, 15, 20
11. _____ 66, 55, 99
12. _____ 27, 21, 45
13. _____ 16, 52
14. _____ 16, 17, 30
15. _____ 24, 54, 36
16. _____ 30, 21, 45

Answer Bank
R. 11
H. 1
T. 4
C. 8
A. 9
S. 3
I. 6
O. 5
F. 7
E. 2

Any positive integer greater than 1 is a prime number or can be expressed as a

product of prime numbers. Except for the order ____ ____   ____ ____ ____

____ ____ ____ ____ ____ ____ ____ ,   ____ ____ ____ ____ expression is unique.

Factors of Monomials and Polynomials

179

Finding the GMF

Just as the greatest common factor of two or more numbers is the largest number that is a factor of the numbers, the *greatest monomial factor, GMF,* is the largest monomial that is a factor of two or more terms. For example, 15 is the greatest common factor of 30 and 45 because 15 is the largest factor of both 30 and 45.

Here is an example of a GMF. $6a^2b$ is the GMF of $12a^3b$ and $18a^2b^2$ because $6a^2b$ is the largest factor of $12a^3b$ and $18a^2b^2$.

Directions: Find the GMF of each group of terms. Match your answers with the answers in the Answer Bank, and write the corresponding letters in the blanks before the problems. Then write the letters above their problem numbers to complete the statement at the end of the activity.

1. _____ $3x$ and $3y$	**Answer Bank**
2. _____ $7x$ and $7x^2$	R. 11
3. _____ $4x$ and $10x$	M. 5
4. _____ $5x^2$ and $10x$	R. 2
5. _____ $6x^2$ and $9x$	F. y^2
6. _____ $8x^2$, $4x$, and 16	A. $4x$
7. _____ x^3, x^2, and x	G. $7x$
8. _____ $10x^2$, $20x$, and 15	P. $2x$
9. _____ $12x$, $8x$, and 6	E. 3
10. _____ $3x^2y$, $5xy$, and $10y$	I. 25
11. _____ $20xy$, $10xy^2$, and $5xy^3$	N. $5xy$
12. _____ $3y^2$, y^3, and y^4	Y. y
13. _____ $8xy^2$, $4x^2$, and $4x$	T. 10
14. _____ $25x^2$ and $100y^2$	L. $5x$
15. _____ $20y^2$, $30y$, and 60	O. x
	H. 4
	S. $3x$

Algebra Teacher's Activities Kit

Finding the GMF

$\overline{}$ $\overline{}$ $\overline{}$ $\quad$ $\overline{}$ $\overline{}$ $\quad$ $\overline{}$ $\overline{}$ $\overline{}$ $\quad$ $\overline{}$ $\overline{}$ $\overline{}$
7   11   1   14   5   15   6   1   2   8   12

$\overline{}$ $\overline{}$ $\quad$ $\overline{}$ $\quad$ $\overline{}$ $\overline{}$ $\overline{}$ $\overline{}$ $\overline{}$
7   12   13   3   9   14   8   1

$\overline{}$ $\overline{}$ $\overline{}$ $\overline{}$ $\overline{}$ $\overline{}$ $\overline{}$ $\overline{}$ $\overline{}$ $\overline{}$.
3   7   4   10   11   7   8   14   13   4

Finding the Missing Factor

Finding the missing factor of a monomial or a polynomial requires division. Here are two examples:

$6a = $ _____ $(2a)$ Divide: $\frac{6a}{2a}$. The quotient is 3.

$3ab + 6a + 12a^2 = $ _____ $(b + 2 + 4a)$ Divide term by term: $\frac{3ab}{b}$, $\frac{6a}{2}$, and $\frac{12a^2}{2a}$

Since all quotients equal 3a, 3a is the missing factor (provided that a or b do not equal 0). To check your answer, simplify $3a(b + 2 + 4a)$.

Directions: Find the missing factor of each expression below. Write the factor in the blank in the term. Then find your answer in the Answer Bank and write its corresponding letter in the blank before the problem. When you have finished, write the letters in order, starting with the first problem, to complete the statement at the end of the activity.

1. _____ $98a = $ _____ $(7a)$

2. _____ $15a = $ _____ (5)

3. _____ $12a^2 = $ _____ $(6a)$

4. _____ $3a^2b = $ _____ (a)

5. _____ $18ab = $ _____ $(9a)$

6. _____ $27a^2b^2 = $ _____ $(3ab)$

7. _____ $6a + 6b = $ _____ $(a + b)$

8. _____ $21a + 28 = $ _____ $(3a + 4)$

9. _____ $42a + 54b = $ _____ $(7a + 9b)$

10. _____ $12a + 3a^2 = $ _____ $(4 + a)$

11. _____ $15a^2 + 12a + 30 = $ _____ $(5a^2 + 4a + 10)$

12. _____ $2b^2 - 2b = $ _____ $(b - 1)$

Algebra Teacher's Activities Kit

Copyright © 2003 John Wiley & Sons, Inc.

Finding the Missing Factor

13. _____ $12a^2b + 18a^2b + 6a =$ _____ $(2ab + 3ab + 1)$

14. _____ $3a^3b^2 - 3a^2b^3 + 3ab^4 =$ _____ $(a^2 - ab + b^2)$

15. _____ $a^3b + 2a^2b^2 + 4ab^3 =$ _____ $(a^2 + 2ab + 4b^2)$

16. _____ $-10ab + 4ab^3 + 14b^4 =$ _____ $(-5a + 2ab^2 + 7b^3)$

17. _____ $a^2b^7 - 2a^2b^6 + a^5b^3 =$ _____ $(b^4 - 2b^3 + a^3)$

18. _____ $-7a + 49a^2 - 14 =$ _____ $(-a + 7a^2 - 2)$

19. _____ $15a^2 - 27a =$ _____ $(5a - 9)$

20. _____ $12a^3 + 30a^2 - 12a =$ _____ $(2a^2 + 5a - 2)$

Answer Bank

A. $3a$	O. $2b$	S. 6	L. $6a$	M. a^2b^3	F. 14	I. 7
Y. $3ab^2$	P. 3	C. $2a$	T. $3ab$	R. $9ab$	N. ab	

You can check your answers for this activity by multiplying each factor.

If one of the ___ ___ ___ ___ ___ ___ ___   ___ ___   ___

___ ___ ___ ___ ___ ___ ___ ___ ___ ___ , you must use the Distributive Property.

Factoring the Difference of Squares

A *perfect square* or a *square number* is a number or term that has two factors that are the same. An example of a square number is 1, whose factors are 1 · 1. Another example is 4, whose factors are 2 · 2. Still other examples are 9, 16, 25, 36, and so on.

Some monomials are also perfect squares. An example is x^2, whose factors are x · x. Another example is x^{10}, whose factors are $x^5 \cdot x^5$, and yet another is $49x^8$, whose factors are $7x^4 \cdot 7x^4$.

The difference of two square numbers can always be factored using the formula $(a^2 - b^2) = (a - b)(a + b)$. This formula only applies to square numbers, and you can always check your answer by multiplying the binomials.

Directions: State whether or not each binomial can be factored. If it can be factored, factor it. If it cannot be factored, write "cannot be factored." Hint: The total number of binomials that cannot be factored can be expressed as the difference of two square numbers.

1. $x^2 - 36 =$ _____

2. $x^2 - 64 =$ _____

3. $x^2 - 1 =$ _____

4. $x^2 + 16 =$ _____

5. $4x^2 - 121 =$ _____

6. $2x^2 - 25 =$ _____

7. $x^4 - 4 =$ _____

8. $16x^2 - 49 =$ _____

9. $x^2y^2 - 9 =$ _____

10. $x^3 - 144 =$ _____

11. $25x^2y^2 - 36 =$ _____

12. $10x^4 - 81 =$ _____

13. $x^6y^4 - 169 =$ _____

14. $x^6y^8 - 100 =$ _____

15. $8x^4y^2 - 25 =$ _____

Finding Factors, Sums, and Differences

Every number, except 1, has at least two factors. *Prime numbers* are numbers that have only two factors. *Composite numbers* are numbers that have more than two factors.

Factors can always be grouped in pairs, even though a number may have an odd number of factors. For example, 16 has five factors: {1, 2, 4, 8, 16}. Yet the pairs of factors are $1 \cdot 16$, $2 \cdot 8$, and $4 \cdot 4$. Always consider the pairs of factors as you complete this activity.

Directions: Find the pairs of factors described below. Find the letter of each factor in the Answer Bank on the next page and write it in the space provided. Starting with the first problem, write the letters to complete the statement at the end of the activity. Be careful, because you might have to switch the order of the letters in some problems. The first problem has been completed for you.

Number	Find the factors of	Sum or difference	Letters of factors	
1	35	sum is 12	M	U
2	72	difference is 6		
3	8	sum is 9		
4	96	difference is 4		
5	18	sum is 11		
6	48	difference is 2		
7	42	sum is 17		
8	26	sum is 15		
9	54	difference is 3		
10	32	difference is 4		
11	8	sum is 6		
12	24	sum is 11		
13	5	difference is 4		
14	140	difference is 4		
15	12	sum is 8		
16	18	difference is 3		

Factors of Monomials and Polynomials

Finding Factors, Sums, and Differences

Answer Bank						
T. 6	C. 9	N. 3	M. 5	O. 14	S. 4	R. 10
P. 1	F. 13	I. 8	L. 12	A. 2	U. 7	

Knowing your M   U ___ ___ ___ ___ ___ ___ ___ ___ ___ ___ ___ ___

___ ___ ___ ___   ___ ___   ___ ___

___ ___ ___ ___ ___ ___ ___ ___ factor in this activity.

Factoring Trinomials I

Factoring trinomials is a skill that is often used to solve equations. It is easy to factor trinomials if you can determine factors of numbers and find sums or differences. To check that the factors you use are correct, simply multiply the binomials.

For example, $x^2 - 2x - 15$ can be factored as $(x - 5)(x + 3)$, because the factors of -15 whose sum equal -2 are -5 and 3.

Here is another example. $x^2 - 7x + 12$ can be factored as $(x - 4)(x - 3)$, because the factors of 12 whose sum equal -7 are -3 and -4.

Directions: Factor each trinomial and write your answer in the space provided. You will likely be correct if each factor is used twice. Check your answers.

1. $x^2 + 5x + 6 =$ _____

2. $x^2 - 6x - 7 =$ _____

3. $x^2 - 12x + 32 =$ _____

4. $x^2 - 4x + 4 =$ _____

5. $x^2 - 9x + 8 =$ _____

6. $x^2 + x - 20 =$ _____

7. $x^2 - x - 30 =$ _____

8. $x^2 - 16x + 60 =$ _____

9. $x^2 - 3x - 28 =$ _____

10. $x^2 - 2x - 15 =$ _____

11. $x^2 + 3x + 2 =$ _____

12. $x^2 - 15x + 36 =$ _____

13. $x^2 - 6x + 5 =$ _____

14. $x^2 - 12x + 27 =$ _____

15. $x^2 - 6x - 40 =$ _____

16. $x^2 - 21x + 108 =$ _____

Factors of Monomials and Polynomials

Factoring Trinomials II

To factor trinomials you must find factors and their sums and differences. If the leading coefficient of a trinomial is a number other than 1, find the factors of the coefficient and the third term. Then examine combinations of the factors to find the sum that is the same as the second term.

For example, to factor $2x^2 - 11x - 12$, first find the factors of 2, then find the factors of -12. Combine these factors so that their products and sums equal -11. $(2 \times -4) + (-3 \times 1) = -11$. Therefore $2x^2 - 11x - 12$ can be factored as $(2x - 3)(x - 4)$. Check this by multiplying the binomials.

Directions: Factor each trinomial. Hint: One factor of each polynomial is a factor of the polynomial in the next problem. Always check your work.

1. $3x^2 - 11x - 4 =$ _____

2. $6x^2 - x - 1 =$ _____

3. $2x^2 + 13x - 7 =$ _____

4. $x^2 - x - 56 =$ _____

5. $x^2 - 5x - 24 =$ _____

6. $4x^2 + 11x - 3 =$ _____

7. $2x^2 + 11x + 15 =$ _____

8. $6x^2 + 11x - 10 =$ _____

9. $12x^2 + x - 6 =$ _____

10. $4x^2 + 15x + 9 =$ _____

11. $x^2 + 12x + 27 =$ _____

12. $5x^2 + 52x + 63 =$ _____

13. $10x^2 - x - 21 =$ _____

14. $12x^2 - 28x + 15 =$ _____

15. $18x^2 - 3x - 10 =$ _____

Algebra Teacher's Activities Kit

Factoring Binomials and Trinomials

Use the following steps when factoring binomials and trinomials:

1. Find the greatest common factor or the greatest monomial factor (if there is one).
2. Write the expression as the product of the factor and a polynomial.
3. Factor the polynomial, if possible.
4. Always check by multiplying.

Directions: Factor each polynomial and write the factors in the space after the polynomial. Find each pair of factors in the Answer Bank on the next page, and write the letters of the factors in the spaces provided before the problem. When you have finished, write the letters, starting with the first problem, in the spaces at the end of the activity to complete a message. Hint: It may be necessary to switch the order of the two letters in each problem to complete the message.

1. ____ ____ $x^2 - x - 6 =$ _____

2. ____ ____ $x^2 - 9x + 20 =$ _____

3. ____ ____ $x^2 + 9x + 14 =$ _____

4. ____ ____ $x^2 - 9x + 8 =$ _____

5. ____ ____ $3x^2 + 16x + 16 =$ _____

6. ____ ____ $x^2 - 13x + 40 =$ _____

7. ____ ____ $x^2 - 6x + 8 =$ _____

8. ____ ____ $x^2 + 2x - 3 =$ _____

9. ____ ____ $x^2 - x - 2 =$ _____

10. ____ ____ $x^2 + 8x + 16 =$ _____

11. ____ ____ $2x^3 - 16x^2 =$ _____

12. ____ ____ $4x + 28 =$ _____

13. ____ ____ $2x^2 - x - 6 =$ _____

14. ____ ____ $2x^3 + 2x^2 =$ _____

15. ____ ____ $x^2 - 11x + 24 =$ _____

16. ____ ____ $6x^2 + 42x =$ _____

Factors of Monomials and Polynomials

Factoring Binomials and Trinomials

Answer Bank

N. $(x + 4)$ O. $(x - 8)$ E. $(x + 7)$ C. $(x + 1)$

P. $(x + 2)$ S. $(x + 3)$ I. $(x - 4)$ M. $(x - 5)$

L. $(x - 1)$ B. 4   R. $(x - 3)$ F. $(2x + 3)$

T. $2x^2$ D. 6x   Y. $(3x + 4)$ A. $(x - 2)$

___ ___ ___ ___ ___

___ ___ ___ ___ ___ ___ ___ ___ ___ ___

___ ___ ___ ___ ___ ___   ___ ___

___ ___ ___ ___ ___ ___ ___ ___.

Algebra Teacher's Activities Kit

Factoring by Grouping

Sometimes the terms of polynomials may already be grouped and then factored. For example, $2(a + 3) + a(a + 3)$ can be written as $(2 + a)(a + 3)$.

At other times it may be necessary for you to group terms and then factor each group of terms. For example, $2a - 4b + a^2 - 2ab$ can be grouped as $(2a - 4b) + (a^2 - 2ab)$. Each group of terms can then be factored: $2(a - 2b) + a(a - 2b) = (2 + a)(a - 2b)$.

Directions: Factor each polynomial. Find each group of factors on the diagram on the next page, and connect the pair of factors with a ruler. When you are finished, you will have drawn fifteen line segments and mastered the skill of factoring by grouping.

1. $5(a + b) + c(a + b) =$ _____

2. $3(a + 2b) + a(a + 2b) =$ _____

3. $c(a - 2b) - (a - 2b) =$ _____

4. $3a(a - 4) + 4(a - 4) =$ _____

5. $a(a - b) + 2b(b - a) =$ _____

6. $5(a + 3) + c(3 + a) =$ _____

7. $c(a + 2b) - (a + 2b) =$ _____

8. $a(a - 2b) + 4(2b - a) =$ _____

9. $3a^2 + 4a - 2b(3a + 4) =$ _____

10. $5a - 20 + ac - 4c =$ _____

11. $a(c - 1) + b(1 - c) =$ _____

12. $3a^2 - ab - 12a + 4b =$ _____

13. $2(a + b) + a^2 + ab + a + b =$ _____

14. $3c - 3 + ac - a =$ _____

15. $15a - 5b - cb + 3ac =$ _____

Factoring by Grouping

$5 + c$

$a - 4$　　　　　$3a - b$　　　$a + b$　　　　　　$3 + a$

$3a + 4$　　　　　$a + 2b$

$a - b$

$a - 2b$　　　　　　　　　$c - 1$

Algebra Teacher's Activities Kit

Factoring the Sum and Difference of Cubes

A number or term raised to the third power is called a cube. Here are some examples: 1 or 1^3, 8 or 2^3, x^3, and $64x^3$ or $(4x)^3$. To factor the sum or difference of cubes, use the procedures below.

$$a^3 + b^3 = (a + b)(a^2 - ab + b^2)$$
$$a^3 - b^3 = (a - b)(a^2 + ab + b^2)$$

Directions: Terms are missing from each of the polynomials written in factored form. Write the missing term in the blank. Beneath each blank is a letter. Write each letter above its corresponding term in the blanks at the end of the activity to complete the statement.

1. $8x^3 - y^3 = (2x - y)(4x^2 + \underline{}_{O} + y^2)$

2. $x^3 + 27 = (x + \underline{}_{C})(x^2 - 3x + 9)$

3. $8 + 125x^3 = (2 + \underline{}_{F})(4 - 10x + 25x^2)$

4. $x^6 + y^6 = (x^2 + \underline{}_{R})(x^4 - x^2y^2 + y^4)$

5. $x^3 - 1 = (\underline{}_{B} - 1)(x^2 + x + 1)$

6. $x^6 - y^3 = (x^2 - y)(x^4 + \underline{}_{Y} + y^2)$

7. $8y^3 - 27x^3 = (2y - 3x)(4y^2 + \underline{}_{E} + 9x^2)$

8. $2x^3 - 2y^3 = \underline{}_{N}(x - y)(x^2 + xy + y^2)$

9. $(x^6 - 1) = (x - 1)(x + \underline{}_{L})(x^4 + x^2 + 1)$

10. $(24x^3 + 81) = 3(2x + 3)(4x^2 - 6x + \underline{}_{U})$

11. $(x - 3)^3 + 27 = x(x^2 - \underline{}_{S} + 27)$

Factoring the Sum and Difference of Cubes

There are ___ ___ ___ ___   ___ ___ ___ ___   ___ ___ ___ ___ ___
         2xy 2 1 x^2y 5x 2xy 9 y^2 3   9   x 6xy 9x

less than one hundred. Name them: _____

Factoring Polynomials Completely

A polynomial is factored completely when it is expressed as a product of prime polynomials or the product of a monomial and a prime polynomial or prime polynomials. (A prime polynomial has a GMF that is equal to 1.)

Use the following checklist to help you factor polynomials completely. If a step does not apply, continue to the next step.

- Find the GMF.
- Check to see whether or not the polynomial is the difference of squares, and factor the polynomial.
- Use the factors of the third term to find the sums and differences (or products of sums and differences if the leading coefficient is a number other than 1).
- If the polynomial has four terms, try to group the terms and factor by grouping.
- Be sure each polynomial is prime.
- Check your work by multiplying each factor.

Directions: Factor each polynomial completely. Each polynomial has at least three factors. All of the factors are included in the Answer Bank.

1. $2x^2 - 6x + 4 =$ _____

2. $x^3 + 3x^2 - 4x =$ _____

3. $3x^2 - 12x - 36 =$ _____

4. $16x^2 + 16x + 4 =$ _____

5. $3x^2 - 27 =$ _____

6. $-x + 4x^3 =$ _____

7. $25x^4 - 100x^2 =$ _____

8. $x^4 - 1 =$ _____

9. $15x^2 - 9x - 6 =$ _____

10. $12x^2 + 38x + 16 =$ _____

11. $30x^3 + 21x^2 + 3x =$ _____

12. $2x^6 - 8 =$ _____

13. $x^4 - y^4 =$ _____

14. $x^2y - 9y + 3x^2 - 27 =$ _____

Factoring Polynomials Completely

Answer Bank

$x + 1$	$3x$	$x - 3$	$x + 4$	$2x - 1$	$x - 2$
$5x + 2$	$x + y$	$25x^2$	$x + 3$	$y + 3$	2
$x^3 + 2$	4	$x - 1$	x	$5x + 1$	$x^3 - 2$
$2x + 1$	$x^2 + 1$	$3x + 8$	3	$x - y$	$x + 2$
$x^2 + y^2$	$x - 6$				

Algebra Teacher's Activities Kit

Reviewing Factoring Skills

All of the skills you need to know about factoring are included on this worksheet. You will need all of them as you complete the problems.

Directions: Read each statement and decide whether it is true or false. If it is true, write "true." If it is false, write "false" and provide an example or an explanation that will make the statement true.

1. 10 is the GCF of 20 and 40. _____

   _____

2. 36 is a square number. _____

   _____

3. $x(x^2 + 1) = x^3 + x$. _____

   _____

4. $x^2 - 16$ cannot be factored. _____

   _____

5. $2x^4$ is the GMF of $10x^4 + 12x^2 + 2$. _____

   _____

6. $(x + 3)$ is a factor of $x^2 + x - 12$. _____

   _____

7. $(2x^2 + 1)(x^2 - 1) = 2x^4 - x^2 - 1$. _____

   _____

8. $x + 1$ is a factor of $x^2 + 1$. _____

   _____

9. The product of two binomials is always a trinomial. _____

   _____

10. 51 is a prime number. _____

   _____

Factors of Monomials and Polynomials

Reviewing Factoring Skills

11. $2x + 1$ is a factor of $6x^2 - 5x - 4$. _____

_____

12. $16x^3$ is a perfect square. _____

_____

13. 1 may be a GMF. _____

_____

14. $x + 3$ is a factor of $x^4 + 3x^3 + x^2 + 3x$. _____

_____

15. $2x^2 - 5x - 12$ cannot be factored. _____

_____

16. $2x^3 + 4x^2 - 16x$ is factored completely as $x(2x^2 + 4x - 16)$. _____

_____

17. $x^3 + 27$ is the sum of two cubes. _____

_____

18. $x^2 + 1x + 3$ cannot be factored. _____

_____

19. $(x^3 - 8) = (x - 2)(x^2 - 2x + 4)$. _____

_____

20. The number of false statements in this exercise is a factor of 20. _____

_____

Functions and Relations

Understanding functions is essential to learning topics found in higher branches of mathematics such as trigonometry and calculus. The twelve activities of this section focus on functions and the application of their terms and notations. Skills, which include constructing T-tables, interpreting graphs, combining functions, and finding domains, ranges, inverses, and values, provide a foundation for further study in mathematics.

Teaching Suggestions for the Activities

7-1   Completing T-Tables

For this activity your students are to complete T-tables. Prerequisite skills include being able to transform equations and solve equations.

Begin the activity by writing $3x + 2y = 10$ on the board or an overhead projector. Ask your students to solve for y if $x = -2$. The answer is $y = 8$. Ask your students to solve for y if $x = \frac{1}{3}$. The answer is $y = 4.5$. Now ask your students to solve for x if $y = 2$. The answer is $x = 2$.

Organize this data in a T-table, pointing out that the values for x are recorded in the first column and that the values for y are shown in the second column. Offer the example of the T-table below on the board or an overhead projector.

X	Y
-2	8
$\frac{1}{3}$	4.5
2	2

Explain that the equation can be transformed as $y = 5 - \frac{3}{2}x$. This makes it easier to solve for y. It can also be rewritten as $x = \frac{10}{3} - \frac{2}{3}y$; this form makes it easier to solve for x.

Review the instructions on the worksheet with your students. Be sure they understand that they must write the letter of the value and read the letters down each table, line by line. Note that some answers will be used more than once.

7-2   Identifying Functions

In this activity your students are asked to complete a T-table and graph the points to determine whether or not the ordered pairs represent a function. To complete this activity successfully, your students should be able to complete T-tables. Activity 7-1 serves as a good foundation. Your students will need graph paper for this activity.

Introduce the activity by writing the following T-tables on the board or an overhead projector:

Example I

X	Y
8	-2
2	-1
0	0
2	1
8	2

Example 2

X	Y
-2	-6
-1	-3
0	0
1	3
2	6

Instruct your students to graph each set of points. Their graphs should look like these:

Graph for Example I   **Graph for Example 2**

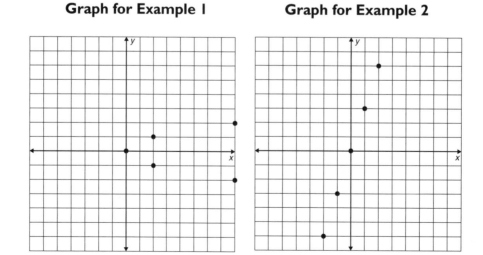

Now ask your students to compare and contrast each set of points. Note that in the first table some values for x have two different values for y. For example, 8 is paired with –2 and 2, and 2 is paired with –1 and 1. In the second table, each value for x is paired with only one value for y. The set of data in the second table is a function.

Review the directions on the worksheet with your students. Note that they should complete the T-tables and then graph the points. There should be ten graphs. Remind them that they are to list the problem numbers of those points that are not a function.

7-3 Finding the Values of Functions

For this activity your students are to find the values of functions. To complete the activity successfully, they should be familiar with the concept of functions. They should also understand the use of the arrow notation and the meaning of f(x).

Begin the activity by reviewing the concept of a function. A function is a set of points and a rule that pairs each value for x with only one value for y.

Explain that sometimes a function cannot be evaluated, because the denominator is zero or a negative number is a radicand (an expression beneath the radical sign). In these cases, a function is undefined and the value is ø.

Review the instructions on the worksheet with your students. Note that some answers will be used more than once.

7-4 Identifying the Domain and Range of a Function

This activity requires students to identify the domain and range of functions by interpreting graphs. Visual perception is an important part of this activity.

Start the activity by explaining that a function consists of two sets, the domain and range, and a rule that assigns to each member of the domain a unique member of the range. Note that the domain of a function consists of all the values for x, while the range of a function consists of all the values for y. Depending on the abilities of your students, you may find it helpful to review the components of the coordinate plane, noting that the x-axis is the horizontal line and that the y-axis is the vertical line.

Discuss the example on the worksheet. Explain that [–3,2] means all real numbers greater than or equal to –3 and less than or equal to 2. Also explain that the domain is the set of all real numbers between –3 and 2 and including –3 and 2. The range [–1,1] is the set of all real numbers between –1 and 1 and including –1 and 1.

Go over the directions on the worksheet with your students. Note that every answer in the Answer Bank will be used and that some answers will be used more than once.

7-5 Finding the Domain of a Function

For this activity your students are given a formula and they must find the domain of a function. To complete this activity successfully, your students should understand that division by zero is undefined and be able to factor polynomials and solve linear equations.

Begin the activity by writing the following expressions on the board or an overhead projector.

$$1.\ f(x) = x \qquad 2.\ f(x) = \frac{1}{x-2} \qquad 3.\ f(x) = \frac{1}{x^2 - 2x - 3}$$

$$4.\ f(x) = \sqrt{x} \qquad 5.\ f(x) = \frac{1}{\sqrt{x}}$$

Instruct your students to compare and contrast these expressions. Their responses may vary, but students should realize the following:

- In three of the expressions, a variable is in the denominator.
- The first expression has neither a denominator nor radicand, and the variable in the first expression can be any number. This means the domain of the function is all real numbers.
- The denominator in the second expression cannot equal zero, because the function is undefined at zero. Therefore, $x - 2 \neq 0$ so $x \neq 2$. This can be expressed as the domain being all real numbers except 2 or $\{x: x \neq 2\}$.
- For the third expression, students must factor the denominator and state $(x - 3)(x + 1) \neq 0$. The domain is all real numbers except 3 or -1 or $\{x: x \neq 3 \text{ or } x \neq -1\}$.
- For the fourth expression, x must be greater than or equal to zero or $\{x: x \geq 0\}$, because it is impossible to find the square root of a negative number.
- For the fifth expression, the domain is all real numbers greater than zero or $\{x: x > 0\}$, because it is impossible to find the square root of a negative number, and division by zero is undefined.
- Some expressions have radicands.

Go over the directions on the worksheet with your students. Make sure that they understand the notation for expressing the domain, and remind them that each domain in the Answer Bank will be used once.

7-6 Using the Basic Operations with Functions

This activity requires your students to perform the four basic operations with functions. To complete the activity successfully, your students should be able to add, subtract, multiply, and divide polynomials.

Begin the activity by writing the following on the board or an overhead projector. (The answers are provided for your information.)

$$(x^2 - 2x - 3) + (x + 1) = \quad x^2 - x - 2$$
$$(x^2 - 2x - 3) - (x + 1) = \quad x^2 - 3x - 4$$
$$(x^2 - 2x - 3)(x + 1) = \quad x^3 - x^2 - 5x - 3$$
$$(x^2 - 2x - 3) \div (x + 1) = \quad x - 3; x \neq -1$$

Explain the basic operations. For the last problem note that since division by zero is undefined, $x \neq -1$.

Extend the concepts illustrated by the examples to functions, and explain to your students that they should treat basic operations with functions in the same way as the operations with polynomials. Next, write the following examples on the board or an overhead projector.

$$\text{If } P(x) = x^2 - 2x - 3 \text{ and } h(x) = x + 1$$
$$(P + h)(x) = P(x) + h(x) = x^2 - x - 2$$
$$(P - h)(x) = P(x) - h(x) = x^2 - 3x - 4$$
$$(P \cdot h)(x) = P(x) \cdot h(x) = x^3 - x^2 - 5x - 3$$
$$(P \div h)(x) = P(x) \div h(x) = x - 3; x \neq -1$$

Note that the domains of the sums, differences, and products are the same as the numbers in the domains of both of the functions with which your students are working, in this case $P(x)$ and $h(x)$. Students must also be sure to restrict the domain, if necessary.

Go over the directions on the worksheet with your students. Note that some answers in the Answer Bank will not be used.

7-7 Finding the Composition of Functions

For this activity your students will be asked to find composite functions. To complete the activity successfully, students should be proficient in working with monomials and polynomials.

Begin the activity by explaining that functions may be combined by using the basic operations and also by substituting one function into another. This activity focuses on substitution.

Discuss the definition and examples on the worksheet. You may find it helpful to write the examples on the board or overhead projector, using different colors of chalk or markers—one color for $g(x)$ and another for $f(x)$. Emphasize the notation using brackets: $(f \circ g)(x) = f[g(x)]$ and note that $g(x)$ in brackets should be used in $f(x)$.

Go over the directions on the worksheet with your students. Note that in most cases $(f \circ g)(x) \neq (g \circ f)(x)$.

7-8 Finding the Inverses of Functions

For this activity your students must match functions with their inverses. Prerequisite skills for this activity include solving equations containing powers and understanding the horizontal line test.

Start the activity by reviewing the horizontal line test with your students. Explain that the test states if no horizontal line intersects the graph of a function more than once, then the inverse is a function. Offer these examples on the board or an overhead projector.

1. $y = x^2$

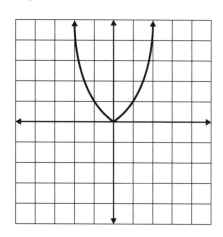

2. $y = \pm\sqrt{x}$

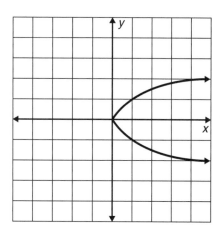

3. $y = x^3$

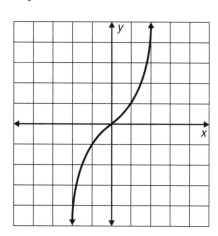

4. $y = \sqrt[3]{x}$

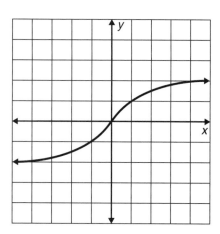

Discuss the graphs and note that the graph of $y = x^2$ does not pass the horizontal line test. If necessary, discuss the process for finding the inverse of a function, and note that students must isolate the value of y before they can find the root of the expression.

Review the directions on the worksheet. Mention that f^{-1} is used to denote the inverse and is read "f inverse." Also mention that each inverse in the Answer Bank is used once.

7-9 Evaluating the Greatest Integer Function

This activity requires your students to evaluate the greatest integer function. Understanding the concepts and skills presented in this activity will help students to solve problems involving functions.

Begin the activity by drawing a number line on the board or an overhead projector. Remind your students that integers are the set of whole numbers and their opposites. {. . . –2, –1, 0, 1, 2 . . .} are integers. Refer to the worksheet, discuss the definition for the greatest integer function, and review the examples.

Go over the instructions on the worksheet with your students. Note that every value in the Answer Bank will be used, and that some will be used more than once.

7-10 Evaluating Piecewise-defined Functions

For this activity your students must express a practical situation in real life as a piecewise-defined function and use this representation to solve word problems. To complete this activity successfully, your students should be able to write equations that model real-life situations. The activity lends itself to small group work.

Start the activity by discussing the definition of a piecewise-defined function, which is a function defined by two or more parts. Discuss the example on the worksheet. Emphasize the two parts of the function: one to use if $x > 0$ and the other to evaluate if $x \leq 0$.

Go over the instructions on the worksheet with your students. Remind them that they will have to write functions that have at least two pieces.

7-11 Identifying Graphs of Families of Functions

This activity requires your students to match functions with their graphs. It provides an introduction to transformations, an important concept in calculus.

Begin the activity by discussing the families of functions on the activity sheet. You may find it helpful to show their graphs on the board or an overhead projector. Depending on the abilities of your students, you may prefer to show points on the graphs by making T-tables or use a graphing calculator to graph each function.

Explain that the graph of each family of functions has essentially the same shape. For example, all absolute value functions will always be v-shaped; however, the size of the "v" and its position on the graph will vary, depending on the specific equation.

Go over the directions on the worksheet with your students. Note that they should identify the family first and write the family name in the blank beneath the graph. They should then focus on functions that belong to the family and use T-tables or a graphing calculator to match the function with its graph. Remind your students that some functions in the Answer Bank will not be used.

7-12 Reviewing the Concepts and Applications of Functions

This activity offers a review of the skills and concepts presented in this section. After having worked on the other activities of this section, most of your students should be able to complete this activity successfully.

Begin the activity by explaining that it is a review exercise. If necessary, explain any concepts or skills your students still may not have fully mastered.

Go over the instructions on the worksheet with your students. Emphasize that they are to rewrite the false statements with examples or explanations to make them true. Explain that the six functions included on the worksheet are to be used as necessary.

Answer Key for Section 7

7-1. 1. T, –1; O, 4   2. C, –3; O, 4   3. M, 9; P, $\frac{1}{4}$ 4. L, 5; E, –5   5. T, –1; E, –5

6. A, 17; T, –1   7. T, –1; A, 17   8. B, –4; L, 5   9. E, –5; I, 2; F, 8   10. Y, –8;

I, 2   11. S, $\frac{1}{2}$; W, $\frac{3}{2}$ 12. R, 3; I, 2; T, –1   13. T, –1; E, –5; N, $\frac{2}{3}$ 14. A, 17;

S, $\frac{1}{2}$ It is easier <u>to complete a T-table if y is written as</u> a function of x.

7-2.

1.

X	Y
– 2	– 4
– 1	– 1
0	2
1	5
2	8

2.

X	Y
– 2	2
– 1	1
0	0
1	– 1
2	– 2

3.

X	Y
– 2	8
– 1	2
0	0
1	2
2	8

4.

X	Y
– 2	2
– 1	1
0	0
1	1
2	2

5.	X	Y
	12	-2
	3	-1
	0	0
	3	1
	12	2

6.	X	Y
	-2	-8
	-1	-1
	0	0
	1	1
	2	8

7.	X	Y
	2	-2
	1	-1
	0	0
	1	1
	2	2

8.	X	Y
	-2	-1
	-1	$-\frac{1}{2}$
	0	0
	1	$\frac{1}{2}$
	2	1

9.	X	Y
	-2	3
	-1	3
	0	3
	1	3
	2	3

10.	X	Y
	5	-2
	5	-1
	5	0
	5	1
	5	2

The set of points in problems 5, 7, and 10 do not represent functions.

7-3. 1. I, ∅ 2. S, –7 3. D, 1 4. E, 0 5. F, –3 6. I, ∅ 7. N, 2 8. E, 0 9. D, 1 10. B, $-\frac{1}{2}$ 11. Y, –1 12. A, $2\frac{1}{2}$ 13. R, 20 14. U, $\frac{1}{25}$ 15. L, –20 16. E, 0 17. I, ∅ 18. N, 2 19. D, 1 20. I, ∅ 21. C, 6 22. A, $2\frac{1}{2}$ 23. T, $\frac{1}{4}$ 24. I, ∅ 25. N, 2 26. G, –13   Function is taken from the Latin term "functio," meaning "to perform." In mathematics a function <u>is defined by a rule indicating</u> what operations must be performed.

7-4. 1. A, [0,3]; F, [1,4] 2. U, [2,5]; N, [–3,2] 3. C, [–3,3]; T, [–4,2] 4. I, [–2,2]; O, [0,2] 5. N, [–3,2]; C, [–3,3] 6. O, [0,2]; N, [–3,2] 7. S, [–4,4]; I, [–2,2] 8. S, [–4,4]; T, [–4,2] 9. S, [–4,4]; O, [0,2] 10. F, [1,4]; T, [–4,2] 11. W, [–4,1]; O, [0,2]   <u>A function consists of two</u> sets, the domain and range, and a rule that assigns to each member of the domain exactly one member of the range.

7-5. 1. L, {x : x ≠ 1} 2. R, {x : x ≠ 1, x ≠ –1} 3. A, {x : x ≥ 0} 4. G, {x : x > 0} 5. U, {x : x ≠ –1, x ≠ 2} 6. I, {x : x ≥ 1} 7. N, {x : x ≠ 0, x ≠ 1} 8. M, {x : x > –1} 9. all real numbers 10. O, {x : x ≠ 0} 11. Y, {x : x ≠ 3, x ≠ –3} 12. B, {x : x ≥ –3} 13. F, {x : x ≥ 3}   In this activity, a function is defined <u>by giving a formula</u>.

7-6. 1. N, $x^2 + x + 1$ 2. E, $x^2 + x - 3$ 3. G, $2x - 2$ 4. A, $x^2 - 2x - 3$ 5. B, $x^3 - 2x^2 + x$ 6. F, x^3 7. Z, $x^2 - x$ 8. O, $-2x + 1$ 9. M, $2x - 1$ 10. U, $x^2 - 3x$ 11. H, $x^2 - 3x + 4$ 12. R, x 13. L, x – 3 14. T, x + 1 15. I, $\frac{x^2 - 2x - 3}{x^2 - 2x + 1}$ 16. S, $\frac{x^2}{x - 3}$ The domains are restricted in Problems 12 through 16 because division by <u>zero has no meaning in the set of real numbers</u>.

7–7. 1. B, $9x^2$ 2. Y, $-6x-1$ 3. S, $-2x^2-1$ 4. U, $3x^3$ 5. O, $4x^2+6x-1$ 6. A, x^4-x^2-3 7. T, $3x^2-3x-9$ 8. L, $-2x^3-1$ 9. D, $-2x^2+2x+5$ 10. F, $3x^2$ 11. W, x^6-x^3-3 12. I, $4x^2+4x+1$ 13. N, $x^4-2x^3-5x^2+6x+9$ 14. H, $27x^3$ 15. R, $9x^2-3x-3$ 16. E, $-6x-3$ The expression f(x) to represent a function <u>was first used by Leonhard Euler</u>.

7-8. 1. N, $f^{-1}(x)=\frac{1}{2}x+2$ 2. S, $f^{-1}(x)=\sqrt[3]{x}$ 3. R, $f^{-1}(x)=\sqrt[5]{x}$ 4. U, $f^{-1}(x)=x$ 5. A, $f^{-1}(x)=\frac{1}{2}x-2$ 6. C, $f^{-1}(x)=\sqrt[3]{2x+4}$ 7. I, $f^{-1}(x)=x-7$ 8. T, $f^{-1}(x)=\frac{1}{3}x+\frac{1}{3}$ 9. L, $f^{-1}(x)=2x-2$ 10. F, $f^{-1}(x)=\sqrt[3]{\frac{x-1}{3}}$ 11. O, $f^{-1}(x)=\sqrt[5]{7x-2}$ 12. E, $f^{-1}(x)=\sqrt[5]{x}$ For each linear function f(x) = mx + b where m ≠ 0, the inverse <u>is a linear function</u>.

7-9. 1. I, –1   2. S, 6   3. A, –4   4. S, 6   5. T, 5   6. E, –14   7. P, –10   8. F, 4   9. U, –8   10. N, –2   11. C, –3   12. T, 5   13. I, –1   14. O, 0   15. N, –2   16. B, 12   17. E, –14   18. C, –3   19. A, –4   20. U, –8   21. S, 6   22. E, –14   The greatest integer function <u>is a step function because</u> its graph resembles a set of stair steps.

7-10. Functions may vary; possible answers follow.

1. t = total time on line in hours per month.

$$f(t)\begin{cases} \$19.95 & \text{if } t \le 50 \\ \$19.95 + \$.99\big[|t-50|\big] & \text{if } t \text{ is an integer} > 50 \\ \$19.95 + \$.99\big[|t-49|\big] & \text{if } t \text{ is not an integer and } t > 50 \end{cases}$$

f(20) = \$19.95; f(55) = \$24.90; f(55.5) = \$25.89

2. t = total time spent on long-distance calls in minutes per month.

$$f(t)\begin{cases} \$29.95 + \$.05\big[|t+1|\big] & \text{if } t \text{ is an integer} \le 30 \\ \$29.95 + \$.05\big[|t|\big] & \text{if } t \text{ is not an integer and } 0 < t < 30 \\ \$31.45 + \$.10\big[|t-30|\big] & \text{if } t \text{ is an integer} > 30 \\ \$31.45 + \$.10\big[|t-29|\big] & \text{if } t \text{ is not an integer and } t > 30 \end{cases}$$

f(15.5) = \$30.75; f(37) = \$32.15

3. t = the number of hours after the park opens.

$$f(t)\begin{cases} \$39.95 & \text{if } t \le 6 \\ \$39.95 - \$10.00 & \text{if } t > 6 \end{cases}$$

f(1) = \$39.95; f(7) = \$29.95

4. t = the total number of hours worked per week.

$$f(t) \begin{cases} \$6.50t & \text{if } t \le 40 \\ \$260 + \$9.75(t-40) & \text{if } t > 40 \end{cases}$$

f(26) = \$169; f(45) = \$308.75

7-11. 1. linear function; f(x) = 2x − 1   2. cubing function; f(x) = x³ + 1   3. squaring function; f(x) = 3x²   4. absolute value function; f(x) = |x − 1| 5. linear function; f(x) = −2   6. square root function; f(x) = $\sqrt{x-1}$ 7. greatest integer function; f(x) = $\llbracket x+1 \rrbracket$ 8. absolute value function; f(x) = |x| + 1   9. square root function; f(x) = $-\sqrt{x}$ 10. cubing function; f(x) = −x³

7-12. Explanations may vary. Problems 2, 5, 7, 8, 11, 13, 15, 19, and 20 are true. 1. false; it depends on the values. If the value represents a function, then there is one "y" for "x."   3. false; f(−1) = −1   4. false; f(x) − g(x) = x + 5   6. false; (g ∘ f)(x) = 6x + 1 or (f ∘ g)(x) = 6x − 7   9. false; f⁻¹(x) is the notation used to express the inverse of f(x)   10. false; g⁻¹(x) = $\frac{x+3}{2}$ 12. false; the range of f(x) is all real numbers greater than or equal to 2   14. false; the graph of x = 4 is a line, but x = 4 is not a function   16. false; $\llbracket 3.5 \rrbracket = 3$ 17. false; G(x) is a function according to the definition of a function   18. false; the domain of G(x) is all real numbers. The range is all real numbers greater than or equal to zero.

Completing T-Tables

A *T-table* is a table used to determine values for x and y that will make an equation true. To complete a T-table, rewrite the equation so that y equals an expression. Then substitute values for x and solve for y. (It is also possible to rewrite the equation so that x equals an expression. Then substitute values for y and solve for x.)

Directions: Complete the T-tables. Find the missing values in the Answer Bank on the next page and write the letter of each value in the corresponding blank in the table. When you have finished, go down each table line by line and write the letters in order to complete the statement at the end of the activity. The first table is completed for you. Some answers will be used more than once.

1. $y = 3x - 1$

X	Y
-2	-7
1	2
0	T
$\frac{5}{3}$	O

2. $y = x$

X	Y
-3	
4	
1	1
-1	-1

3. $y = x^2$

X	Y
3	
-2	4
-1	1
$\frac{1}{2}$	

4. $y = \frac{1}{2}x$

X	Y
10	
-1	$-\frac{1}{2}$
6	3
-10	

5. $y = \frac{x}{4} - 3$

X	Y
8	
0	-3
-8	
1	$-2\frac{3}{4}$

6. $3y = 4x + 1$

X	Y
$12\frac{1}{2}$	
0	$\frac{1}{3}$
-1	
-4	-5

7. $2x = y + 1$

X	Y
1	1
	-3
4	7
9	

8. $x + y = 10$

X	Y
0	10
-1	11
	14
5	

9. $xy = 4$

X	Y
	$-\frac{4}{5}$
1	4
2	
$\frac{1}{2}$	

Completing T-Tables

10. $y = x^3$

X	Y
-1	-1
-2	
	8
0	0

11. $y = \frac{1}{x}$

X	Y
	2
3	$\frac{1}{3}$
$\frac{2}{3}$	
2	$\frac{1}{2}$

12. $y = -x + 5$

X	Y
0	5
2	
3	
	6

13. $3x + y = 0$

X	Y
	3
$\frac{5}{3}$	
2	-6
	-2

14. $-2x + y = 10$

X	Y
$3\frac{1}{2}$	
-6	-2
	11
4	18

Answer Bank

Y. -8	I. 2	E. -5	O. 4	A. 17	P. $\frac{1}{4}$
B. -4	S. $\frac{1}{2}$	W. $\frac{3}{2}$	C. -3	F. 8	T. -1
R. 3	M. 9	N. $\frac{2}{3}$	L. 5		

It is easier _T_ _O_ __ __ __ __ __ __ __ __ __ __ __-__ __ __ __ __

__ __ __ __ __ __ __ __ __ __ __ __ __ __ a function of x.

Identifying Functions

A *relation* is any set of ordered pairs. A *function* is a special type of relation in which each value for x is paired with only one value for y.

A T-table and graph can be used to organize ordered pairs to determine if a set of points is a function.

Directions: Complete each T-table. Then graph the ordered pairs. (You should have ten separate graphs.) When you have finished, list the problem numbers of the sets of points that are *not* functions.

1. $y = 3x + 2$

X	Y
−2	
−1	
0	
1	
2	

2. $y = -x$

X	Y
−2	
−1	
0	
1	
2	

3. $y = 2x^2$

X	Y
−2	
−1	
0	
1	
2	

4. $y = |x|$

X	Y
−2	
−1	
0	
1	
2	

5. $x = 3y^2$

X	Y
	−2
	−1
	0
	1
	2

6. $y = x^3$

X	Y
−2	
−1	
0	
1	
2	

7. $x = |y|$

X	Y
	−2
	−1
	0
	1
	2

8. $y = \frac{1}{2}x$

X	Y
−2	
−1	
0	
1	
2	

9. $y = 3$

X	Y
−2	
−1	
0	
1	
2	

10. $x = 5$

X	Y
	−2
	−1
	0
	1
	2

The set of points in problem numbers _____ *do not* represent functions.

Finding the Values of Functions

A *function* is a set of points and a rule that pairs each value for x with only one value for y. Functions can be described in two ways, examples of which follow:

- f:x → 3x − 4, which means that the function f pairs x with 3x − 4. If x = 3, then 3 is paired with 5. This is written f(3) = 5.
- h(x) = −5x + 2, which means that the function h pairs x with −5x + 2. If x = 3, then 3 is paired with −13. This is written h(3) = −13.

Some functions cannot be evaluated if the denominator is zero or a negative number is under the radical symbol. The value of such functions cannot be found and the value is ø.

Directions: Find the value of each function, if possible, and write it in the blank after the problem. Then find the value in the Answer Bank and write the letter of the value in the blank before the problem. When you have finished, write the letters in order, starting with the first problem, to complete the statement at the end of the activity.

$$f{:}x \rightarrow 3x - 4 \qquad P{:}x \rightarrow x^2 \qquad h(x) = -5x + 2$$

$$F(x) = \frac{10}{x} \qquad H(x) = \frac{x+2}{x^2-4} \qquad g(x) = \sqrt{x}$$

1. _____ F(0) = _____

2. _____ f(−1) = _____

3. _____ F(10) = _____

4. _____ P(0) = _____

5. _____ f($\frac{1}{3}$) = _____

6. _____ g(−1) = _____

7. _____ h(0) = _____

8. _____ h($\frac{2}{5}$) = _____

9. _____ P(1) = _____

10. _____ H(0) = _____

11. _____ f(1) = _____

12. _____ h($-\frac{1}{10}$) = _____

13. _____ F($\frac{1}{2}$) = _____

14. _____ P($\frac{1}{5}$) = _____

15. _____ F($-\frac{1}{2}$) = _____

16. _____ g(0) = _____

17. _____ H(2) = _____

18. _____ g(4) = _____

19. _____ P(−1) = _____

20. _____ H(−2) = _____

21. _____ g(36) = _____

22. _____ F(4) = _____

23. _____ P($\frac{1}{2}$) = _____

24. _____ g(−4) = _____

25. _____ F(5) = _____

26. _____ f(−3) = _____

Finding the Values of Functions

<table>
<tr><td colspan="4" align="center">**Answer Bank**</td></tr>
<tr><td>U. $\frac{1}{25}$</td><td>E. 0</td><td>D. 1</td><td>L. −20</td></tr>
<tr><td>A. $2\frac{1}{2}$</td><td>Y. −1</td><td>I. ø</td><td>R. 20</td></tr>
<tr><td>N. 2</td><td>T. $\frac{1}{4}$</td><td>F. −3</td><td>G. −13</td></tr>
<tr><td>S. −7</td><td>B. $-\frac{1}{2}$</td><td>C. 6</td><td></td></tr>
</table>

Function is taken from the Latin term "functio," meaning "to perform." In mathematics

a function __ __   __ __ __ __ __ __ __   __ __   __

__ __ __ __   __ __ __ __ __ __ __ __ __

what operations must be performed.

Algebra Teacher's Activities Kit

Copyright © 2003 John Wiley & Sons, Inc.

Identifying the Domain and Range of a Function

Linear functions whose graphs are straight lines continue infinitely in two directions. x can be any real number and y can be any real number. The *domain* includes the values of x, and the *range* includes the values of y. The domain and range of a linear function are all real numbers.

Sometimes the domain of a function is not all real numbers. To find the domain of a linear function by looking at a graph, consider the x-axis and determine what values are graphed.

To find the range of a linear function by looking at a graph, consider the y-axis and determine what values are graphed.

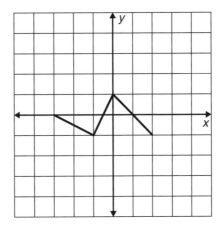

In the example above, the domain is any real number greater than or equal to –3 and less than or equal to 2. This can be written as [–3,2]. The range is any real number greater than or equal to –1 and less than or equal to 1. This can be written as [–1,1].

Directions: For each graph on the following pages, find the domain and range. Match your answers with the answers in the Answer Bank. Write the letter of the domain and then the letter of the range in the spaces below each graph. Then write the letters in order, starting with those of the first graph, to complete the statement at the end of the activity.

Identifying the Domain and Range of a Function

1.

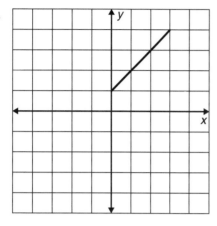

Domain: _____

Range: _____

2.

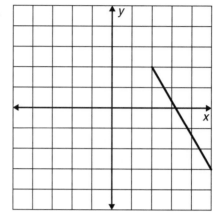

Domain: _____

Range: _____

3.

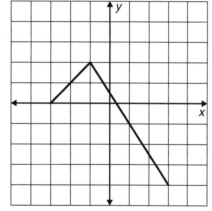

Domain: _____

Range: _____

4.

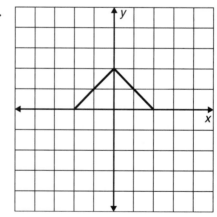

Domain: _____

Range: _____

Algebra Teacher's Activities Kit

Identifying the Domain and Range of a Function

5.

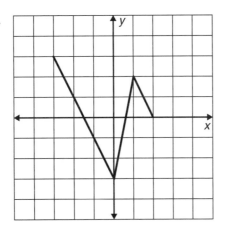

Domain: _____

Range: _____

6.

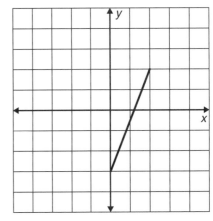

Domain: _____

Range: _____

7.

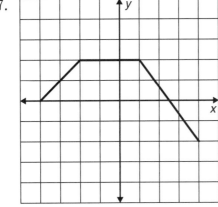

Domain: _____

Range: _____

8.

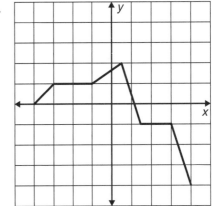

Domain: _____

Range: _____

Identifying the Domain and Range of a Function

9.

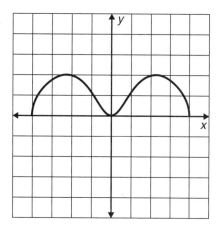

Domain: _____

Range: _____

10.

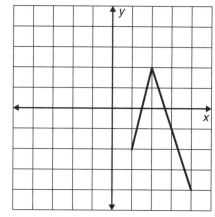

Domain: _____

Range: _____

11.

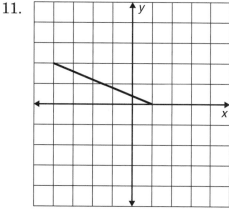

Domain: _____

Range: _____

Answer Bank				
C. [–3,3]	I. [–2,2]	S. [–4,4]	A. [0,3]	O. [0,2]
F. [1,4]	U. [2,5]	N. [–3,2]	T. [–4,2]	W. [–4,1]

___ ___ ___ ___ ___ ___ ___ ___ ___ ___ ___ ___   ___ ___ ___ ___ ___ ___ ___ ___ ___

___ ___   ___ ___ ___ sets, the domain and range, and a rule that assigns to each member of the domain exactly one member of the range.

Algebra Teacher's Activities Kit

Finding the Domain of a Function

Some functions have no meaning because the denominator equals zero or the radicand is a negative number. To find the domain of these functions, you must find the real numbers for which the functions *have* meaning.

   If the domain is all real numbers, x can be any real number and the function will have meaning.

   If the function has a variable in the denominator, then the domain is all real numbers that will make the denominator any number except zero.

   If the function has a variable in the radicand, then the domain is all real numbers that will make the radicand greater than or equal to zero.

Directions: Find the domain of each function, and match your answers with the answers in the Answer Bank. Write the letter of the domain in the blank after its corresponding function. When you have finished, write each letter above its problem number to complete the statement at the end of the activity.

1. $f(x) = \dfrac{1}{x-1}$ _____

2. $f(x) = \dfrac{1}{x^2-1}$ _____

3. $f(x) = \sqrt{3x}$ _____

4. $f(x) = \dfrac{1}{\sqrt{2x}}$ _____

5. $f(x) = \dfrac{1}{x^2-x-2}$ _____

6. $f(x) = \sqrt{x-1}$ _____

7. $f(x) = \dfrac{1}{x^2-x}$ _____

8. $f(x) = \dfrac{1}{\sqrt{x+1}}$ _____

9. $f(x) = \dfrac{1}{x^2+1}$ _____

10. $f(x) = \dfrac{1}{2x}$ _____

11. $f(x) = \dfrac{1}{x^2-9}$ _____

12. $f(x) = \sqrt{x+3}$ _____

13. $f(x) = \sqrt{x-3}$ _____

Answer Bank

N. $\{x : x \neq 0, x \neq 1\}$	Y. $\{x : x \neq 3, x \neq -3\}$	R. $\{x : x \neq 1, x \neq -1\}$
G. $\{x : x > 0\}$	L. $\{x : x \neq 1\}$	A. $\{x : x \geq 0\}$
B. $\{x : x \geq -3\}$	I. $\{x : x \geq 1\}$	F. $\{x : x \geq 3\}$
O. $\{x : x \neq 0\}$	U. $\{x : x \neq -1, x \neq 2\}$	V. all real numbers
		M. $\{x : x > -1\}$

In this activity, a function is defined $\underline{}\ \underline{}$ $\underline{}\ \underline{}\ \underline{}\ \underline{}\ \underline{}\ \underline{}$ $\underline{}$
                                                            12   11   4   6   9   6   7   4   3

$\underline{}\ \underline{}\ \underline{}\ \underline{}\ \underline{}\ \underline{}\ \underline{}$.
13   10   2   8   5   1   3

Using the Basic Operations with Functions

Functions, like monomials and polynomials, can be added, subtracted, multiplied, and divided. The same procedures apply.

- To add or subtract, combine similar terms.
- To multiply monomials, multiply the coefficients and add the exponents if the bases are the same.
- To multiply polynomials or polynomials and monomials, use the Distributive Property repeatedly.
- To divide monomials, divide the coefficients and subtract the exponents.
- To divide polynomials or polynomials and monomials, factor, if possible, and simplify.

When working with functions, remember that the domains of the sums, differences, and products are the numbers that are in the domains of both functions. The value of the denominator cannot equal zero, so the domain of a quotient may be restricted.

Directions: Find each sum, difference, product, or quotient. Match your answers with the expressions in the Answer Bank and write the letter of your answer in the blank after each problem. Then write the letter above its problem number to complete the statement at the end of the activity. Not all expressions in the Answer Bank will be used.

$$f(x) = x^2 \qquad P(x) = x^2 - 2x - 3 \qquad h(x) = x + 1$$
$$F(x) = x - 3 \qquad G(x) = x \qquad H(x) = x^2 - 2x + 1$$

1. $(f + h)(x) =$ _____

2. $(f + F)(x) =$ _____

3. $(F + h)(x) =$ _____

4. $(h \cdot F)(x) =$ _____

5. $(G \cdot H)(x) =$ _____

6. $(f \cdot G)(x) =$ _____

7. $(f - G)(x) =$ _____

8. $(H - f)(x) =$ _____

9. $(f - H)(x) =$ _____

10. $(P - F)(x) =$ _____

11. $(H - F)(x) =$ _____

12. $(f \div G)(x); x \neq 0 =$ _____

13. $(P \div h)(x); x \neq -1 =$ _____

14. $(P \div F)(x); x \neq 3 =$ _____

15. $(P \div H)(x); x \neq 1 =$ _____

16. $(f \div F)(x); x \neq 3 =$ _____

Algebra Teacher's Activities Kit

Copyright © 2003 John Wiley & Sons, Inc.

7-6
(continued)

Using the Basic Operations with Functions

Answer Bank

R. x

H. $x^2 - 3x + 4$

O. $-2x + 1$

C. $x^3 - x^2 - x + 1$

B. $x^3 - 2x^2 + x$

N. $x^2 + x + 1$

I. $\dfrac{x^2 - 2x - 3}{x^2 - 2x + 1}$

K. $2x + 2$

G. $2x - 2$

Z. $x^2 - x$

E. $x^2 + x - 3$

A. $x^2 - 2x - 3$

L. $x - 3$

M. $2x - 1$

U. $x^2 - 3x$

T. $x + 1$

S. $\dfrac{x^2}{x - 3}$

F. x^3

The domains are restricted in Problems 12 through 16 because division by

$\overline{7}\ \overline{2}\ \overline{12}\ \overline{8}\quad \overline{11}\ \overline{4}\ \overline{16}\quad \overline{1}\ \overline{8}\quad \overline{9}\ \overline{2}\ \overline{4}\ \overline{1}\ \overline{15}\ \overline{1}\ \overline{3}\quad \overline{15}\ \overline{1}$

$\overline{14}\ \overline{11}\ \overline{2}\quad \overline{16}\ \overline{2}\ \overline{14}\quad \overline{8}\ \overline{6}\quad \overline{12}\ \overline{2}\ \overline{4}\ \overline{13}\quad \overline{1}\ \overline{10}\ \overline{9}\ \overline{5}\ \overline{2}\ \overline{12}\ \overline{16}$.

Finding the Composition of Functions

The *Composition of Functions* refers to a way of combining two functions. If f and g are functions, f ∘ g is the composite function, which is also called the composition of f and g. $(f \circ g)(x) = f(g(x)) = f[g(x)]$.

Suppose $g(x) = 4x$ and $f(x) = x^3$. To find the composite function $(f \circ g)(x)$, substitute $g(x)$ or $4x$ into $f(x)$ so $f(4x) = (4x)^3 = 64x^3$. This can also be written as $f[g(x)] = f(4x) = 64x^3$.

To find $(g \circ f)(x)$, substitute $f(x)$ or x^3 into $g(x)$ so that $g(x^3) = 4x^3$. This can also be written as $g[f(x)] = g(x^3) = 4x^3$.

Directions: Find each composite function. Match your answers with the answers in the Answer Bank and write the letter of your answers in the spaces provided. Then write each letter above its corresponding problem number to complete the statement at the end of the activity.

$$g(x) = 3x \qquad f(x) = x^2 \qquad F(x) = -2x - 1$$
$$G(x) = x^2 - x - 3 \qquad h(x) = x^3$$

1. $(f \circ g)(x) =$ _____   2. $(F \circ g)(x) =$ _____
3. $(F \circ f)(x) =$ _____   4. $(g \circ h)(x) =$ _____
5. $(G \circ F)(x) =$ _____   6. $(G \circ f)(x) =$ _____
7. $(g \circ G)(x) =$ _____   8. $(F \circ h)(x) =$ _____
9. $(F \circ G)(x) =$ _____   10. $(g \circ f)(x) =$ _____
11. $(G \circ h)(x) =$ _____   12. $(f \circ F)(x) =$ _____
13. $(f \circ G)(x) =$ _____   14. $(h \circ g)(x) =$ _____
15. $(G \circ g)(x) =$ _____   16. $(g \circ F)(x) =$ _____

Answer Bank

R. $9x^2 - 3x - 3$	I. $4x^2 + 4x + 1$	W. $x^6 - x^3 - 3$
S. $-2x^2 - 1$	D. $-2x^2 + 2x + 5$	Y. $-6x - 1$
N. $x^4 - 2x^3 - 5x^2 + 6x + 9$	O. $4x^2 + 6x - 1$	E. $-6x - 3$
L. $-2x^3 - 1$	F. $3x^2$	U. $3x^3$
B. $9x^2$	H. $27x^3$	
T. $3x^2 - 3x - 9$	A. $x^4 - x^2 - 3$	

The expression f(x) to represent a function ___ ___ ___   ___ ___ ___ ___ ___
                                           11 6   3   10 12 15 3   7

___ ___ ___ ___   ___ ___   ___ ___ ___ ___ ___ ___ ___ ___   ___ ___ ___ ___ ___.
 4   3 16   9   1   2   8 16   5 13 14   6 15   9   16   4   8 16 15

Finding the Inverses of Functions

Every function has an inverse, but not every inverse is a function. If a horizontal line intersects a graph more than once, then the inverse of the function is not a function. Functions whose inverses are not functions have even numbers as exponents.

To find the inverse of a function, replace f(x) with y, switch x and y, and solve for y. Study the examples below.

$$f(x) = 7x - 10$$
$$y = 7x - 10$$
$$x = 7y - 10$$
$$x + 10 = 7y$$
$$\frac{x+10}{7} = y = f^{-1}(x)$$

$$f(x) = 4x^3 + 2$$
$$y = 4x^3 + 2$$
$$x = 4y^3 + 2$$
$$x - 2 = 4y^3$$
$$\sqrt[3]{\frac{x-2}{4}} = y = f^{-1}(x)$$

Directions: Find the inverse of each function and match your answers with the answers in the Answer Bank. Write the letter of each answer in the space after the function. Then write each letter over its problem number to complete the statement at the end of the activity.

1. $f(x) = 2x - 4$ _____

2. $f(x) = x^3$ _____

3. $f(x) = x^5$ _____

4. $f(x) = x$ _____

5. $f(x) = 2x + 4$ _____

6. $f(x) = \frac{1}{2}x^3 - 2$ _____

7. $f(x) = x + 7$ _____

8. $f(x) = 3x - 1$ _____

9. $f(x) = \frac{1}{2}x + 1$ _____

10. $f(x) = 3x^3 + 1$ _____

11. $f(x) = \frac{x^5 + 2}{7}$ _____

12. $f(x) = x^7$ _____

Answer Bank		
O. $f^{-1}(x) = \sqrt[5]{7x - 2}$	S. $f^{-1}(x) = \sqrt[3]{x}$	I. $f^{-1}(x) = x - 7$
A. $f^{-1}(x) = \frac{1}{2}x - 2$	L. $f^{-1}(x) = 2x - 2$	N. $f^{-1}(x) = \frac{1}{2}x + 2$
E. $f^{-1}(x) = \sqrt[7]{x}$	R. $f^{-1}(x) = \sqrt[5]{x}$	F. $f^{-1}(x) = \sqrt[3]{\frac{x-1}{3}}$
T. $f^{-1}(x) = \frac{1}{3}x + \frac{1}{3}$	C. $f^{-1}(x) = \sqrt[3]{2x + 4}$	U. $f^{-1}(x) = x$

For each linear function f(x) = mx + b where m ≠ 0, the inverse $\overline{}\ \overline{}$
 7 2

$\overline{}\ \ \overline{}\ \overline{}\ \overline{}\ \overline{}\ \overline{}\ \overline{}\ \ \overline{}\ \overline{}\ \overline{}\ \overline{}\ \overline{}\ \overline{}\ \overline{}\ \overline{}$.
  5   9   7   1 12   5   3   10   4   1   6   8   7   11   1

Evaluating the Greatest Integer Function

The *greatest integer function* is a function defined as the largest integer less than or equal to x. It is denoted as $f(x) = [|x|]$. For example, $[|0.5|] = 0$, $[|3.7|] = 3$, $[|4|] = 4$, and $[|-2.2|] = -3$. The graph of this function is shown below.

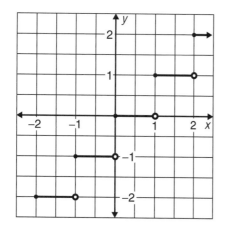

$$[|x|] = \begin{cases} \vdots \\ -2 \text{ if } -2 \leq x < -1 \\ -1 \text{ if } -1 \leq x < 0 \\ 0 \text{ if } 0 \leq x < 1 \\ 1 \text{ if } 1 \leq x < 2 \\ 2 \text{ if } 2 \leq x < 3 \\ \vdots \end{cases}$$

To evaluate a function means to find the value of the function at a particular point. To find the value of the greatest integer function, substitute the value for x. Treat the greatest integer symbol as a grouping symbol and simplify the expression within the symbol. Then find the greatest integer less than or equal to that value.

Directions: Evaluate each function and write its value after the function. Then match the value with the values in the Answer Bank on the next page. Write the corresponding letter of each value in the space before the function. When you have finished, write the letters in order, starting with the first function, to complete the statement at the end of the activity.

$$g(x) = [|x|]$$

$$g(x) = [|2x|]$$

1. _____ g(–1) = _____

4. _____ g(3.4) = _____

2. _____ g(6.5) = _____

5. _____ g(2.5) = _____

3. _____ g(–4) = _____

6. _____ g(–7) = _____

Algebra Teacher's Activities Kit

Evaluating the Greatest Integer Function

$$g(x) = 2\big[|x|\big]$$

7. _____ g(–4.5) = _____

8. _____ g(2.1) = _____

9. _____ g(–3.5) = _____

$$g(x) = \big[|x|\big] - 2$$

10. _____ g(0.5) = _____

11. _____ g(–0.5) = _____

12. _____ g(7.4) = _____

$$g(x) = \big[|x - 2|\big]$$

13. _____ g(1.6) = _____

14. _____ g(2.7) = _____

15. _____ g(0.2) = _____

$$g(x) = -\big[|x|\big]$$

16. _____ g(–11.9) = _____

17. _____ g(14.5) = _____

18. _____ g(3) = _____

$$g(x) = 4\big[|x + 2|\big]$$

19. _____ g(–2.8) = _____

20. _____ g(–3.2) = _____

$$g(x) = 4\big[|x|\big] + 2$$

21. _____ g(1.2) = _____

22. _____ g(–3.8) = _____

Answer Bank					
P. –10	S. 6	U. –8	B. 12	T. 5	E. –14
O. 0	A. –4	I. –1	F. 4	N. –2	C. –3

The greatest integer function __ __   __   __ __ __ __

__ __ __ __ __ __ __   __ __ __ __ __ __ __ its graph resembles

a set of stair steps.

Evaluating Piecewise-Defined Functions

A *piecewise-defined function* is a function defined by two or more parts. Piecewise-defined functions have several practical applications. Before you can use a piecewise-defined function, you must determine which part to use, depending on the value of x.

Consider the piecewise-defined function.

$$f(x) = \begin{cases} 3x & \text{if } x > 0 \\ 2x & \text{if } x \le 0 \end{cases}$$

To determine which expression to use, consider the value of x.

$$f(3) = 3 \times 3 = 9 \qquad \text{(because } x > 0\text{)}$$
$$f(0) = 2 \times 0 = 0 \qquad \text{(because } x \le 0\text{)}$$
$$f(-2) = 2(-2) = -4 \qquad \text{(because } x \le 0\text{)}$$

Directions: Each of the following situations can be modeled as a piecewise-defined function. Write the function and use the function to find the value at the given point.

1. An Internet service provider charges $19.95 per month for the first 50 hours of being on line. An additional charge of $0.99 is applied for each additional hour or portion thereof. Let t equal the number of hours spent using the on-line service per month. Write the function and find the charge for 20 hours, 55 hours, and 55.5 hours.

   f(t) =   f(20) = _____

                              f(55) = _____

                              f(55.5) = _____

2. A telephone company has a special rate plan: a monthly charge of $29.95 for unlimited local calls and a $.05 per minute (or portion thereof) charge for the first 30 minutes of long-distance calls. After the first 30 minutes of long-distance calls, a charge of $.10 per minute (or portion thereof) is applied for each additional minute. The long-distance charges are added to the charges for the local calls at the end of the month. Let t equal the total time spent on long distance calls in minutes per month. Write this function and determine the total cost of the January bill that included 15.5 minutes of long-distance time, and the February bill, which included 37 minutes of long-distance time.

   f(t) =   f(15.5) = _____ for January's bill

                     f(37) = _____ for February's bill

Algebra Teacher's Activities Kit

Evaluating Piecewise-Defined Functions

3. A local amusement park is open from 10 A.M. to 10 P.M. each day. The daily admission charge for an adult is $39.95. The admission is $10 less if an adult visits the park after 4 P.M. Let t equal the number of hours after the park opens. Write this function and find the cost if an adult enters the park at 11 A.M. and another adult enters the park at 5 P.M.

f(t) =

f(1) = _____

f(7) = _____

4. You have decided to accept a job this summer that pays $6.50 per hour and time and a half for overtime. (Overtime is the time you work that exceeds 40 hours per week.) Let t equal the total number of hours worked per week. Write the function and use it to find your earnings if you work just 26 hours one week, and 45 hours another week.

f(t) =

f(26) = _____

f(45) = _____

Identifying Graphs of Families of Functions

A *family of functions* is a collection of functions whose equations are related. The equations differ by a single constant called a *parameter*. Each family of functions has the same shape. The size and position of the graph will vary, depending on the parameter.

Six families of functions and their graphs are shown below.

Linear Function	**Squaring Function**	**Square Root Function**
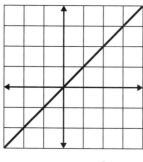	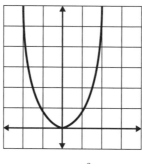	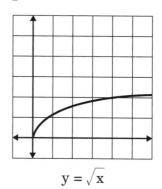
$y = mx + b$	$y = x^2$	$y = \sqrt{x}$

Cubing Function	**Absolute Value Function**	**Greatest Integer Function**
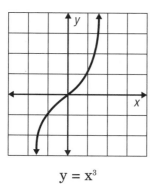	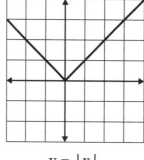	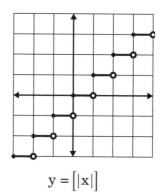
$y = x^3$	$y = |x|$	$y = \left[\,|x|\,\right]$

Directions: On the following ten graphs, identify the family to which each function belongs. Write the name of the family beneath the graph. Next, match the graphs with the equations in the Answer Bank at the end of this activity, and write the equation under the family name. Some equations will not be used.

Algebra Teacher's Activities Kit

Copyright © 2003 John Wiley & Sons, Inc.

Identifying Graphs of Families of Functions

1.

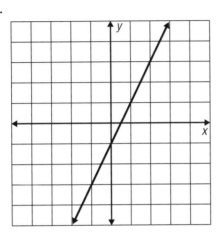

_____

_____

2.

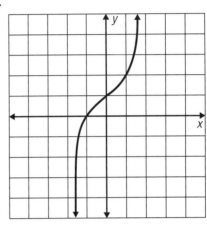

_____

_____

3.

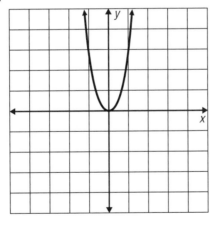

_____

_____

4.

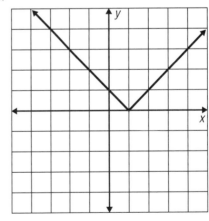

_____

_____

Identifying Graphs of Families of Functions

5.

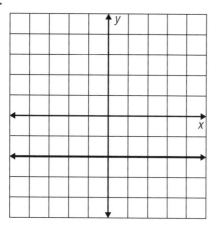

_____

_____

6.

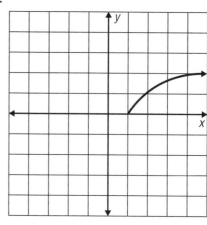

_____

_____

7.

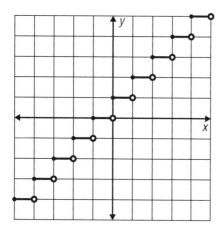

_____

_____

8.

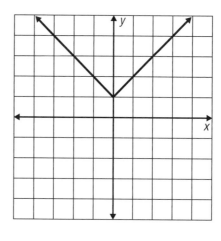

_____

_____

Identifying Graphs of Families of Functions

9.

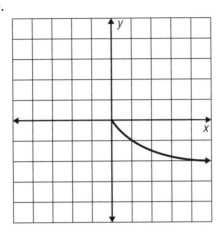

10.

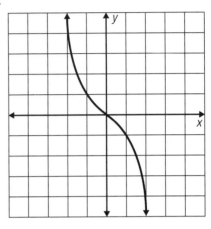

_____

_____

Answer Bank

$f(x) = \big[\lvert x + 1 \rvert\big]$ $f(x) = 3x^2$ $f(x) = \lvert x - 1 \rvert$

$f(x) = \lvert x \rvert + 1$ $f(x) = x^3 + 1$ $f(x) = -x^3$

$f(x) = \big[\lvert x \rvert\big] + 2$ $f(x) = x^2 + 3$ $f(x) = x - 2$

$f(x) = \sqrt{x - 1}$ $f(x) = 2x - 1$ $f(x) = -\sqrt{x}$

                                                       $f(x) = -2$

Reviewing the Concepts and Applications of Functions

Many of the concepts you need to know about functions are included on this worksheet. You will need to apply them to specific functions or functions in general.

Directions: Read each statement and decide whether it is true or false. If it is true, write "true." If it is false, write "false" and provide an example or an explanation that will make the statement true. Use the functions listed below if a specific function is mentioned.

$$f(x) = 3x + 2 \qquad g(x) = 2x - 3 \qquad h(x) = \frac{2}{x}$$

$$F(x) = x^2 + 2 \qquad G(x) = |x| \qquad H(x) = \sqrt{x - 5}$$

1. The values for x and y, organized in a T-table, always represent a function.

   _____

   _____

2. $f(x)$ is a function. _____

   _____

3. $f(-1) = 1.$ _____

   _____

4. $f(x) - g(x) = x - 1.$ _____

   _____

5. $f(x) \cdot g(x) = 6x^2 - 5x - 6.$ _____

   _____

6. $(f \circ g)(x) = 6x + 1.$ _____

   _____

7. The domain of $h(x)$ is all real numbers except 0. _____

   _____

8. The inverse of a function may be a function. _____

   _____

9. f^{-1} means the reciprocal of $f(x)$. _____

   _____

Reviewing the Concepts and Applications of Functions

10. $g^{-1}(x) = \dfrac{x-3}{2}$. _____ ___

_____

11. The graph of the absolute value of x is shaped like a V. _____

_____

12. The range of F(x) is all real numbers greater than 2. _____

_____

13. The domain of H(x) is all real numbers greater than or equal to 5.

_____

14. x = 4 is an example of a linear function. _____

_____

15. H(30) = 5. _____

_____

16. $\left[\lvert 3.5 \rvert\right] = 4$. _____

_____

17. G(–2) = 2 and G(2) = 2, therefore G(x) is not a function.

_____

_____

18. The domain of G(x) is all real numbers greater than or equal to zero since the

absolute value is never negative. _____

_____

19. The domains of f(x), g(x), and F(x) are all real numbers. _____

_____

20. The number of true statements on this worksheet is the same as g(6).

_____

Complex Numbers

The activities in this section begin with real numbers and extend to using imaginary numbers. Topics include classifying real numbers, writing rational numbers, finding real roots, using the four operations to simplify radicals, simplifying imaginary numbers, and using complex numbers to simplify expressions. Mastery of the skills presented in this section are necessary to solve the equations included in the next section.

Teaching Suggestions for the Activities

8-1 Identifying Subsets of Real Numbers

For this activity your students are to classify numbers and place them in the smallest subset of the real numbers. To complete this activity successfully, students will need to recognize various types of numbers, including whole numbers, fractions, decimals, square roots, and pi.

Begin the activity by discussing ways things can be classified. For example, objects may be classified according to type, size, color, or shape. Note that there are many kinds of numbers, of which real numbers constitute a major set.

Refer to the different sets of numbers presented on the worksheet. Depending on the abilities of your students, you may find it helpful to define each group.

Review the directions on the worksheet with your students, and remind them that they are to fill in the blanks below the subsets. Also note that each number will be used once.

8-2 Expressing Fractions as Repeating Decimals and Repeating Decimals as Fractions

As its title indicates, this activity involves two important skills associated with fractions and decimals. All numbers used in the activity can be written as repeating decimals.

Start the activity by converting a fraction such as $\frac{3}{4}$ to a decimal. If necessary, write the conversion on the board or an overhead projector. $3 \div 4 = 0.75$. Note that the same procedure is used if a digit repeats.

Refer your students to the example on the worksheet and explain that $\frac{3}{11} = 3 \div 11$, which equals $0.272727\ldots$ or $0.\overline{27}$. Be sure that your students understand the notation.

Next, review the procedures outlined on the worksheet. Note that $0.\overline{86} \times 100 = 86.\overline{86}$. Explain the reasoning: $0.868686\ldots \times 100 = 86.\overline{86}$. Emphasize that the pair of numbers still repeats.

Go over the instructions on the worksheet with your students. Caution them that not all of the answers in the Answer Bank will be used.

8-3 Simplifying Square Roots

This activity focuses on square roots and word problems. Students are to express their answers in radical form and as a decimal rounded to a specific place.

Introduce the activity by explaining that formulas containing square roots can be used to determine the speed of an object. Discuss the two examples on the worksheet, and make sure that your students understand the process of simplifying square roots.

Review the directions on the worksheet and point out that there are two sets of instructions. Note that for Problems 1 through 16, students are to round their answers to the nearest tenth, and that for Problems 17 through 20, they are to round answers to the nearest whole number.

8-4 Finding the Nth Root of a Number

For this activity your students must expand the concept of the square root to other roots and find various roots of numbers. To complete this activity successfully, your students should be able to find the square roots of numbers.

Begin the activity by discussing the meanings of finding a square root and squaring a number. Offer the following examples on the board or an overhead projector.

If $a^2 = b$, then $\sqrt{b} = a$ and if $\sqrt{b} = a$, then $a^2 = b$. For example, $6^2 = 36$, therefore $\sqrt{36} = 6$.

Extend this concept to finding the cube root and cubing a number. Offer this example.

If $a^3 = b$, then $\sqrt[3]{b} = a$ and if $\sqrt[3]{b} = a$, then $a^3 = b$. For example, $2^3 = 8$, therefore $\sqrt[3]{8} = 2$.

Continue this process to include the fourth and fifth roots. Explain that the notation $\sqrt[n]{b} = a$ is the principal root of the nth root of b. Also explain that n is the index of the radical expression. If there is no index, the index is understood to be 2. If a variable is in the radicand, it is assumed that the variable represents a nonnegative number.

Discuss the examples on the worksheet, emphasizing that finding the nth root of a number is the inverse of multiplying the number n times. Be sure that your students understand the examples before assigning the activity.

Review the directions on the worksheet, and note that every answer will be used at least once. Also emphasize to your students that a statement will be revealed, and that they are to follow the directions in the blanks provided and write an explanation.

8-5 Multiplying and Dividing Radicals

In this activity your students are required to multiply or divide radicals, simplify products and quotients, and express answers in radical form. They do not have to rationalize the denominator. To complete this activity successfully, your students should be able to simplify radicals.

Begin the activity by explaining the following rules for multiplying and dividing radicals:

$$\text{Product Rule: } \sqrt{x}\sqrt{y} = \sqrt{xy} \quad x \geq 0, y \geq 0$$

$$\text{Quotient Rule: } \sqrt{\frac{x}{y}} = \frac{\sqrt{x}}{\sqrt{y}} \quad x \geq 0, y > 0$$

These rules can be simply stated: the product of two radicals is the radical of the products; the quotient of two radicals is the radical of the quotients. Students must be aware of the restrictions on the variables.

Discuss the examples on the worksheet. Depending on the abilities of your students, you may find it helpful to offer more examples on the board or an overhead projector.

Review the instructions on the worksheet. Note that every answer in the Answer Bank will be used, and that some answers will be used more than once.

8-6 Rationalizing the Denominator

For this activity your students must simplify products and quotients of radicals by rationalizing the denominator, which is the process of writing the expression without a radical in the denominator. To complete this activity successfully, your students should be able to multiply and divide rational numbers. Activity 8-5 is a helpful prerequisite for this activity.

Begin the activity by reviewing the concept of multiplying and dividing radicals. Present and discuss the following examples on the board or an overhead projector:

$$\sqrt{\frac{48}{3}} = \sqrt{16} = 4 \qquad \sqrt{\frac{3}{8}}\sqrt{\frac{2}{8}} = \frac{\sqrt{6}}{\sqrt{64}} = \frac{\sqrt{6}}{8}$$

Next, discuss the examples on the worksheet. Explain the steps, emphasizing how students will know if an expression is simplified. Depending on the abilities of your students, you may find it helpful to provide additional examples.

Review the directions on the worksheet with your students. Note that some answers in the Answer Bank will be used more than once.

8-7 Simplifying Sums and Differences of Radicals

This activity requires your students to add and subtract radicals. Students must be proficient in simplifying radicals before attempting to complete the activity.

Begin the activity by discussing the process for simplifying radicals. Remind your students that a radical is in simplest form if no radicand has a perfect square as a factor (except 1).

Write the following examples on the board or an overhead projector and instruct your students to simplify. (The answers are provided for you.)

$$\sqrt{18} = 3\sqrt{2} \qquad \sqrt{32} = 4\sqrt{2} \qquad \sqrt{50} = 5\sqrt{2}$$

Next, discuss the examples on the worksheet, noting that only like radicands can be added or subtracted. Students should realize that the final sums and differences cannot be simplified.

Review the directions on the worksheet. Note that every answer will be used at least once.

8-8 Simplifying Products That Contain Radicals

In this activity your students will use the Distributive Property or use FOIL to multiply expressions that contain radicals. To complete the activity successfully, your students should be able to simplify, multiply, and add radicals. The activity not only builds on these skills but serves as a review.

Start the activity by reviewing the Distributive Property and applying it to the multiplication of binomials. Offer the following example on the board or an overhead projector:

$$\sqrt{3}\left(\sqrt{10} + \sqrt{6}\right) = \sqrt{30} + \sqrt{18} = \sqrt{30} + 3\sqrt{2}$$

Explain the process, noting that the answer is simplified. Emphasize that all radicals must be simplified and that only radicals with the same number under the radical sign can be added or subtracted. Now offer the next example.

$$\left(\sqrt{5} + \sqrt{10}\right)\left(\sqrt{5} - 2\right) = \sqrt{25} - 2\sqrt{5} + \sqrt{50} - 2\sqrt{10} = 5 - 2\sqrt{5} + 5\sqrt{2} - 2\sqrt{10}$$

Discuss the steps in detail to ensure that students understand the procedure. Also discuss the examples on the worksheet, noting that the answers are in simplest form.

Go over the directions on the worksheet with your students. Your students may find it helpful if you simplify the first problem as a class exercise.

8-9 Using Conjugates to Simplify Products and Quotients

For this activity your students are to simplify products and quotients using conjugates. To complete this activity successfully, your students should be able to multiply and simplify radicals, and rationalize a denominator that has only one radical.

Start the activity by offering examples of conjugates on the board or an overhead projector:

$$\sqrt{3} + 2 \text{ and } \sqrt{3} - 2 \qquad 2\sqrt{7} + 6 \text{ and } 2\sqrt{7} - 6 \qquad 7\sqrt{3} + 2\sqrt{5} \text{ and } 7\sqrt{3} - 2\sqrt{5}$$

Note that a conjugate consists of the sum of two numbers and the difference of two numbers. Refer your students to the definition of a conjugate on the worksheet, then discuss the example. Note that they should simplify all radicals. Also note that they have to multiply both the numerator and denominator by the conjugate of the denominator in order to simplify quotients.

Review the directions on the worksheet with your students. Remind them that all products and quotients must be simplified and that each answer is used once.

8-10 Using i

This activity extends the concept of square roots to include finding the square roots of negative numbers. To complete this activity successfully, your students should be able to simplify square roots if the radicand is greater than or equal to zero.

Introduce the activity by reviewing the process of simplifying square roots such as $\sqrt{64} = 8$, $\sqrt{48} = 4\sqrt{3}$, and $\sqrt{90} = 3\sqrt{10}$. Note that all of these are real numbers.

Explain that the imaginary number i was introduced so that equations such as $x^2 = -5$ could be solved. Discuss the definition $i^2 = -1$, which is the same as $i = \sqrt{-1}$. Offer the following examples on the board or an overhead projector, and explain the concepts and procedures.

$$-\sqrt{-36} = -6i \qquad (5i)^2 = 25i^2 = -25 \qquad -(2i)(6i) = -12i^2 = 12$$

Review the directions on the worksheet with your students. Note that all answers will be used once except for one answer, which will be used twice.

8-11 Using Complex Numbers to Simplify Expressions

For this activity your students must add, subtract, multiply, and divide complex numbers. To complete this activity successfully, your students should be able to use the Distributive Property to multiply binomials, and also be able to use conjugates.

Introduce complex numbers by explaining that these numbers include both real and imaginary numbers. If necessary, review examples of imaginary numbers such as $\sqrt{-10} = i\sqrt{10}$, $2i$, $3 + 2i$, and $-i\sqrt{2}$. Also, review simplifying expressions such as $(3i)(4i) = 12i^2$ or -12 (since $i^2 = -1$).

Discuss the examples on the worksheet, emphasizing that it is necessary to simplify radicals before adding, subtracting, multiplying, and dividing. Remind your students to use conjugates such as $3 - 6i$ and $3 + 6i$ when rationalizing the denominator.

Review the directions on the worksheet. Note that some answers will not be used.

8-12 Reviewing Concepts and Skills Related to Complex Numbers

This multiple-choice activity reviews the concepts and skills presented in this section. Although only a minimal amount of instruction should be necessary, you may wish to review any material in the preceding eleven activities that your students found difficult to master.

Go over the directions on the worksheet with your students. Note that some problems have more than one correct answer.

Answer Key for Section 8

8-1. Opposites of Natural Numbers: $-6, -\sqrt{9} = -3$ Zero: 0   Odd Numbers: $3, \sqrt{25} = 5$ Even Numbers: 16 $\sqrt{4} = 2$ Terminating Decimals: $0.27, \frac{2}{5}$ Repeating Decimals: $0.\overline{27}, 0.33\frac{1}{3}, \frac{2}{9}$ Irrational Numbers: $\pi, \sqrt{2}$

8-2. 1. A, $0.\overline{2}$ 2. B, $\frac{2}{3}$ 3. S, $\frac{14}{99}$ 4. L, $0.\overline{153846}$ 5. E, $0.1\overline{6}$ 6. T, $0.\overline{857142}$
7. M, $0.\overline{3}$ 8. H, $\frac{4}{9}$ 9. U, $\frac{8}{11}$ 10. Y, $0.8\overline{3}$ 11. D, $0.\overline{285714}$ 12. R, $\frac{8}{9}$
13. I, $\frac{1}{11}$ 14. O, $0.\overline{63}$ The correct name for the fraction <u>bar is the solidus symbol. (/)</u>

8-3. 1. $2\sqrt{6}, 4.9$ 2. $4\sqrt{3}, 6.9$ 3. $2\sqrt{3}, 3.5$ 4. $5\sqrt{2}, 7.1$ 5. $3\sqrt{6}, 7.3$ 6. $2\sqrt{14}, 7.5$ 7. $2\sqrt{15}, 7.7$ 8. $5\sqrt{3}, 8.7$ 9. $7\sqrt{2}, 9.9$ 10. $2\sqrt{26}, 10.2$ 11. $2\sqrt{22}, 9.4$
12. $4\sqrt{2}, 5.7$ 13. $2\sqrt{5}, 4.5$ 14. $3\sqrt{14}, 11.2$ 15. $5\sqrt{10}, 15.8$ 16. $6\sqrt{2}, 8.5$
17. 53 miles per hour   18. 43 miles per hour   19. 91 miles per hour
20. The daredevil in Problem 9 traveled 11 miles per hour faster.

8-4. 1. E, 4   2. X, -11 3. P, n   4. L, -10 5. A, 6   6. I, 3   7. N, n^3 8. W, -4
9. H, -5 10. Y, -3 11. I, 3   12. T, 2   13. I, 3   14. S, 5   15. P, n   16. O, n^2 17. S, 5   18. S, 5   19. I, 3   20. B, -2 21. L, -10 22. E, 4   23. T, 2
24. O, n^2 25. F, -8 26. I, 3   27. N, n^3 28. D, 7   29. T, 2   30. H, -5
31. E, 4   <u>Explain why it is possible to find the</u> nth root of a negative number if n is odd, but not if n is even. Explanations may vary. A possible explanation is that a negative number multiplied by itself an odd number of times is negative, but a negative number multiplied by itself an even number of times is positive.

8-5. 1. C, $3\sqrt{2}$ 2. H, $\sqrt{70}$ 3. R, $4\sqrt{5}$ 4. I, $2\sqrt{15}$ 5. S, $\sqrt{7}$ 6. T, $2\sqrt{6}$ 7. O, 9
8. F, 4   9. F, 4   10. R, $4\sqrt{5}$ 11. U, 2   12. D, $\frac{\sqrt{3}}{2}$ 13. O, 9   14. L, $4\sqrt{6}$
15. F, 4   16. F, 4   17. W, $\sqrt{6}$ 18. A, $\frac{\sqrt{11}}{5}$ 19. S, $\sqrt{7}$ 20. T, $2\sqrt{6}$ 21. H, $\sqrt{70}$
22. E, $3\sqrt{5}$ In the early part of the 16th century, <u>Christoff Rudolff was the</u> first person to use the radical symbol as we use it today.

8-6. 1. O, $\frac{\sqrt{15}}{3}$ 2. F, $2\sqrt{2}$ 3. T, $2\sqrt{3}$ 4. H, $\frac{\sqrt{2}}{4}$ 5. E, $\sqrt{2}$ 6. N, $\frac{\sqrt{10}}{4}$ 7. U, $\frac{\sqrt{2}}{2}$
8. M, $\frac{\sqrt{70}}{7}$ 9. B, $\sqrt{14}$ 10. E, $\sqrt{2}$ 11. R, $\frac{4\sqrt{7}}{7}$ 12. I, $\frac{\sqrt{7}}{7}$ 13. S, $\frac{\sqrt{15}}{5}$
14. C, $\frac{5\sqrt{3}}{3}$ 15. H, $\frac{\sqrt{2}}{4}$ 16. A, $\frac{3\sqrt{2}}{10}$ 17. N, $\frac{\sqrt{10}}{4}$ 18. G, $\frac{\sqrt{5}}{2}$ 19. E, $\sqrt{2}$

20. D, $\frac{\sqrt{2}}{3}$ When a denominator is rationalized, the value of the expression is not changed. Only the form <u>of the number is changed</u>.

8-7. 1. O, $5\sqrt{2}$ 2. F, $\sqrt{6}$ 3. T, $6\sqrt{2}$ 4. H, $9\sqrt{2}$ 5. E, $-\sqrt{6}$ 6. L, $-\sqrt{30}$ 7. A, $9\sqrt{3}$ 8. T, $6\sqrt{2}$ 9. I, $3\sqrt{5}$ 10. N, $\sqrt{3}$ 11. W, $\sqrt{11}$ 12. O, $5\sqrt{2}$ 13. R, $5\sqrt{3}$ 14. D, $-\sqrt{5}$ 15. R, $5\sqrt{3}$ 16. A, $9\sqrt{3}$ 17. D, $-\sqrt{5}$ 18. I, $3\sqrt{5}$ 19. X, 16   20. M, 4   21. E, $-\sqrt{6}$ 22. A, $9\sqrt{3}$ 23. N, $\sqrt{3}$ 24. I, $3\sqrt{5}$ 25. N, $\sqrt{3}$ 26. G, 7   27. R, $5\sqrt{3}$ 28. O, $5\sqrt{2}$ 29. O, $5\sqrt{2}$ 30. T, $6\sqrt{2}$ The radical sign, $\sqrt{}$, is a modified form of the letter "r," which is taken from the first letter <u>of the Latin word "radix," meaning "root."</u>

8-8. 1. incorrect, $\sqrt{6}+3$ 2. incorrect, $5\sqrt{2}+2\sqrt{10}$ 3. incorrect, $2\sqrt{6}+10\sqrt{3}$ 4. correct   5. incorrect, -1 6. correct   7. correct   8. correct   9. incorrect, $17+8\sqrt{2}$ 10. incorrect, $-6+5\sqrt{3}$

8-9. 1. C, 4   2. E, 7   3. N, -1 4. O, 2   5. S, -8 6. F, -46 7. A, $\dfrac{\sqrt{5}-1}{4}$ 8. P, $4\sqrt{2}+4$ 9. G, $-6-3\sqrt{5}$ 10. R, $\dfrac{2\sqrt{3}+3\sqrt{2}}{-3}$ 11. J, $\dfrac{11+\sqrt{33}}{8}$ 12. D, $\dfrac{2+3\sqrt{2}}{14}$ 13. H, $-9+4\sqrt{5}$ 14. U, $\dfrac{-19+8\sqrt{3}}{-13}$ 15. T, $-1-\sqrt{2}$ 16. W, $\dfrac{\sqrt{15}+5}{-2}$ <u>The product of two conjugates</u> will always be an integer.

8-10. 1. W, $7i$ 2. A, $i\sqrt{15}$ 3. S, $2i\sqrt{6}$ 4. I, -2 5. N, -9 6. T, 6   7. R, -6 8. O, $-4\sqrt{2}$ 9. D, -12 10. U, $12i$ 11. C, 9   12. E, 12   13. D, -12 14. B, $2i\sqrt{14}$ 15. Y, $-3\sqrt{2}$ The expression "imaginary number" <u>was introduced by</u> René Descartes in the 17th century.

8-11. 1. A, $7-4i$ 2. N, $11-10i$ 3. O, $3+10i$ 4. Y, $-2-10i$ 5. B, $-10+i$ 6. S, $-12+6i$ 7. R, 2   8. L, 34   9. M, $23-11i$ 10. W, $-7-24i$ 11. P, $-5+2i\sqrt{6}$ 12. U, $11-i\sqrt{5}$ 13. E, $\dfrac{3+i}{10}$ 14. X, $\dfrac{16+15i}{13}$ 15. C, $\dfrac{11-4i\sqrt{3}}{13}$ The sum, difference, product, and quotient of two complex numbers is <u>always a complex number</u>.

8-12. 1. W, irrational numbers   2. I, 0.5   3. T, $\dfrac{2}{9}$ 4. H, $2\sqrt{6}$ 5. P, 15; O, 0   6. I, $2\sqrt{3}+\sqrt{5}$ 7. N, 3   8. T, $5\sqrt{2}$ 9. S, $\dfrac{2\sqrt{5}}{5}$ 10. O, 7   11. N, -1 12. A, 16   13. N, -5; U, 5   14. M, $9i\sqrt{2}$ 15. B, $3-\sqrt{5}$ 16. E, $-1+\sqrt{2}$ 17. R, $\dfrac{3}{4}$ 18. L, $\sqrt{-5}$; I, $-\sqrt{-5}$ 19. N, 8   20. E, $3\sqrt{2}+4\sqrt{3}$ Imaginary numbers cannot be paired <u>with points on a number line</u>.

Identifying Subsets of Real Numbers

It is common to classify things that share similar characteristics. For example, books may be broadly classified as fiction or nonfiction, animals may be vertebrates or invertebrates, and plants may be flowers, bushes, or trees. In algebra, numbers can be classified according to the following chart.

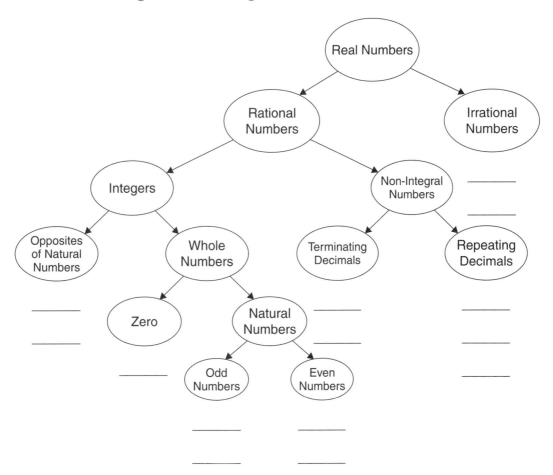

Directions: Write each number that follows in the space below each subset of the real numbers so that each of the seven smallest subsets contains at least one example.

−6	16	0	$0.\overline{27}$	0.27	$\sqrt{2}$	3
$0.33\frac{1}{3}$	$\sqrt{4}$	$-\sqrt{9}$	π	$\frac{2}{9}$	$\frac{2}{5}$	$\sqrt{25}$

8-2

Expressing Fractions as Repeating Decimals and Repeating Decimals as Fractions

Every rational number can be expressed as a fraction and a decimal. Sometimes one form of the number is easier to use. Although the equivalent forms of a number may appear to be different, the value of the number remains the same.

To change a fraction to a decimal, divide the numerator by the denominator. Here is an example:

$$\frac{3}{11} = 3 \div 11 \text{ or } 0.\overline{27}$$

To change a repeating decimal to a fraction, do the following:

1. Let n = the number.
2. If one digit repeats, multiply by 10. If two digits repeat, multiply by 100. If three digits repeat, multiply by 1,000, and so on.
3. Subtract the original number from the number you have multiplied by 10, 100, 1,000, and so on.
4. Solve for n.

Study the example:

$$n = 0.\overline{86}$$
$$100n = 86.\overline{86}$$
$$-n = -0.\overline{86}$$
$$99n = 86$$
$$n = \frac{86}{99}$$

Directions: Match each number with its equivalent form. Find each answer in the Answer Bank, then write its corresponding letter above its problem number to complete the statement at the end of the activity. Not all of the answers will be used.

1. $\frac{2}{9}$ 2. $0.\overline{6}$

3. $0.\overline{14}$ 4. $\frac{2}{13}$

5. $\frac{1}{6}$ 6. $\frac{6}{7}$

Expressing Fractions as Repeating Decimals and Repeating Decimals as Fractions

7. $\frac{1}{3}$ 8. $0.\overline{4}$

9. $0.\overline{72}$ 10. $\frac{5}{6}$

11. $\frac{2}{7}$ 12. $0.\overline{8}$

13. $0.\overline{09}$ 14. $\frac{7}{11}$

Answer Bank

K. $\frac{5}{9}$	R. $\frac{8}{9}$	M. $0.\overline{3}$	L. $0.\overline{153846}$ A. $0.\overline{2}$		B. $\frac{2}{3}$
U. $\frac{8}{11}$	H. $\frac{4}{9}$	O. $0.\overline{63}$	S. $\frac{14}{99}$	D. $0.\overline{285714}$	
G. $0.8\overline{1}$	Y. $0.8\overline{3}$	E. $0.1\overline{6}$	I. $\frac{1}{11}$	T. $0.\overline{857142}$	

The correct name for the fraction $\underline{\quad}\ \underline{\quad}\ \underline{\quad}\quad \underline{\quad}\ \underline{\quad}\quad \underline{\quad}\ \underline{\quad}\ \underline{\quad}$
                                           2   1 12   13 3   6   8   5

$\underline{\quad}\ \underline{\quad}\ \underline{\quad}\ \underline{\quad}\ \underline{\quad}\ \underline{\quad}\ \underline{\quad}\quad \underline{\quad}\ \underline{\quad}\ \underline{\quad}\ \underline{\quad}\ \underline{\quad}\ \underline{\quad}$. (/)
  3 14 4 13 11 9   3   3 10 7   2 14 4

Simplifying Square Roots

Square roots can be used in formulas to find the speed of an object. Two of those formulas are described below.

Suppose an object falls from a ten-story building. Since a story is about 12 feet high, the distance the object falls is 120 feet. You can find how fast the object falls by using the formula $V = 8\sqrt{h}$, where V equals the velocity (rate of speed) of the object in miles per hour and h is the distance the object falls in feet.

$$V = 8\sqrt{120}$$
$$V = 8\sqrt{4}\sqrt{30}$$
$$V = 16\sqrt{30}$$
$$V \approx 88 \text{ mi/hr}$$

The object falls at a rate of approximately 88 miles per hour.

Square roots can also be used to determine the speed of a car prior to an accident or an abrupt stop. By measuring the length of skid marks, and using the formula $S = 2\sqrt{5d}$, where S equals the speed of the car in miles per hour and d equals the length of the skid marks in feet, police can find out how fast the car was traveling. If, for example, the skid marks are 100 feet, the car was traveling at about 45 miles per hour. (This formula applies to dry pavement only.)

Directions: Simplify each expression. Express your answers in radical form and as a decimal rounded to the nearest tenth. Then answer the questions on the next page.

1. $\sqrt{24} =$ _____ or _____   2. $\sqrt{48} =$ _____ or _____

3. $\sqrt{12} =$ _____ or _____   4. $\sqrt{50} =$ _____ or _____

5. $\sqrt{54} =$ _____ or _____   6. $\sqrt{56} =$ _____ or _____

7. $\sqrt{60} =$ _____ or _____   8. $\sqrt{75} =$ _____ or _____

9. $\sqrt{98} =$ _____ or _____   10. $\sqrt{104} =$ _____ or _____

11. $\sqrt{88} =$ _____ or _____   12. $\sqrt{32} =$ _____ or _____

13. $\sqrt{20} =$ _____ or _____   14. $\sqrt{126} =$ _____ or _____

15. $\sqrt{250} =$ _____ or _____   16. $\sqrt{72} =$ _____ or _____

Algebra Teacher's Activities Kit

Copyright © 2003 John Wiley & Sons, Inc.

Simplifying Square Roots

Directions: Use the formulas at the beginning of the worksheet to solve the following problems. Round your answers to the nearest whole number.

17. At the scene of an automobile accident, police measured the skid marks of a car before it ran off the road. The skid marks were 140 feet on dry pavement. About how fast was the car going just before the accident?

18. The skid marks of a second car at the same accident were 92 feet. About how fast was this car going?

19. A daredevil bungee-jumps from a high bridge and falls 130 feet before the cord slows his fall and draws him back. About how fast was this daredevil traveling downward?

20. Another daredevil bungee-jumps from a bridge. He falls 100 feet before the cord slows his fall. Which daredevil traveled faster? What is the difference in their speeds?

Finding the Nth Root of a Number

Other than square roots of numbers, you may find cube roots, fourth roots, fifth roots, and so on. Following are some examples.

$$\sqrt{81} = 9 \text{ because } 9^2 = 81$$
$$\sqrt[3]{512} = 8 \text{ because } 8^3 = 512$$
$$\sqrt[3]{-27} = -3 \text{ because } (-3)^3 = -27$$
$$-\sqrt{49} = -7 \text{ because } -(7)^2 = -49$$
$$\sqrt{n^2} = n \text{ because } (n)^2 = n^2 \quad (n \geq 0)$$
$$\sqrt[3]{n^{15}} = n^5 \text{ because } (n^5)^3 = n^{15}$$
$$\sqrt{-4} \text{ is not a real number}$$

Directions: Find the indicated root and match your answers with the answers in the Answer Bank. Write the letter of each answer in the blank before its problem. When you have finished, write the letters in order, starting with the first problem, to complete the statement at the end of the activity. For all problems assume n > 0.

1. _____ $\sqrt{16} =$

2. _____ $-\sqrt{121} =$

3. _____ $\sqrt[3]{n^3} =$

4. _____ $-\sqrt{100} =$

5. _____ $\sqrt[3]{216} =$

6. _____ $\sqrt{9} =$

7. _____ $\sqrt[2]{n^6} =$

8. _____ $-\sqrt{16} =$

9. _____ $-\sqrt{25} =$

10. _____ $\sqrt[3]{-27} =$

11. _____ $\sqrt[4]{81} =$

12. _____ $\sqrt[3]{8} =$

13. _____ $\sqrt[5]{243} =$

14. _____ $\sqrt{25} =$

15. _____ $\sqrt{n^2} =$

16. _____ $\sqrt[3]{n^6} =$

17. _____ $\sqrt[3]{125} =$

18. _____ $\sqrt[4]{625} =$

19. _____ $\sqrt[3]{27} =$

20. _____ $\sqrt[5]{-32} =$

21. _____ $\sqrt[3]{-1000} =$

22. _____ $\sqrt[4]{256} =$

23. _____ $\sqrt[5]{32} =$

24. _____ $\sqrt[5]{n^{10}} =$

25. _____ $-\sqrt{64} =$

26. _____ $\sqrt[6]{729} =$

27. _____ $\sqrt[3]{n^9} =$

28. _____ $\sqrt[3]{343} =$

29. _____ $\sqrt[4]{16} =$

30. _____ $-\sqrt[3]{125} =$

31. _____ $\sqrt[3]{64} =$

Finding the Nth Root of a Number

<table>
<tr><td colspan="6" align="center">**Answer Bank**</td></tr>
<tr><td>H. -5</td><td>F. -8</td><td>E. 4</td><td>P. n</td><td>W. -4</td><td>N. n^3</td></tr>
<tr><td>I. 3</td><td>A. 6</td><td>D. 7</td><td>S. 5</td><td>B. -2</td><td>T. 2</td></tr>
<tr><td>Y. -3</td><td>L. -10</td><td>O. n^2</td><td>X. -11</td><td></td><td></td></tr>
</table>

— — — — — — — — — —   — — —   — —   — —

— — — — — — — — — —   — —   — — — —   — — ___ nth root

of a negative number if n is odd, but not if n is even.

_____

_____

_____

_____

Multiplying and Dividing Radicals

Follow the rules below to multiply and divide radicals. Always simplify your answers.

- The product of two radicals is the radical of the products. Each of the two radicands must be greater than or equal to zero. (A *radicand* is the number beneath the radical symbol.)

$$\text{Example: } \sqrt{10}\sqrt{5} = \sqrt{50} = \sqrt{25}\sqrt{2} = 5\sqrt{2}$$

- The quotient of two radicals is the radical of the quotients. The radicand in the numerator must be greater than or equal to zero, and the radicand in the denominator must be greater than zero.

$$\text{Example: } \sqrt{\frac{30}{2}} = \sqrt{15}$$

Directions: Simplify each product or quotient. Then find each answer in the Answer Bank, and write its corresponding letter in the blank before its problem. When you have finished, write the letters in order, starting with the first problem, to complete the statement at the end of the activity. Some answers will be used more than once.

1. _____ $\sqrt{6}\sqrt{3} =$

2. _____ $\sqrt{35}\sqrt{2} =$

3. _____ $\sqrt{40}\sqrt{2} =$

4. _____ $\sqrt{5}\sqrt{12} =$

5. _____ $\sqrt{\frac{28}{4}} =$

6. _____ $\sqrt{3}\sqrt{8} =$

7. _____ $\sqrt{27}\sqrt{3} =$

Algebra Teacher's Activities Kit

Multiplying and Dividing Radicals

8. _____ $\sqrt{\dfrac{48}{3}} =$

9. _____ $\sqrt{8}\sqrt{2} =$

10. _____ $\sqrt{\dfrac{400}{5}} =$

11. _____ $\sqrt{\dfrac{144}{36}} =$

12. _____ $\sqrt{\dfrac{3}{4}} =$

13. _____ $\sqrt{\dfrac{243}{3}} =$

14. _____ $\sqrt{8}\sqrt{12} =$

15. _____ $\sqrt{4}\sqrt{4} =$

16. _____ $\sqrt{\dfrac{32}{2}} =$

17. _____ $\sqrt{\dfrac{3}{5}}\sqrt{10} =$

18. _____ $\sqrt{\dfrac{11}{25}} =$

19. _____ $\sqrt{\dfrac{49}{7}} =$

20. _____ $\sqrt{\dfrac{48}{2}} =$

21. _____ $\sqrt{\dfrac{700}{10}} =$

22. _____ $\sqrt{\dfrac{90}{2}} =$

Answer Bank
F. 4
D. $\dfrac{\sqrt{3}}{2}$
U. 2
H. $\sqrt{70}$
A. $\dfrac{\sqrt{11}}{5}$
S. $\sqrt{7}$
L. $4\sqrt{6}$
T. $2\sqrt{6}$
I. $2\sqrt{15}$
W. $\sqrt{6}$
E. $3\sqrt{5}$
O. 9
R. $4\sqrt{5}$
C. $3\sqrt{2}$

In the early part of the 16th century, __ __ __ __ __ __ __ __ __

__ __ __ __ __ __ __ __ __ __ __ __ __ first to use the radical

symbol as we use it today.

Rationalizing the Denominator

An expression involving radicals is in simplified form if:

- No radicand has a perfect square as a factor (except 1.)
- No fractions are under the radical sign.
- No radicals are in the denominator.

Rationalizing the denominator is the process of rewriting an expression that <u>has</u> a radical in the denominator as an expression that <u>does not have</u> a radical in the denominator.

To rationalize a denominator, multiply the numerator and denominator by a radical so that the denominator is a perfect square. Then simplify. Here are some examples:

$$\frac{9}{\sqrt{6}}\frac{\sqrt{6}}{\sqrt{6}}=\frac{9\sqrt{6}}{\sqrt{36}}=\frac{9\sqrt{6}}{6}=\frac{3\sqrt{6}}{2} \qquad \sqrt{\frac{1}{7}}\sqrt{\frac{1}{2}}=\sqrt{\frac{1}{14}}=\frac{1\sqrt{14}}{\sqrt{14}\sqrt{14}}=\frac{\sqrt{14}}{14} \qquad \sqrt{\frac{11}{5}}=\frac{\sqrt{11}}{\sqrt{5}}\frac{\sqrt{5}}{\sqrt{5}}=\frac{\sqrt{55}}{5}$$

Directions: Simplify each expression. Find each answer in the Answer Bank and write the corresponding letter in the space before the problem. When you have finished, write the letters in order, starting with the first problem, to complete the statement at the end of the activity.

1. _____ $\dfrac{5}{\sqrt{15}}=$

2. _____ $\dfrac{4}{\sqrt{2}}=$

3. _____ $\dfrac{12}{\sqrt{12}}=$

4. _____ $\sqrt{\dfrac{1}{8}}=$

5. _____ $\dfrac{\sqrt{6}}{\sqrt{3}}=$

6. _____ $\dfrac{\sqrt{5}}{\sqrt{8}}=$

7. _____ $\sqrt{\dfrac{1}{2}}=$

8. _____ $\sqrt{\dfrac{10}{7}}=$

9. _____ $\sqrt{\dfrac{7}{5}}\sqrt{10}=$

10. _____ $\sqrt{\dfrac{2}{3}}\sqrt{3}=$

11. _____ $\sqrt{\dfrac{16}{7}}=$

12. _____ $\sqrt{\dfrac{1}{10}}\sqrt{\dfrac{10}{7}}=$

13. _____ $\sqrt{\dfrac{3}{5}}=$

14. _____ $\dfrac{5}{\sqrt{3}}=$

15. _____ $\dfrac{1}{2}\sqrt{\dfrac{1}{2}}=$

16. _____ $\dfrac{3}{\sqrt{50}}=$

17. _____ $\sqrt{\dfrac{1}{2}}\sqrt{\dfrac{10}{8}}=$

18. _____ $\sqrt{\dfrac{40}{32}}=$

19. _____ $\dfrac{\sqrt{16}}{2\sqrt{2}}=$

20. _____ $\sqrt{\dfrac{1}{11}}\sqrt{\dfrac{22}{9}}=$

Rationalizing the Denominator

Answer Bank

N. $\dfrac{\sqrt{10}}{4}$ H. $\dfrac{\sqrt{2}}{4}$ F. $2\sqrt{2}$ S. $\dfrac{\sqrt{15}}{5}$ R. $\dfrac{4\sqrt{7}}{7}$ C. $\dfrac{5\sqrt{3}}{3}$

M. $\dfrac{\sqrt{70}}{7}$ A. $\dfrac{3\sqrt{2}}{10}$ D. $\dfrac{\sqrt{2}}{3}$ G. $\dfrac{\sqrt{5}}{2}$ I. $\dfrac{\sqrt{7}}{7}$ B. $\sqrt{14}$

U. $\dfrac{\sqrt{2}}{2}$ N. $\dfrac{\sqrt{10}}{4}$ O. $\dfrac{\sqrt{15}}{3}$ E. $\sqrt{2}$ T. $2\sqrt{3}$

When a denominator is rationalized, the value of the expression is not changed.

Only the form __ __   __ __ __   __ __ __ __ __ __   __ __

__ __ __ __ __ __ __.

Simplifying Sums and Differences of Radicals

To add or subtract radicals, the numbers under the radical symbol must be the same. In some cases, radicals will need to be simplified before adding or subtracting. Study the examples that follow.

$$4\sqrt{3} + \sqrt{5} + 2\sqrt{3} = 6\sqrt{3} + \sqrt{5}$$

$$\sqrt{12} + \sqrt{20} - \sqrt{75} = 2\sqrt{3} + 2\sqrt{5} - 5\sqrt{3} = 2\sqrt{5} - 3\sqrt{3}$$

$$\sqrt{10} - \sqrt{16} + \sqrt{40} = \sqrt{10} - 4 + 2\sqrt{10} = 3\sqrt{10} - 4$$

Directions: Find the sum or difference of each expression and write the answer in the space after the problem. Next, match each answer with the answers in the Answer Bank and write its corresponding letter in the space before each problem. When you have finished, write the letters in order, starting with the first problem, to complete the statement at the end of the activity. Some answers will be used more than once.

1. _____ $6\sqrt{2} - \sqrt{2} =$ _____

2. _____ $3\sqrt{6} - 2\sqrt{6} =$ _____

3. _____ $\sqrt{98} - \sqrt{2} =$ _____

4. _____ $\sqrt{32} + \sqrt{50} =$ _____

5. _____ $3\sqrt{6} - 4\sqrt{6} =$ _____

6. _____ $\sqrt{30} - \sqrt{120} =$ _____

7. _____ $\sqrt{75} + \sqrt{48} =$ _____

8. _____ $\sqrt{32} + \sqrt{8} =$ _____

9. _____ $4\sqrt{5} - \sqrt{5} =$ _____

10. _____ $3\sqrt{3} - 2\sqrt{3} =$ _____

11. _____ $\sqrt{44} - \sqrt{11} =$ _____

12. _____ $\sqrt{18} + \sqrt{8} =$ _____

Algebra Teacher's Activities Kit

Copyright © 2003 John Wiley & Sons, Inc.

Simplifying Sums and Differences of Radicals

13. _____ $\sqrt{108} - \sqrt{3} =$ _____

14. _____ $\sqrt{20} - \sqrt{45} =$ _____

15. _____ $\sqrt{12} + \sqrt{27} =$ _____

16. _____ $\sqrt{12} + \sqrt{147} =$ _____

17. _____ $\sqrt{125} - \sqrt{180} =$ _____

18. _____ $\sqrt{20} + \sqrt{5} =$ _____

19. _____ $\sqrt{121} + \sqrt{25} =$ _____

20. _____ $\sqrt{16} + \sqrt{12} + \sqrt{75} =$ _____ $+ 7\sqrt{3}$

21. _____ $\sqrt{6} - \sqrt{24} =$ _____

22. _____ $\sqrt{27} + \sqrt{108} =$ _____

23. _____ $\sqrt{147} - \sqrt{108} =$ _____

24. _____ $\sqrt{15} + \sqrt{45} = \sqrt{15} +$ _____

25. _____ $\sqrt{10} - \sqrt{27} + \sqrt{48} = \sqrt{10} +$ _____

26. _____ $\sqrt{49} + \sqrt{32} =$ _____ $+ 4\sqrt{2}$

27. _____ $\sqrt{120} + \sqrt{75} = 2\sqrt{30} +$ _____

28. _____ $\sqrt{32} + \sqrt{2} =$ _____

29. _____ $\sqrt{50} + \sqrt{27} =$ _____ $+ 3\sqrt{3}$

30. _____ $\sqrt{12} + \sqrt{72} = 2\sqrt{3} +$ _____

Answer Bank

O. $5\sqrt{2}$

I. $3\sqrt{5}$

G. 7

N. $\sqrt{3}$

H. $9\sqrt{2}$

M. 4

F. $\sqrt{6}$

D. $-\sqrt{5}$

T. $6\sqrt{2}$

L. $-\sqrt{30}$

A. $9\sqrt{3}$

X. 16

R. $5\sqrt{3}$

W. $\sqrt{11}$

E. $-\sqrt{6}$

The radical sign, $\sqrt{}$, is a modified form of the letter "r," which is taken from the first

letter __ __   __ __ __   __ __ __ __   __ __ __ __

" __ __ __ __ __ ,"   __ __ __ __ __ __ __ __   " __ __ __ ."

Simplifying Products That Contain Radicals

To simplify products that contain radicals, follow these steps: Use the Distributive Property if a binomial is multiplied by a monomial. If two binomials must be multiplied, use FOIL. Then express the product in simplest form. Study these examples.

$$\sqrt{6}\left(\sqrt{3}+\sqrt{5}\right)=\sqrt{18}+\sqrt{30}=3\sqrt{2}+\sqrt{30}$$

$$\left(\sqrt{6}+\sqrt{2}\right)\left(\sqrt{6}-\sqrt{5}\right)=\sqrt{36}-\sqrt{30}+\sqrt{12}-\sqrt{10}=6-\sqrt{30}+2\sqrt{3}-\sqrt{10}$$

Directions: Of the problems below, some products are correct and are expressed in simplest form. Others contain errors in multiplication or the products are not simplified. If a product is correct, write "correct" on the line that follows it. If there is an error, write "incorrect" and write the correct answer. Hint: There are only $\left(\sqrt{5}-1\right)\left(\sqrt{5}+1\right)$ correct answers.

1. $\sqrt{3}\left(\sqrt{2}+\sqrt{3}\right)=\sqrt{6}+\sqrt{9}$ _____

2. $\sqrt{5}\left(\sqrt{10}+\sqrt{8}\right)=2\sqrt{5}+10\sqrt{2}$ _____

3. $2\sqrt{3}\left(\sqrt{2}+5\right)=2\sqrt{6}+2\sqrt{15}$ _____

4. $2\sqrt{3}\left(3\sqrt{2}+2\sqrt{3}\right)=6\sqrt{6}+12$ _____

5. $\left(\sqrt{3}-2\right)\left(\sqrt{3}+2\right)=5$ _____

6. $\left(2-\sqrt{3}\right)\left(2+\sqrt{3}\right)=1$ _____

7. $\left(\sqrt{3}-1\right)^2=4-2\sqrt{3}$ _____

8. $\left(\sqrt{3}+1\right)^2=4+2\sqrt{3}$ _____

9. $\left(5+\sqrt{2}\right)\left(3+\sqrt{2}\right)=17+15\sqrt{2}$ _____

10. $\left(3+4\sqrt{3}\right)\left(2-\sqrt{3}\right)=6-9\sqrt{3}$ _____

Using Conjugates to Simplify Products and Quotients

Conjugates are numbers of the form $a\sqrt{b}+c\sqrt{d}$ and $a\sqrt{b}-c\sqrt{d}$ where a, b, c, and d are integers, and b and d are greater than 0. Conjugates are used to rationalize the denominator if the denominator is the sum or difference of two radicals, or the sum or difference of a radical and an integer.

To find the product of two conjugates, use the FOIL method: First terms, Outer terms, Inner terms, Last terms. Then simplify. For example:

$$\left(3\sqrt{2}+\sqrt{5}\right)\left(3\sqrt{2}-\sqrt{5}\right)=9\sqrt{4}-3\sqrt{10}+3\sqrt{10}-\sqrt{25}=18-5=13$$

To find a quotient, multiply the numerator and denominator by the conjugate of the denominator. Then simplify. For example:

$$\frac{\sqrt{2}}{3\sqrt{2}+\sqrt{5}}=\frac{\sqrt{2}}{\left(3\sqrt{2}+\sqrt{5}\right)}\frac{\left(3\sqrt{2}-\sqrt{5}\right)}{\left(3\sqrt{2}-\sqrt{5}\right)}=\frac{3\sqrt{4}-\sqrt{10}}{13}=\frac{6-\sqrt{10}}{13}$$

Directions: Simplify each product or quotient and write your answer in the blank. Find each answer in the Answer Bank, then write the letter of the answer above its problem number to complete the statement at the end of the activity.

1. $\left(3+\sqrt{5}\right)\left(3-\sqrt{5}\right)=$ _____

2. $\left(3-\sqrt{2}\right)\left(3+\sqrt{2}\right)=$ _____

3. $\left(\sqrt{3}+2\right)\left(\sqrt{3}-2\right)=$ _____

4. $\left(\sqrt{5}+\sqrt{3}\right)\left(\sqrt{5}-\sqrt{3}\right)=$ _____

5. $\left(\sqrt{3}-\sqrt{11}\right)\left(\sqrt{3}+\sqrt{11}\right)=$ _____

6. $\left(\sqrt{3}+7\right)\left(\sqrt{3}-7\right)=$ _____

7. $\dfrac{1}{\sqrt{5}+1}=$ _____

8. $\dfrac{4}{\sqrt{2}-1}=$ _____

9. $\dfrac{3}{2-\sqrt{5}}=$ _____

10. $\dfrac{\sqrt{2}}{\sqrt{6}-3}=$ _____

11. $\dfrac{\sqrt{11}}{\sqrt{11}-\sqrt{3}}=$ _____

12. $\dfrac{\sqrt{2}+1}{\sqrt{2}+4}=$ _____

13. $\dfrac{2-\sqrt{5}}{2+\sqrt{5}}=$ _____

14. $\dfrac{4-\sqrt{3}}{\sqrt{3}+4}=$ _____

15. $\dfrac{\sqrt{3}}{\sqrt{3}-\sqrt{6}}=$ _____

16. $\dfrac{\sqrt{5}}{\sqrt{3}-\sqrt{5}}=$ _____

Using Conjugates to Simplify Products and Quotients

Answer Bank

F. -46 N. -1 G. $-6-3\sqrt{5}$ H. $-9+4\sqrt{5}$

W. $\dfrac{\sqrt{15}+5}{-2}$ U. $\dfrac{-19+8\sqrt{3}}{-13}$ J. $\dfrac{11+\sqrt{33}}{8}$ E. 7

C. 4 A. $\dfrac{\sqrt{5}-1}{4}$ R. $\dfrac{2\sqrt{3}+3\sqrt{2}}{-3}$ T. $-1-\sqrt{2}$

O. 2 D. $\dfrac{2+3\sqrt{2}}{14}$ P. $4\sqrt{2}+4$ S. -8

$\overline{}$ $\overline{}$ $\overline{}$ $\overline{}$ $\overline{}$ $\overline{}$ $\overline{}$ $\overline{}$ $\overline{}$ $\overline{}$ $\overline{}$ $\overline{}$ $\overline{}$ $\overline{}$ $\overline{}$
15 13 2   8 10 4 12 14 1 15   4 6   15 16 4

$\overline{}$ $\overline{}$ $\overline{}$ $\overline{}$ $\overline{}$ $\overline{}$ $\overline{}$ $\overline{}$ $\overline{}$ $\overline{}$ will always be an integer.
1   4   3   11 14 9   7 15 2   5

Algebra Teacher's Activities Kit

Copyright © 2003 John Wiley & Sons, Inc.

NAME _____ DATE _____ SECTION _____

Using *i*

$\sqrt{-25}$ is not a real number because –25 does not have two identical factors. To find the square root of –25 and other negative numbers, the imaginary number *i* is used.

By definition $i^2 = -1$ or $i = \sqrt{-1}$.
This definition can be used to simplify $\sqrt{-25}$ as $5i$ and simplify products such as $(3i)(7i)$ as $21i^2$ or –21.

Directions: Simplify each expression and write your answer on the space after the problem. Match your answers with the answers in the Answer Bank, and write the corresponding letter of each answer in the blank before the problem. When you have finished, write the letters in order, starting with the first problem, to complete the statement at the end of the activity. Each answer will be used once, but one answer will be used twice.

1. _____ $\sqrt{-49} =$ _____   2. _____ $\sqrt{-15} =$ _____

3. _____ $\sqrt{-24} =$ _____   4. _____ $2i^2 =$ _____

5. _____ $(3i)^2 =$ _____   6. _____ $-6i^2 =$ _____

7. _____ $-\sqrt{36} =$ _____   8. _____ $-\sqrt{32} =$ _____

9. _____ $(-3i)(-4i) =$ _____   10. _____ $\sqrt{-144} =$ _____

11. _____ $(3i)(-3i) =$ _____   12. _____ $-12i^2 =$ _____

13. _____ $12i^2 =$ _____   14. _____ $\sqrt{-56} =$ _____

15. _____ $-\sqrt{18} =$ _____

Answer Bank

T. 6	A. $i\sqrt{15}$	C. 9	B. $2i\sqrt{14}$	W. $7i$
U. $12i$	O. $-4\sqrt{2}$	D. –12	E. 12	S. $2i\sqrt{6}$
R. –6	Y. $-3\sqrt{2}$	I. –2	N. –9	

The expression "imaginary number" ___ ___ ___

___ ___ ___ ___ ___ ___ ___ ___ ___ ___ ___

René Descartes in the 17th century.

Complex Numbers

Using Complex Numbers to Simplify Expressions

The *real numbers* and *imaginary numbers* form the set of *complex numbers*. A complex number can written as a + bi where a and b are real numbers. The a is the real part of the complex number and b is the imaginary part.

To add and subtract complex numbers, combine the real parts and the imaginary parts. For example:

$$(3 + 2i) + (6 - 4i) = 3 + 6 + (2 - 4)i = 9 - 2i$$
$$(3 + 2i) - (6 - 4i) = 3 - 6 + (2 + 4)i = -3 + 6i$$

To multiply two complex numbers, use FOIL and then substitute −1 for i^2. For example:

$$(3 + 2i)(6 - 4i) = 18 - 12i + 12i - 8i^2 = 18 - 8(-1) = 26$$

To divide two complex numbers, multiply the numerator and the denominator by the conjugate of the denominator. Here is an example:

$$\frac{3 + 2i}{(6 - 4i)} = \frac{(3 + 2i)}{(6 - 4i)} \frac{(6 + 4i)}{(6 + 16i)} = \frac{18 + 24i - 8}{36 - 16i^2} = \frac{10 + 24i}{52} = \frac{5 + 12i}{26}$$

Directions: Simplify each expression on the next page. Find the answer in the Answer Bank and write the letter of your answer in the blank before the problem. Then write each letter above its corresponding problem number to complete the statement at the end of the activity. Some answers will not be used.

Algebra Teacher's Activities Kit

Copyright © 2003 John Wiley & Sons, Inc.

NAME   DATE   SECTION

Using Complex Numbers to Simplify Expressions

Answer Bank
R. 2
B. $-10 + i$
W. $-7 - 24i$
M. $23 - 11i$
O. $3 + 10i$
D. $\dfrac{33 + 2i\sqrt{3}}{39}$
U. $11 - i\sqrt{5}$
A. $7 - 4i$
C. $\dfrac{11 - 4i\sqrt{3}}{13}$
Y. $-2 - 10i$
N. $11 - 10i$
T. $\dfrac{16 - 5i}{13}$
X. $\dfrac{16 + 15i}{13}$
S. $-12 + 6i$
L. 34
P. $-5 + 2i\sqrt{6}$
E. $\dfrac{3 + i}{10}$

1. _____ $(4 + 3i) + (3 - 7i) =$

2. _____ $(6 - 8i) + (5 - 2i) =$

3. _____ $(5 + 4i) - (2 - 6i) =$

4. _____ $(2 - 3i) - (4 + 7i) =$

5. _____ $(4 + 3i) - 2(7 + i) =$

6. _____ $2i(3 + 6i) =$

7. _____ $(1 + i)(1 - i) =$

8. _____ $(5 + 3i)(5 - 3i) =$

9. _____ $(5 + i)(4 - 3i) =$

10. _____ $(3 - 4i)^2 =$

11. _____ $(1 + i\sqrt{6})^2 =$

12. _____ $(2 - \sqrt{-5})(3 + \sqrt{-5}) =$

13. _____ $\dfrac{1}{3 - i} =$

14. _____ $\dfrac{6 + i}{3 - 2i} =$

15. _____ $\dfrac{6 - i\sqrt{3}}{6 + i\sqrt{3}} =$

The sum, difference, product, and quotient of two complex numbers is

$\overline{}$ $\overline{}$ $\overline{}$ $\overline{}$ $\overline{}$ $\overline{}$ $\overline{}$ $\overline{}$ $\overline{}$ $\overline{}$ $\overline{}$ $\overline{}$ $\overline{}$
1   8 10   1   4   6   1   15   3   9 11   8 13 14

$\overline{}$ $\overline{}$ $\overline{}$ $\overline{}$ $\overline{}$ $\overline{}$.
2   12   9   5 13   7

Reviewing Concepts and Skills of Complex Numbers

This activity focuses on a variety of concepts and skills associated with complex numbers. All of the problems are multiple choice and some have more than one answer.

Directions: Circle the answer, or answers, to each problem below. Then write the letters of the circled answers in order, starting with the first problem, to complete the statement at the end of the activity.

1. π, $\sqrt{2}$, and $\sqrt{3}$ are all examples of _____.

        A. rational numbers

        W. irrational numbers

        S. whole numbers

2. Which of the following is not an integer?

        I. 0.5   H. 0   L. 3

3. Which of the following is equivalent to $0.\overline{2}$?

        A. $\frac{1}{5}$ M. $\frac{22}{100}$ T. $\frac{2}{9}$

4. $\sqrt{24}$ written in simplest form equals _____.

        H. $2\sqrt{6}$ I. $6\sqrt{2}$ M. $8\sqrt{3}$

5. Which of the following are whole numbers?

        P. 15   O. 0   S. –3

6. $\sqrt{3} + \sqrt{5} + \sqrt{3}$ equals _____.

        S. $\sqrt{11}$ M. $\sqrt{45}$ I. $2\sqrt{3} + \sqrt{5}$

7. $\left(\sqrt{3}\right)^{2}$ written in simplest form is _____.

        D. $\sqrt{9}$ T. 9   N. 3

8. $\sqrt{5}\sqrt{10}$ written in simplest form is _____.

        A. $\sqrt{50}$ S. $2\sqrt{5}$ T. $5\sqrt{2}$

9. $\frac{2}{\sqrt{5}}$ written in simplest form is _____.

        R. $\frac{2\sqrt{5}}{25}$ S. $\frac{2\sqrt{5}}{5}$ H. $\frac{\sqrt{5}}{2}$

Reviewing Concepts and Skills of Complex Numbers

10. $\left(3+\sqrt{2}\right)\left(3-\sqrt{2}\right)$ equals _____.

    S. $7+6\sqrt{2}$ I. $7-6\sqrt{2}$ O. 7

11. i^2 equals _____.

    D. 1 N. -1 F. $\sqrt{-1}$

12. $15 - i^2$ equals _____.

    A. 16 R. 14 O. $15-\sqrt{-1}$

13. If $n^2 = 25$, then n equals _____.

    B. 625 N. -5 U. 5

14. $3i\sqrt{2} + 6i\sqrt{2}$ equals _____.

    E. $-9i\sqrt{2}$ D. $18i^2\sqrt{2}$ M. $9i\sqrt{2}$

15. The conjugate of $3+\sqrt{5}$ is _____.

    B. $3-\sqrt{5}$ R. $\sqrt{5}+3$ S. $\sqrt{3}+5$

16. $\dfrac{1}{1+\sqrt{2}}$ equals _____.

    T. $1-\sqrt{2}$ E. $-1+\sqrt{2}$ I. -1

17. $\left(\dfrac{\sqrt{3}}{2}\right)^2$ written in simplest form is _____.

    A. $\dfrac{9}{4}$ R. $\dfrac{3}{4}$ F. $\dfrac{\sqrt{9}}{4}$

18. Which of the following numbers are imaginary?

    E. $-\sqrt{5}$ L. $\sqrt{-5}$ I. $-\sqrt{-5}$

19. $\left(5+i\sqrt{2}\right)+3-\sqrt{-2}$ equals _____.

    M. $8-2i\sqrt{2}$ R. $8-4i$ N. 8

20. $\sqrt{18}+\sqrt{75}-\sqrt{3}$ equals _____.

    T. $10\sqrt{3}$ E. $3\sqrt{2}+4\sqrt{3}$ D. $6\sqrt{3}$

Imaginary numbers cannot be paired __ __ __ __　__ __ __ __ __ __

__ __　__　__ __ __ __ __ __ __　__ __ __ __ .

Polynomial, Exponential, and Logarithmic Functions

The thirteen activities of this section explore various types of functions, ranging from quadratic functions to logarithmic functions. Skills necessary for solving equations related to these functions are addressed. Activities with real-life applications include calculating monthly loan payments and compound interest.

Teaching Suggestions for the Activities

9-1 Solving Quadratic Equations by Factoring

All of the quadratic equations in this activity can be solved by factoring. For some, students will have to find binomial factors and for others they will need to find the greatest monomial factor.

Begin the activity by reviewing the definition of a quadratic equation, which is a polynomial equation of degree two. Emphasize that a polynomial of degree two means that the polynomial is simplified and the highest degree of any term is two.

Review the procedures for factoring and discuss the Zero-Product Property, which states that if a product is zero, then one of the factors or both of the factors are zero. Explain the examples on the worksheet and offer additional examples if necessary.

Review the directions on the worksheet with your students. Note that all answers in the Answer Bank will be used, and that some will be used more than once. Also mention that some letters in some problems may need to be reversed when placed in the blanks at the end of the activity.

9-2 Solving Simple Quadratic Equations

This activity requires your students to simplify radicals and solve equations. Some equations involve only a squared term while others involve a binomial squared.

Begin the activity by instructing your students to solve $x^2 = 25$. Most of your students will say that the answer is 5 because $5 \times 5 = 25$. Encourage your students to find another solution so that the same number squared equals 25. Students should realize that -5×-5 also equals 25.

Discuss the Square Root Property that states the solution set of $x^2 = k$ is $\pm\sqrt{k}$. Remind students of the meaning of the symbol $\pm$, and note that if $k > 0$, both solutions are real. If $k < 0$, then both solutions are imaginary. Emphasize that the square root of a negative number does not exist in the set of real numbers.

Discuss the examples provided on the worksheet. Explain the steps necessary to finding the solutions and make sure your students understand the procedure.

Review the directions on the worksheet. Note that all terms will be used once.

9-3 Solving a Quadratic Equation by Completing the Square

This activity requires your students to complete the square in order to solve quadratic equations. To complete the activity successfully, students should be able to simplify square roots, factor trinomials, and work with polynomials.

Begin the activity by reviewing how to solve equations such as $x^2 = 7$ ($x = \pm 7$) and $(x - 2)^2 = 5$ ($x = 2 \pm\sqrt{5}$). Note that the $\pm$ symbol means "plus or minus."

Discuss the example on the worksheet, making certain that your students understand the process. Note that they will always add $a\left(\dfrac{b}{2a}\right)^2$ to both sides of the equation. Doing so creates a perfect square. (In the example $a = 1$.)

If necessary, offer the following example on the board or an overhead projector:

$$4x^2 - 8x + 1 = 0 \qquad a = 4, b = -8, c = 1$$
$$4x^2 - 8x = -1 \qquad \text{variables must be on one side}$$
$$4(x^2 - 2x) = -1 \qquad \text{factor the left-hand side}$$
$$4(x^2 - 2x + 1) = -1 + 4 \qquad \text{add } a\left(\dfrac{b}{2a}\right)^2 \text{ to each side}$$

$$4(x - 1)^2 = -1 + 4 \qquad \text{write a perfect square}$$

$$4(x - 1)^2 = 3 \qquad \text{simplify}$$

$$(x - 1)^2 = \frac{3}{4} \qquad \text{simplify}$$

$$x - 1 = \pm\sqrt{\frac{3}{4}} \qquad \text{take the square root}$$

$$x = 1 \pm \frac{\sqrt{3}}{2} \qquad \text{simplify}$$

$$x = \frac{2 \pm \sqrt{3}}{2} \qquad \text{simplify}$$

Emphasize the third step, adding 4 to each side, and note the use of parentheses. Even though 1 is written in parentheses, students are actually adding 4.

Go over the directions on the worksheet with your students. Note that the Value Bank contains the number that is added in each problem. One value will be used twice. The Answer Bank contains the solutions to the problems.

9-4 Using the Quadratic Formula

For this activity your students will use the quadratic formula to solve equations. To complete the activity successfully, your students should be able to simplify radicals.

Begin the activity by reviewing the meaning of the $\pm$ symbol and the steps for simplifying radicals. Discuss the formula on the worksheet, providing examples if necessary. Explain the use of the discriminate and how it is used to find the number and types of solutions to an equation.

Review the directions on the worksheet with your students. Caution them that not only must they identify incorrect solutions but correct them as well.

9-5 Using Equations to Describe Parabolas

In this activity your students are given equations and must identify the axis of symmetry, vertex, and x- and y-intercepts of parabolas. To complete this activity successfully, your students must be able to graph parabolas by constructing T-tables.

Start the activity by discussing the concept of a quadratic equation such as $y = ax^2 + bx + c$. Use a T-table to sketch the equation of the parabola on the activity sheet. Explain the meanings of the axis of symmetry, vertex, x-intercepts and y-intercepts, and discuss the formulas and examples on the worksheet. If necessary, sketch some parabolas based on equations and demonstrate how to use the axis of symmetry and other important points.

Go over the instructions on the worksheet. Emphasize that each answer in the Answer Bank can be paired with one equation. Remind your students to state the relationship between each pair.

9-6 Classifying Polynomial Functions

This activity requires your students to simplify polynomial functions and then classify them as a constant, linear, quadratic, or cubic function. To complete this activity successfully, your students should be able to simplify polynomials.

Begin the activity by explaining that the degree of a polynomial is the greatest degree of its terms after it has been simplified. Next, discuss the examples of the constant, linear, quadratic, and cubic functions that are presented on the activity sheet. Depending on the abilities of your students, you may wish to review combining similar terms, the Distributive Property, and the steps for multiplying binomials.

Go over the instructions on the worksheet. Remind your students that they are to simplify and classify the functions. You may wish to caution them to be aware that some functions may already be simplified.

9-7 Using Synthetic Division

This activity requires your students to use synthetic division to factor polynomials. Synthetic division is used to find roots of polynomial functions.

Begin the activity by explaining that synthetic division is a type of mathematical shorthand that provides an abbreviated way of dividing polynomials. You may find it helpful to use long division to divide $x^3 + x^2 - 5x - 2$ and compare this to the example on the worksheet, which uses synthetic division. Such comparisons enable some students to more easily understand the relationship between the two methods.

Explain that when using synthetic division, the divisor must be of the form $x - c$. If the divisor is $x - 2$, then the polynomial must be divided by 2. If the divisor is $x + 2$, the polynomial must be divided by -2. Note that the polynomial must be written in descending order. Zeroes must be included to preserve this order. For example, $2 - 3x^2 + 4x^3$ must be rewritten as $4x^3 - 3x^2 + 0x + 2$. Emphasize that the coefficients are 4, -3, 0, and 2.

Depending on the level of your students, you may wish to include an example that has a remainder such as $\frac{3x^2 + 4x + 2}{x + 2}$. (The quotient is $3x - 2 + \frac{6}{x + 2}$.)

Review the directions on the worksheet with your students. Note that after completing the statement at the end of the activity, they are to write an explanation.

9-8 Using Synthetic Division to Factor Polynomials

For this activity your students are to factor polynomials through the use of synthetic division. To complete the activity successfully, students should be able to simplify polynomials.

Start the activity by reviewing synthetic division. Emphasize that synthetic division can only be used if the divisor is of the form x – c. Note that if there is no remainder when students divide by c, then x – c is a factor. If there is no remainder when students divide by –c, then x + c is a factor.

Explain to your students that they should use practical choices when selecting a divisor. The number they choose should be a factor of the third term. If a factor is found, students should then factor the resulting polynomials, remembering that not all polynomials can be factored.

Go over the directions on the worksheet with your students. Note that all of the factors are included in the Answer Bank; some factors will be used more than once.

9-9 Finding the Zeroes of Polynomial Functions

For this activity your students must find the zeroes of polynomial functions by writing the corresponding equation and solving for x. This involves several prerequisite skills, including finding the GMF, factoring the difference of squares, solving quadratic equations, using synthetic division, factoring by grouping, and factoring the sum and difference of cubes. This activity lends itself well to students working in small groups.

Introduce the activity by explaining that the zeroes of a function are the same as the solutions to the corresponding equation. For example, the function $f(x) = x^2 - 2x - 24$ can be written as $x^2 - 2x - 24 = 0$ with the solutions of $x = 6$ or $x = -4$. These two solutions are the zeroes of the function. Note that if the degree of the function is n, there are n roots (including multiple roots) in the complex number system.

Discuss the guidelines for solving polynomial equations, which are shown on the worksheet. Emphasize that the guidelines serve as a checklist students should refer to as they solve the equations.

Go over the instructions of the activity. Remind your students that the domain is the complex number system that includes imaginary numbers.

9-10 Solving Exponential Equations

This activity requires your students to solve exponential equations. The problems in the activity do not require factoring. To complete this activity successfully, your students must be familiar with the laws of exponents.

Begin the activity by reviewing numbers written in exponential form such as $2^4 = 16$, $2^3 = 8$, $3^2 = 9$, $3^3 = 27$, and so on. Explain that an exponential equation is an equation that has a variable as an exponent. Note that in order to solve these equations, students must rewrite one or both sides of the equation so that the bases are the same. They then must follow the laws of exponents to solve the equation. Discuss the laws of exponents, which are shown on the worksheet, and go over the examples.

Review the directions on the worksheet. Remind your students to explain the pattern at the end of the activity.

9-11 Solving Equations Involving Logarithms

For this activity your students are required to solve equations with logarithms. To complete the activity successfully, students will need to be able to convert equations from exponential form to logarithmic form and from logarithmic form to exponential form.

Start the activity by discussing the examples on the worksheet. Depending on the abilities of your students, you may find it helpful to provide more examples.

Review the directions on the worksheet, stressing that students must write the equations in exponential form and then solve. Note that all of the answers in the Answer Bank will be used, and that one answer will be used twice.

9-12 Borrowing and Repaying Money (with Interest)

This activity requires students to determine the monthly payment of an item purchased with credit. To complete this activity successfully, students should understand the Order of Operations, exponents, and fractions.

Begin the activity by asking your students if they, or their parents, have ever bought something on credit. It is likely that most have. Explain that lending institutions rely on formulas for determining the monthly payments that will be necessary to repay the loan.

Discuss the formula on the worksheet with your students. Point out the variables, and make sure that students understand how to use the formula, which can appear to be quite complex. However, if students are deliberate and careful with their work, they should be able to utilize the formula competently.

Review the instructions with your students. Remind them to round their answers to the nearest cent.

9-13 Calculating Compound Interest

For this activity your students are to calculate compound interest using a formula. To complete the activity successfully, they should understand the Order of Operations, fractions, and exponents.

Introduce the activity by discussing the interest paid on savings accounts, money market accounts, and certificates of deposit. Explain that interest is the fee a financial institution, for example, a bank or savings and loan, pays the account holder for keeping funds in the account, which the financial institution may then lend to others. (When the financial institution lends the money to another party at a higher rate of interest, the company earns a profit.) The interest paid on accounts is generally compounded, meaning that it is calculated on the principal as well as the money in the account that is earned. Explain that interest may be compounded semiannually, twice a year, quarterly, four times a year, or daily.

Review the directions on the worksheet with your students. Note that they should assume that no additions or withdrawals have been made. Students should round their answers to the nearest cent.

Answer Key for Section 9

9-1. 1. Y, 3; E, 2 2. T, –5; A, 4 3. L, –2; L –2 4. O, 0; F, 10 5. T, –5; H, –3 6. E, 2; T, –5 7. Y, 3; P, $\frac{1}{2}$ 8. E, 2; I, $-\frac{1}{2}$ 9. S, $\frac{5}{2}$; O, 0 10. N, –1; T, –5 11. H, –3; E, 2 12. S, $\frac{5}{2}$; A, 4 13. M, $-\frac{3}{4}$; E, 2 14. L, –2; I, $-\frac{1}{2}$ 15. N, –1; E, 2   Although René Descartes first used raised numbers for powers in 1637, he continued to write x^2 as xx because xx uses the same amount of space as x^2 <u>yet all of the type is on the same line</u>.

9-2. 1. G, $\pm\sqrt{5}$ 2. H, $\pm\sqrt{15}$ 3. L, $\pm2\sqrt{5}$ 4. D, $\pm4\sqrt{3}$ 5. T, ±7 6. O, ±10 7. R, $-3\pm\sqrt{10}$ 8. W, $7\pm\sqrt{14}$ 9. I, $-4\pm4\sqrt{2}$ 10. M, no real number solution 11. U, $\frac{8\pm\sqrt{5}}{2}$ 12. A, $\frac{-15\pm\sqrt{30}}{3}$ 13. E, 6 or 0 <u>William Oughtred</u> introduced the $\pm$ symbol in his book *Clavis Mathematicae*, published in 1631.

9-3. 1. A, 16; R, $4 \pm \sqrt{3}$ 2. E, 4; K, $2 \pm \sqrt{3}$ 3. N, $\frac{1}{4}$; O, $\frac{-1 \pm \sqrt{5}}{2}$ 4. W, 9; N, $-3 \pm 3\sqrt{2}$ 5. V, 12; A, $\frac{6 \pm \sqrt{21}}{3}$ 6. L, 3; U, $\frac{3 \pm \sqrt{39}}{3}$ 7. E, 4; S, $-2 \pm 2\sqrt{5}$ Thanks to Francois Viète (1540–1603), equations such as $ax^2 + bx + c$ can be solved by writing a formula if a, b, and c <u>are known values</u>.

9-4. 1. incorrect; $x = \frac{-5 \pm \sqrt{57}}{2}$ 2. correct   3. incorrect; no real solutions or $-1 \pm i\sqrt{7}$ 4. incorrect; $-1 \pm \sqrt{3}$ 5. incorrect; $x = \frac{5}{2}$; $x = -1$ 6. correct   7. correct   8. correct   9. incorrect; $x = \frac{-3 \pm 2\sqrt{6}}{3}$ 10. incorrect; $x = 4 \pm \sqrt{3}$

9-5. 1. $x = \frac{3}{2}$; axis of symmetry   2. $\left(\frac{5}{2}, -\frac{9}{4}\right)$; vertex   3. $(0, -6)$; y-intercept   4. $\varnothing$; no x-intercept   5. $x = 0$; axis of symmetry   6. $(0, -15)$; y-intercept   7. $(0, -3)$; y-intercept   8. $\left(\frac{1}{2}, -\frac{3}{2}\right)$; vertex   9. $x = \frac{2}{3}$; axis of symmetry   10. $(0, 6)$; y-intercept

9-6. 1. can't be simplified; quadratic   2. can't be simplified; constant   3. $f(x) = 3x^2 + 4x + 2$; quadratic   4. $f(x) = 7x + 4$; linear   5. $f(x) = x^2 + x - 2$; quadratic   6. $f(x) = x^3 - x$; cubic   7. $f(x) = 3x^3 + 15x^2 + 12x$; cubic   8. $f(x) = x^2 + x$; quadratic   9. $f(x) = 8x^3 + 7$; cubic   10. $f(x) = x^2 + 4x + 4$; quadratic   11. $f(x) = x^2 + 3x + 2$; quadratic   12. $f(x) = 8x$; linear   13. $f(x) = x^3 + 6x^2 + 12x + 8$; cubic   14. $f(x) = 5$; constant   15. $f(x) = 10x$; linear

9-7. 1. O, $x^2 - 2x + 2$ 2. I, $x^2 - 5x + 9$ 3. T, $2x^2 - x + 6$ 4. A, $-5x^2 - x + 13 + \frac{22}{x-2}$ 5. C, $2x^2 - x + 4 + \frac{1}{x+1}$ 6. F, $4x^2 + 2x + 6 + \frac{6}{x-3}$ 7. N, $4x^3 - 3x^2 + 4x - 4$ 8. L, $x^2 + 2x + 4 - \frac{2}{x-2}$ 9. G, $3x^2 + 1$ 10. U, $2x^2 - 3x + 9 - \frac{8}{x-2}$ 11. R, $x^3 + 2x + 1 + \frac{4}{x+1}$ 12. E, $x^3 - x^2 + 3x - 9 + \frac{30}{x+3}$ Synthetic means <u>not genuine; artificial</u>. Explanations may vary. A possible explanation is that synthetic division is not really long division. It is a shorthand method of division because only the coefficients are included.

9-8. 1. $(x + 5)(x + 3)(x - 2)$ 2. $(x - 4)(x - 2)(x + 1)$ 3. $(x + 2)(x - 3)(x + 1)$ 4. $(x - 1)^2(x + 1)$ 5. $(x - 3)(x + 2)(x - 1)(x + 3)$ 6. $(x - 1)(x - 4)(x - 5)$ 7. $(x + 1)^2(x - 1)(x - 3)$ 8. $(x - 4)(x^2 + 4x + 2)$

9-9. 1. $x = \pm 3$ 2. $x = 5$, $x = -1$ 3. $x = 0$, $x = 3$, $x = 6$ 4. $x = -3$, $x = 1$, $x = -2$ 5. $x = 5 \pm \sqrt{19}$ 6. $x = \pm 2$, $x = \pm 2i$ 7. $x = 0$, $x = \pm 2$ 8. $x = 2.5$ (a double root)   9. $x = \frac{5 \pm \sqrt{21}}{2}$ 10. $x = \frac{\pm\sqrt{5}}{2}$, $x = -3$

9-10. 1. $x = -5$ 2. $x = -4$ 3. $x = -3$ 4. $x = -2$ 5. $x = -\frac{7}{4}$ 6. $x = -\frac{3}{8}$ 7. $x = \frac{1}{9}$

8. $x = \frac{1}{6}$ 9. $x = \frac{1}{4}$ 10. $x = \frac{1}{3}$ 11. $x = \frac{5}{4}$ 12. $x = 2\frac{1}{3}$ 13. $x = 4$

14. $x = 4\frac{2}{3}$ 15. $x = 6$ The answers are in ascending order.

9-11. 1. J, 64   2. O, 4   3. H, $\frac{1}{8}$ 4. N, 9   5. N, 9   6. A, $\frac{1}{25}$ 7. P, $\frac{1}{243}$ 8. I, 2

9. E, 3   10. R, 125   The term "logarithm" was first used by <u>John Napier</u> in 1616.

9-12. 1. $95.40   2. $100.10   3. $70.97   4. $176.14

9-13. 1. $541.43   2. No, she will only have $1,236.27.   3. $105.25
4. $14,600.78

Solving Quadratic Equations by Factoring

A *quadratic equation* is a polynomial equation of degree two. Following are some examples:

$$x^2 + 2x + 1 \qquad x^2 - 16 \quad x^2 - 2x - 15 \qquad 2x^2 + 7x + 3$$

To solve a quadratic equation by factoring, first find the factors. If the product of two numbers is 0, one or both factors must equal 0. Then solve for x. For example:

$$x^2 - 2x - 15 = 0$$
$$(x - 5)(x + 3) = 0$$
$$x - 5 = 0 \text{ or } (x + 3) = 0$$
$$x = 5 \text{ or } x = -3$$

Directions: Solve each equation and write the solutions in the spaces provided after the equations. Then match your answers with the answers in the Answer Bank. Write the corresponding letters of the answers in the spaces before the equations. When you have finished, write the letters, starting with the first problem, to complete the statement at the end of the activity. You may have to reverse the order of some letters in each problem.

1. _____ _____ $x^2 - 5x + 6 = 0$ x = _____ or x = _____

2. _____ _____ $x^2 + x - 20 = 0$ x = _____ or x = _____

3. _____ _____ $x^2 + 4x + 4 = 0$ x = _____ or x = _____

4. _____ _____ $x^2 - 10x = 0$ x = _____ or x = _____

5. _____ _____ $x^2 + 8x + 15 = 0$ x = _____ or x = _____

6. _____ _____ $x^2 + 3x - 10 = 0$ x = _____ or x = _____

7. _____ _____ $2x^2 - 7x + 3 = 0$ x = _____ or x = _____

8. _____ _____ $2x^2 - 3x - 2 = 0$ x = _____ or x = _____

9. _____ _____ $2x^2 - 5x = 0$ x = _____ or x = _____

10. _____ _____ $x^2 + 6x + 5 = 0$ x = _____ or x = _____

11. _____ _____ $x^2 + x - 6 = 0$ x = _____ or x = _____

12. _____ _____ $2x^2 - 13x + 20 = 0$ x = _____ or x = _____

13. _____ _____ $4x^2 - 5x - 6 = 0$ x = _____ or x = _____

14. _____ _____ $2x^2 + 5x + 2 = 0$ x = _____ or x = _____

15. _____ _____ $x^2 - x - 2 = 0$ x = _____ or x = _____

Algebra Teacher's Activities Kit

Copyright © 2003 John Wiley & Sons, Inc.

Solving Quadratic Equations by Factoring

Answer Bank

E. 2   P. $\frac{1}{2}$ Y. 3   L. –2   T. –5   I. $-\frac{1}{2}$ O. 0

F. 10   M. $-\frac{3}{4}$ S. $\frac{5}{2}$ A. 4   H. –3   N. –1

Although René Descartes first used raised numbers for powers in 1637, he continued to write x^2 as xx because xx uses the same amount of space as x^2 ___ ___ ___

___ ___ ___   ___ ___   ___ ___ ___   ___ ___ ___ ___   ___ ___   ___ ___ ___

___ ___ ___   ___ ___ ___ ___   ___ ___ ___ ___.

Solving Simple Quadratic Equations

Some quadratic equations cannot be solved by factoring. Many of these equations may be solved by using the Square Root Property.

This property states that if $x^2 = k$, then the solution set is $\sqrt{k}$ or $-\sqrt{k}$, which can be abbreviated as $\pm\sqrt{k}$. To solve simple quadratic equations by using the Square Root Property, do the following:

- Isolate the squared term or binomial.
- Take the square root of each side.
- Solve for x.
- Simplify your answer.

Study these two examples:

$$(x + 7)^2 = 28 \qquad\qquad 5(x - 3)^2 = 15$$
$$x + 7 = \pm\sqrt{28} \qquad\qquad (x - 3)^2 = \frac{15}{5} = 3$$
$$x = -7 \pm 2\sqrt{7} \qquad\qquad x - 3 = \pm\sqrt{3}$$
$$x = 3 \pm \sqrt{3}$$

Directions: Solve each quadratic equation and match your answer with the answers in the Answer Bank. Write the corresponding letter of each answer in the space before the equation. Then write the letters above their problem numbers to complete the statement at the end of the activity.

Algebra Teacher's Activities Kit

Copyright © 2003 John Wiley & Sons, Inc.

Solving Simple Quadratic Equations

1. _____ $x^2 = 5$

2. _____ $x^2 = 15$

3. _____ $x^2 = 20$

4. _____ $x^2 = 48$

5. _____ $x^2 = 49$

6. _____ $x^2 = 100$

7. _____ $(x + 3)^2 = 10$

8. _____ $(x - 7)^2 = 14$

9. _____ $(x + 4)^2 = 3^2$

10. _____ $(x - 5)^2 = -50$

11. _____ $(x - 4)^2 = \dfrac{5}{4}$

12. _____ $(x + 5)^2 = \dfrac{10}{3}$

13. _____ $2(x - 3)^2 = 18$

Answer Bank

I. $-4 \pm 4\sqrt{2}$

A. $\dfrac{-15 \pm \sqrt{30}}{3}$

W. $7 \pm \sqrt{14}$

R. $-3 \pm \sqrt{10}$

H. $\pm\sqrt{15}$

T. ± 7

G. $\pm\sqrt{5}$

E. 6 or 0

L. $\pm 2\sqrt{5}$

D. $\pm 4\sqrt{3}$

M. no real number
   solutions

O. ± 10

U. $\dfrac{8 \pm \sqrt{5}}{2}$

___ ___ ___ ___ ___ ___ ___   ___ ___ ___ ___ ___ ___ ___ ___ introduced
 8 9 3 3 9 12 10   6 11 1 2 5 7 13 4

the $\pm$ symbol in his book *Clavis Mathematicae,* published in 1631.

Solving a Quadratic Equation by Completing the Square

One way to solve quadratic equations is by completing the square. The example below shows the steps necessary when solving for x.

$x^2 + 6x - 12 = 0$	$a = 1, b = 6, c = -12$
$x^2 + 6x = 12$	variables must be on one side
$x^2 + 6x + 9 = 12 + 9$	add a $\left(\dfrac{b}{2a}\right)^2$
$x^2 + 6x + 9 = 21$	simplify
$(x + 3)^2 = 21$	rewrite the trinomial as a perfect square
$x + 3 = \pm\sqrt{21}$	take the square root
$x = -3 \pm \sqrt{21}$	isolate the variable

Directions: Solve each equation by completing the square. Match the value you add to each equation with the values under the Values Bank, and match your answers with the answers under the Answer Bank. For each problem, write the corresponding letter of the value you added in the first space after the problem number, then write the corresponding letter of the answer in the space directly before the problem. When you have finished, write the letters in order, starting with the first problem, to complete the statement at the end of the activity. One value will be used twice.

1. _____ _____ $x^2 - 8x + 13 = 0$

2. _____ _____ $x^2 - 4x + 1 = 0$

3. _____ _____ $x^2 + x - 1 = 0$

4. _____ _____ $x^2 + 6x - 9 = 0$

5. _____ _____ $3x^2 - 12x + 5 = 0$

6. _____ _____ $3x^2 - 6x - 10 = 0$

7. _____ _____ $x^2 + 4x - 16 = 0$

Values Bank
V. 12
N. $\dfrac{1}{4}$
E. 4
L. 3
W. 9
A. 16

Answer Bank
A. $\dfrac{6 \pm \sqrt{21}}{3}$
S. $-2 \pm 2\sqrt{5}$
R. $4 \pm \sqrt{3}$
N. $-3 \pm 3\sqrt{2}$
K. $2 \pm \sqrt{3}$
U. $\dfrac{3 \pm \sqrt{39}}{3}$
O. $\dfrac{-1 \pm \sqrt{5}}{2}$

Thanks to Francois Vietè (1540–1603), equations such as $ax^2 + bx + c$ can be solved by writing a formula if a, b, and c ___ ___ ___   ___ ___ ___ ___ ___

___ ___ ___ ___ ___ ___.

Algebra Teacher's Activities Kit

Copyright © 2003 John Wiley & Sons, Inc.

Using the Quadratic Formula

The *quadratic formula* shown below may always be used to solve second-degree equations of the form $ax^2 + bx + c = 0$, $a \neq 0$.

$$x = \frac{-b \pm \sqrt{b^2 - 4ac}}{2a}$$

The expression $b^2 - 4ac$ is called the *discriminate*. It is used to find the number and type of solutions of a quadratic equation.

- An equation has two real solutions if $b^2 - 4ac > 0$.
- An equation has one real solution if $b^2 - 4ac = 0$.
- An equation has no real solutions if $b^2 - 4ac < 0$.

Directions: Use the quadratic formula to solve each equation. Compare your answers to the answers that are provided. If a solution is correct, write "correct" on the line that follows. If a solution is incorrect, correct it. Hint: Six solutions are incorrect.

1. $x^2 + 5x - 8 = 0$ $x = -5 \pm \dfrac{\sqrt{57}}{2}$ _____

2. $x^2 + 5x - 4 = 0$ $x = \dfrac{-5 \pm \sqrt{41}}{2}$ _____

3. $x^2 + 2x + 8 = 0$ $x = -1 \pm \sqrt{7}$ _____

4. $x^2 + 2x - 2 = 0$ $x = 1 \pm \sqrt{3}$ _____

5. $2x^2 - 3x - 5 = 0$ $x = \dfrac{-5}{2}, x = 1$ _____

6. $4x^2 - 12x + 9 = 0$ $x = \dfrac{3}{2}$ _____

7. $2x^2 + 12x + 5 = 0$ $x = \dfrac{-6 \pm \sqrt{26}}{2}$ _____

8. $x^2 + 12x - 27 = 0$ $x = -6 \pm 3\sqrt{7}$ _____

9. $3x^2 + 6x - 5 = 0$ $x = -1 \pm 2\sqrt{6}$ _____

10. $x^2 - 8x + 13 = 0$ $x = \dfrac{8 \pm 3\sqrt{2}}{2}$ _____

Using Equations to Describe Parabolas

A *parabola* is a U-shaped curve. The graph of the equation $y = ax^2 + bx + c$ is a parabola. It has a line of symmetry called the axis of symmetry. The equation of the axis of symmetry is $x = \frac{-b}{2a}$.

The vertex, which is the highest or lowest point, is:

$$\left(\frac{-b}{2a}, f\left(\frac{-b}{2a}\right)\right)$$

The y-intercept, the point where the line crosses the y-axis, is $(0, f(0))$.

A parabola may have two x-intercepts, one x-intercept, or no x-intercept, depending on the specific function. The x-intercept, or intercepts, can be found by using the quadratic formula. (They can also sometimes be found by factoring.)

For example:

$y = x^2 + 3x + 2$	$a = 1, b = 3, c = 2$
axis of symmetry	$x = \frac{-b}{2a}$ or $x = \frac{-3}{2}$
vertex	$\left(\frac{-b}{2a}, f\left(\frac{-b}{2a}\right)\right)$ or $\left(\frac{-3}{2}, \frac{-1}{4}\right)$
y-intercept	$(0, f(0))$ or $(0, 2)$
x-intercepts	$(-2, 0)\ (-1, 0)$

Here is the graph for the above equation:

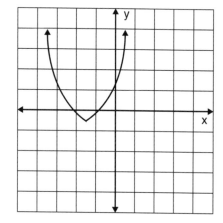

Now go to the next page.

Using Equations to Describe Parabolas

Directions: Consider each quadratic equation. One of the four important features of each graph is listed in the Answer Bank. Match each equation with the correct feature. Write the feature on the line after the equation, then write whether the feature is the axis of symmetry, vertex, y-intercept, or no x-intercept(s).

1. $y = x^2 - 3x - 4$ _____   _____

2. $y = x^2 - 5x + 4$ _____   _____

3. $y = x^2 + x - 6$ _____   _____

4. $y = x^2 - 4x + 5$ _____   _____

5. $y = x^2 - 49$ _____   _____

6. $y = x^2 - 2x - 15$ _____   _____

7. $y = 2x^2 - 5x - 3$ _____   _____

8. $y = 2x^2 - 2x - 1$ _____   _____

9. $y = 3x^2 - 4x + 1$ _____   _____

10. $y = 4x^2 - 11x + 6$ _____   _____

Answer Bank				
$(0,-3)$	$(0,-6)$	$x = 0$	$(0,-15)$	$x = \frac{3}{2}$
$\left(\frac{5}{2}, -\frac{9}{4}\right)$	$\left(\frac{1}{2}, -\frac{3}{2}\right)$	$x = \frac{2}{3}$	$\varnothing$	$(0,6)$

Classifying Polynomial Functions

A *polynomial function* is a function of the form:

$$f(x) = a_n x^n + a_{n-1} x^{n-1} + \ldots + a_1 x + a_0 \qquad a_n \neq 0$$

n is a nonnegative integer and $a_n, a_{n-1} \ldots a_0$ are real numbers.
Polynomial functions can be classified as a constant function of degree zero, a linear function of degree one, a quadratic function of degree two, and a cubic function of degree three. Some examples include:

- $f(x) = 3$, degree zero, constant function
- $f(x) = x^2 + 3x - x^2 + 4 = 3x + 4$, degree one, linear function
- $f(x) = x^2 + 4x - 3x = x^2 + x$, degree two, quadratic function
- $f(x) = 4x^3 - 3x + 7x^3 - 4x^2 + 8 = 11x^3 - 4x^2 - 3x + 8$, degree three, cubic function

Directions: Simplify, if possible, then classify each function as constant, linear, quadratic, or cubic. Hint: Two functions are constant, three are linear, six are quadratic, and four are cubic.

1. $f(x) = 3x^2 + 2x$ _____

2. $f(x) = 7$ _____

3. $f(x) = 3x^2 + 7x + 2 - 3x$ _____

4. $f(x) = 3x^2 + 7x + 4 - 3x^2$ _____

5. $f(x) = (x + 2)(x - 1)$ _____

6. $f(x) = x(x + 1)(x - 1)$ _____

7. $f(x) = 3x(x + 1)(x + 4)$ _____

8. $f(x) = x(x + 2) - x$ _____

9. $f(x) = 8x^3 + 4x - 4x + 7$ _____

10. $f(x) = (x + 2)^2$ _____

11. $f(x) = (x + 2)^2 - (x + 2)$ _____

12. $f(x) = (x + 2)^2 - (x - 2)^2$ _____

13. $f(x) = (x + 2)^3$ _____

14. $f(x) = 8 - 3$ _____

15. $f(x) = 2x(4 + 1)$ _____

Algebra Teacher's Activities Kit

Using Synthetic Division

Synthetic division is a type of mathematical shorthand for dividing polynomials. It is useful for factoring polynomials and can be used to find the roots of functions. Synthetic division can only be used if the divisor is a binomial in the form of $x - c$.

The procedure is simple:

1. Write the polynomial in descending order.
2. Write the coefficients.
3. Place "c" in the divisor.
4. Multiply.
5. Add.
6. Continue to multiply and add.
7. Write the coefficient. (Each coefficient in the quotient is one degree less than the degree of the original polynomial.)
8. Write the last number (if it is $\neq 0$) over the original divisor.

Here is an example: $\dfrac{x^3 + x^2 - 5x - 2}{x - 2}$

$$
\begin{array}{r|rrrr}
2 & 1 & 1 & -5 & -2 \\
  &   & 2 & 6 & 2 \\
\hline
  & 1 & 3 & 1 & 0
\end{array}
$$

The quotient is $x^2 + 3x + 1$.

Directions: Use synthetic division to divide each polynomial on the next page. Match each quotient with the answers in the Answer Bank, then write the letter of each answer in the blank above its problem number to complete the statement at the end of the activity. Finally, explain how the statement relates to synthetic division.

Using Synthetic Division

1. $\dfrac{x^3 - 3x^2 + 4x - 2}{x - 1} =$

2. $\dfrac{x^3 - 3x^2 - x + 18}{x + 2} =$

3. $\dfrac{2x^3 + 3x^2 + 4x + 12}{x + 2} =$

4. $\dfrac{-5x^3 + 9x^2 + 15x - 4}{x - 2} =$

5. $\dfrac{2x^3 + x^2 + 3x + 5}{x + 1} =$

6. $\dfrac{4x^3 - 10x^2 - 12}{x - 3} =$

7. $\dfrac{4x^4 + x^3 + x^2 - 4}{x + 1} =$

8. $\dfrac{x^3 - 10}{x - 2} =$

9. $\dfrac{3x^3 + 12x^2 + x + 4}{x + 4} =$

10. $\dfrac{x^2 + 3x + 2x^3 + 10}{x + 2} =$

11. $\dfrac{x^4 + x^3 + 2x^2 + 3x + 5}{x + 1} =$

12. $\dfrac{3 + x^4 + 2x^3}{x + 3} =$

Answer Bank

G. $3x^2 + 1$

A. $-5x^2 - x + 13 + \dfrac{22}{x - 2}$

F. $4x^2 + 2x + 6 + \dfrac{6}{x - 3}$

U. $2x^2 - 3x + 9 - \dfrac{8}{x - 2}$

C. $2x^2 - x + 4 + \dfrac{1}{x + 1}$

N. $4x^3 - 3x^2 + 4x - 4$

L. $x^2 + 2x + 4 - \dfrac{2}{x - 2}$

E. $x^3 - x^2 + 3x - 9 + \dfrac{30}{x + 3}$

T. $2x^2 - x + 6$

R. $x^3 + 2x + 1 + \dfrac{4}{x + 1}$

I. $x^2 - 5x + 9$

O. $x^2 - 2x + 2$

Synthetic means $\overline{}\ \overline{}\ \overline{}\quad \overline{}\ \overline{}\ \overline{}\ \overline{}\ \overline{}\ \overline{}\ \overline{}$;

                   7   1   3   9   12   7   10   2   7   12

$\overline{}\ \overline{}\ \overline{}\ \overline{}\ \overline{}\ \overline{}\ \overline{}\ \overline{}\ \overline{}\ \overline{}$.

4   11   3   2   6   2   5   2   4   8

Explanation: _____

_____

_____

_____

Using Synthetic Division to Factor Polynomials

Synthetic division can be used to factor polynomials, especially if there is no familiar pattern. By considering the factors and using trial and error, a factor of the polynomial may be found. The resulting polynomial may be factored easily, or it may not be factored at all.

If you use "c" as the divisor and there is no remainder, then x – c is a factor. If you divide by –c and there is no remainder, then x + c is a factor.

For an example, factor $x^3 - 6x + 9$. The factors of 9 are $1 \times 9, -1 \times -9, 3 \times 3$, and -3×-3. Use trial and error. Check to see if x – 3 is a factor by dividing by 3.

$$
\begin{array}{r|rrr}
3 & 1 & 0 & -6 & 9 \\
  &   & 3 & 9 & 9 \\
\hline
  & 1 & 3 & 3 & 18
\end{array}
\quad x^2 + 3x + 3 + \frac{18}{x-3}
$$

x – 3 is not a factor because there is a remainder.

Use trial and error to check if x + 3 is a factor. Divide by –3.

$$
\begin{array}{r|rrr}
-3 & 1 & 0 & -6 & 9 \\
   &   & -3 & 9 & -9 \\
\hline
   & 1 & -3 & 3 & 0
\end{array}
\quad x^2 - 3x + 3
$$

$$x^3 - 6x + 9 = (x + 3)(x^2 - 3x + 3)$$

Directions: Use synthetic division to factor the polynomials. All factors are included in the Answer Bank. Some will be used more than once.

1. $x^3 + 6x^2 - x - 30 =$ _____

2. $x^3 - 5x^2 + 2x + 8 =$ _____

3. $x^3 - 7x - 6 =$ _____

4. $x^3 - x^2 - x + 1 =$ _____

5. $x^4 + x^3 - 11x^2 - 9x + 18 =$ _____

6. $x^3 - 10x^2 + 29x - 20 =$ _____

7. $x^4 - 2x^3 - 4x^2 + 2x + 3 =$ _____

8. $x^3 - 14x - 8 =$ _____

Answer Bank
$(x - 2)$
$(x^2 + 4x + 2)$
$(x - 4)$
$(x + 3)$
$(x + 2)$
$(x + 5)$
$(x + 1)$
$(x - 3)$
$(x - 1)$
$(x - 5)$

Finding the Zeroes of Polynomial Functions

The *zeroes of a polynomial function* are the values of x for which $f(x) = 0$. To find the zeroes of a polynomial function, write the corresponding polynomial equation and solve for x. The number of zeroes is the same as the degree of the polynomial function. Use the following guidelines to help you solve polynomial equations.

1. Factor the GMF if possible. Then consider the remaining polynomial.

2. If the polynomial has two terms, check whether or not the polynomial is the difference of squares, difference of cubes, or the sum of cubes; then use the appropriate formula.

   $a^2 - b^2 = (a - b)(a + b)$

   $a^3 - b^3 = (a - b)(a^2 + ab + b^2)$

   $a^3 + b^3 = (a + b)(a^2 - ab + b^2)$

3. If the remaining polynomial has three terms, check whether or not the polynomial is a quadratic. If it is, try to factor, complete the square, or use the quadratic formula:

   $$x = \frac{-b \pm \sqrt{b^2 - 4ac}}{2a}$$

4. If the remaining polynomial has three or more terms, try to use synthetic division.

5. If the remaining polynomial has four terms, try to factor by grouping.

Note: After factoring, set each factor equal to zero and solve for x.

Directions: Find the zeroes of each polynomial function.

1. $f(x) = x^2 - 9$ _____

2. $f(x) = x^2 - 4x - 5$ _____

3. $f(x) = x^3 - 9x^2 + 18x$ _____

4. $f(x) = x^3 + 4x^2 + x - 6$ _____

5. $f(x) = x^2 - 10x + 6$ _____

6. $f(x) = x^4 - 16$ _____

7. $f(x) = x^3 - 4x$ _____

8. $f(x) = 4x^2 - 20x + 25$ _____

9. $f(x) = x^2 - 5x + 1$ _____

10. $f(x) = 4x^3 + 12x^2 - 5x - 15$ _____

NAME   DATE   SECTION

Solving Exponential Equations

An *exponential function* is an equation in which a variable is an exponent. An exponential function with base a is denoted by $f(x) = a^x$ where $a > 0$, $a \neq 1$, and x is a real number.

To solve the exponential equations in this activity, both sides of the equation must be expressed as a power of the same base. To write both sides as a power of the same base, use the laws of exponents shown below:

$$(a^x)^y = a^{xy} \qquad a^x \cdot a^y = a^{x+y} \qquad \frac{a^x}{a^y} = a^{x-y} \qquad (ab)^x = a^x b^x \qquad \left(\frac{a}{b}\right)^x = \frac{a^x}{b^x}$$

$$a^{-x} = \frac{1}{a^x} \qquad \frac{1}{a^{-x}} = a^x \qquad b^x = b^y \rightarrow x = y \qquad a^x = b^x \rightarrow a = b \qquad a^0 = 1$$

To solve $9^{x+1} = \sqrt{27}$ use the laws of exponents to write each expression as a power of 3.

$$\left(3^2\right)^{x+1} = \left(3^3\right)^{\frac{1}{2}}$$
$$3^{2x+2} = 3^{\frac{3}{2}}$$

Then solve for x. $x = -\dfrac{1}{4}$

Directions: Solve each exponential equation. If you solve each correctly, you will notice a pattern to your answers. Explain this pattern at the end of the activity.

1. $7^{6x} = 7^{2x-20}$ _____

2. $8^{2x} = 16^{x-2}$ _____

3. $36^x = 6^{x-3}$ _____

4. $16^3 = 64^{5x+12}$ _____

5. $4^{x+1} = 8^{2x+3}$ _____

6. $12^{2x+1} = \sqrt[4]{12}$ _____

7. $16^{6x} = 4^{3x+1}$ _____

8. $2^{3x-1} = \left(\dfrac{1}{8}\right)^x$ _____

9. $49^x = 7^{\frac{1}{2}}$ _____

10. $3^x = \sqrt[3]{3}$ _____

11. $49^x = \left(\sqrt{7}\right)^5$ _____

12. $3^4 = 27^{x-1}$ _____

13. $3^{x-1} = 27$ _____

14. $6^{3x-8} = 216^2$ _____

15. $2^{x-1} = 32$ _____

Describe the pattern indicated by the answers. _____

_____

Solving Equations Involving Logarithms

The inverse of the exponential function $f(x) = b^x$ is called the *logarithmic function*: $y = \log_b x$ if and only if $x = b^y$ for all positive real numbers x and b, b ≠ 0.

It is easy to convert from exponential to logarithmic form by using the definition. For example:

$$8^2 = 64 \text{ can be written as } \log_8 64 = 2.$$
$$\sqrt{25} = 5 \text{ can be written as } \log_{25} 5 = \frac{1}{2}.$$

It is also easy to convert from logarithmic form to exponential form.

$$\log_2 8 = 3 \text{ can be written as } 2^3 = 8.$$
$$\log_{10} 100 = 2 \text{ can be written as } 10^2 = 100.$$

To solve equations involving logarithms, convert the expression to exponential form and solve for x. For example:

$$\log_2 16 = x \qquad \log_3 x = 2$$
$$2^x = 16 \qquad 3^2 = x$$
$$x = 4 \qquad x = 9$$

Directions: Solve each logarithmic equation. Match each answer with the answers in the Answer Bank, then write the corresponding letters in the spaces before the problems. Write the letters in order, starting with the first problem, to complete the statement at the end of the activity. One answer is used twice.

1. _____ $\log_8 x = 2$

2. _____ $\log_{16} x = \frac{1}{2}$

3. _____ $\log_4 x = -\frac{3}{2}$

4. _____ $\log_3 x = 2$

5. _____ $\log_x 27 = \frac{3}{2}$

6. _____ $\log_x 5 = -\frac{1}{2}$

7. _____ $\log_3 x = -5$

8. _____ $\log_{12} 144 = x$

9. _____ $\log_{\frac{1}{9}} x = -\frac{1}{2}$

10. _____ $\log_5 x = 3$

Answer Bank

N. 9   P. $\frac{1}{243}$ O. 4   H. $\frac{1}{8}$ R. 125

A. $\frac{1}{25}$ I. 2   J. 64 E. 3

The term "logarithm" was first used by ___ ___ ___ ___ ___ ___ ___ ___ ___ ___ in 1616.

Borrowing and Repaying Money (with Interest)

When you make an expensive purchase—for example, a home entertainment center, a car, or a house—you may need to borrow money from a bank. In order to use the bank's money, you must agree to pay a fee, called interest, which is usually calculated in with the repayment of the loan. Following is a formula you can use to calculate monthly payments necessary to repay borrowed money.

$$M = \frac{A\left(\frac{r}{12}\right)\left(1 + \frac{r}{12}\right)^n}{\left(1 + \frac{r}{12}\right)^n - 1}$$

M = monthly payment, A = amount borrowed, r = annual rate of interest, n = the number of months of the loan.

Directions: Using the formula, calculate the monthly payment for the following purchases. Round all answers to the nearest cent.

1. **An entertainment center.** The amount borrowed is $3,000 at an annual rate of interest of 9% for three years (or 36 months).

2. **Furniture.** The amount borrowed is $4,500 at an annual rate of interest of 12% for 5 years.

3. **A motorcycle.** The amount borrowed is $3,500 at an annual rate of interest of 8% for 5 years.

4. **A used car.** The amount borrowed is $7,500 at an annual rate of interest of 6% for 4 years.

Calculating Compound Interest

Money deposited in an interest-bearing account such as a savings account, money market fund, or certificate of deposit not only pays interest on the amount of money invested, but also on the interest earned. The amount of money in the account (assuming there have been no additional deposits or any withdrawals) depends on the following:

- The principal, which is the original amount of money invested.
- The rate of interest.
- The number of times the interest is compounded per year.
- The number of years.

The formula below is used to calculate the amount of money in an account that bears compound interest.

$$A = P\left(1 + \frac{r}{n}\right)^{nt}$$

A = amount of money in account, P = the original investment, r = rate of interest, n = the number of times the interest is compounded per year, and t = the number of years.

Directions: Solve each problem. Assume there are no additional deposits or withdrawals. Round your answers to the nearest cent.

1. Terrel received $500 for his sixteenth birthday. He deposited this money into an account that pays 4% interest compounded quarterly. How much money will he have on his eighteenth birthday?

Algebra Teacher's Activities Kit

Calculating Compound Interest

2. After working all summer, Margaret placed $1,200 in a savings account. She left the money in the account for one year at a rate of 3% interest, compounded semiannually. After the one year is up, will she have enough money to buy a car for $1,500?

3. How much more interest is earned after three years if $10,000 is deposited in an account that offers an interest rate of 8% compounded monthly than an account that bears 8% compounded annually?

4. The Santos deposited $10,000 in a savings account at an interest rate of 6%, compounded semiannually. They then opened another account with a deposit of $1,000 at an interest rate of 3%, compounded monthly. Find the total amount of money that would be in the two accounts after five years.

Potpourri

The twenty activities of this section use algebraic skills and thinking in one way or another, but they do not fit neatly into any of the previous sections. They are somewhat freewheeling and fun, and you might find it most appropriate to use them as extra credit or simply make them available as challenges to your students.

Teaching Suggestions for the Activities

10-1 Know the Rules

The procedures and operations of algebra, like many other branches of mathematics, are founded on properties, which serve as rules when solving problems. For this activity your students must match various properties with their examples.

Go over the instructions on the worksheet with your students, noting that not all properties will be used. Also caution them that some of the presumed properties listed are not real properties. Remind them that matching the properties and examples correctly will enable them to complete the message at the end of the activity.

10-2 Cracking a Code

This activity provides your students practice with simplifying expressions. Review the instructions on the worksheet with them and emphasize that correct answers will match a letter of the alphabet. This will enable them to figure out the coded message. Note that they will need to break the letters of the message into words.

10-3 Simplifying Expressions

This activity provides your students with practice in simplifying a variety of expressions. Go over the instructions with your students and note that answers will match a phrase that is associated with a number. Point out the first problem as an example. Remind your students that not all phrases will be used.

10-4 Following Instructions

This activity requires your students to use clues to identify words related to algebra. Go over the instructions on the worksheet with your students, noting that they are to follow the directions and select specific letters. The letters will enable them to complete a statement. Remind your students that they must break the letters of the statement into words.

10-5 Following Algebraic Directions

For this activity your students are required to follow specific directions and solve equations. If they complete the activity correctly, they will identify a special number.

Review the instructions on the worksheet with your students and go over the first problem together. Caution them to follow the directions precisely and be careful to avoid careless mistakes. A mistake in one problem will lead to mistakes in the problems that follow.

10-6 Scrambled Algebra

This activity contains twenty "scrambled" words related to algebra. Your students are to unscramble the words. As an extension, you may have them write other scrambled algebra words, which they may ask their friends to unscramble.

10-7 Getting from A to B

This activity requires your students to identify the mathematical steps needed to complete equations. Since they are required to use the Order of Operations, the activity serves well as a review. Go over the instructions on the worksheet. If necessary, discuss the first problem, which is done as an example.

10-8 Building an Algebra Vocabulary Chain

For this activity you may prefer to have your students work in pairs. Go over the instructions on the worksheet and review the four words that serve as examples of the beginning of an algebra word chain. Encourage your students to create chains of as many words as they can.

10-9 Finding Equal Values

For this activity your students are required to match equivalent expressions. Review the instructions on the worksheet, noting that different expressions represent the same number. Emphasize to your students that they must pay close attention to find those that are equivalent. Remind them that correct answers will enable them to complete the statement at the end of the activity.

10-10 Finding Algebra Words

This activity is a word search that contains words related to algebra. Explain to your students that the puzzle contains sixteen words, which may be written horizontally, vertically, forward, and backward. After finding the words in the puzzle, they are to write the words on the lines that follow.

10-11 The Words of Algebra

For this activity you may prefer to have your students work in pairs. Using the letters contained in the statement at the top of the worksheet, students are to list as many words related to algebra as they can. Not permitting them to refer to their texts or math reference sources will make the activity more challenging.

10-12 Creating Equations with Variables

This activity requires your students to write equations, using given variables. Review the instructions on the worksheet and discuss the first problem as an example. Caution your students to pay close attention to the Order of Operations as they complete the worksheet.

10-13 Is It True or False?

This activity requires your students to determine whether statements related to algebra are true or false. Correct answers will reveal a word that indicates they have completed the worksheet correctly. Review the instructions with your students, emphasizing that they are to write the letters of the true statements in order from last to first in the blanks at the end of the worksheet.

10-14 Algebra and Interesting Facts

In this activity your students are given sentences in which a fact is missing. They are then presented with two possible answers, each of which is related to an algebra statement. The correct statement identifies the correct fact to complete the sentence. Go over the instructions with your students, noting that the first problem is completed for them as an example.

10-15 Who Used It First?

Most students take the symbols we use in math for granted. They do not realize that someone developed each one. This activity requires your students to research several mathematicians to find the symbol(s) or notation(s) they originated in the form we use today. This activity serves well as an extra-credit assignment.

10-16 Algebra Stumpers

This activity serves well as a review. Your students are to create five problems or questions, which you may refer to as "stumpers," on a topic in algebra. You provide the topic, which may be review material or material your students are currently studying. After students have created their stumpers, they are to share them with friends and try to solve each other's stumpers. Encourage your students to create material in the form of equations, word problems, or problems that require multiple steps to solve. Go over the instructions and remind your students that they must provide an answer key on the back of their sheets.

10-17 Famous Mathematicians and Algebra

For this activity your students are to research mathematicians and match them with their contributions to the study and advancement of algebra. Review the instructions on the worksheet and suggest that they use a variety of sources, including math texts, math reference books, encyclopedias, and sources on the Internet.

For an extension, you might have your students select a mathematician, conduct additional research, and present their findings in an oral or written report.

10-18 Who Wrote It?

This activity encourages students to research individuals who have contributed to the advancement of algebra. Your students are to match each mathematician with his or her work. Explain that many of the titles are presented in their native language with the translation included.

Review the instructions on the worksheet with your students. Suggest that they consult various sources, including math texts and references, encyclopedias, and sources on the Internet to find the information they need.

For an extension, you may wish to encourage your students to select a mathematician and conduct more research about his or her life.

10-19 An Algebra Research Paper

This activity serves well as a formal part of your program or as an extra-credit assignment. Your students are to select a mathematician who has made an impact on algebra and write a report. You may find it beneficial to work with your students' English teachers, who may offer guidance in the research and development of material. While a list of possible mathematicians is provided on the worksheet, you may add more, based on your program and the abilities of your students. Remind your students to include the highlights of the career of the individual they research.

10-20 An Algebra Essay

For a culminating activity for the year, you may wish to have your students write a short essay that focuses on their opinions and impressions of algebra. Encourage them to consider the importance of algebra and how algebra relates to everyday life. Also encourage them to use solid writing and good grammar.

Answer Key for Section 10

10-1. 1. Y 2. O 3. U 4. A 5. R 6. E 7. R 8. I 9. G 10. H 11. T
<u>You are right.</u>

10-2. 1. Y, 25 2. O, 15 3. U, 21 4. D, 4 5. E, 5 6. C, 3 7. I, 9 8. P, 16
9. H, 8 10. E, 5 11. R, 18 12. E, 5 13. D, 4 14. T, 20 15. H, 8
16. E, 5 17. C, 3 18. O, 15 19. D, 4 20. E, 5 <u>You deciphered the code.</u>

10-3. 2. 4 quarters in a dollar 3. 365.25 days in a year 4. 13 items in a
baker's dozen 5. 12 inches in a foot 6. 5,280 feet in a mile 7. 1,000
millimeters in a meter 8. 64 small squares on a checkerboard 9. 9
planets in the solar system 10. 24 hours in a day 11. 16 ounces in a
pound 12. 60 seconds in a minute

10-4. 1. exponent 2. operations 3. matrices 4. simplify 5. coordinate
6. solution 7. inverse 8. linear 9. formula 10. whole 11. positive
12. graph 13. absolute value 14. origin 15. set 16. binomial
17. radical sign <u>Express yourself with algebra!</u>

10-5. 2. 2.4, 4.6 3. 24.4, 4.6 4. 16, 20.6 5. 8, 12.6 6. 3, 4.2 7. 6, 4.2
8. 0.36, 4.2 9. 4.8, 9 10. 1.4, 9 11. 0.3, 9 12. 25, 34 13. 34, 34
14. 18, 16 15. 15, 1 <u>Special Number = 1</u> Explanations may vary. A
possible answer is that 1 is a special number because a number multiplied or divided by 1 remains the same.

10-6. 1. factor 2. positive 3. graph 4. quadrant 5. monomial 6. radical
7. variable 8. reciprocal 9. absolute value 10. expression 11. slope
12. coordinate 13. proportion 14. square root 15. negative
16. polynomial 17. origin 18. function 19. exponent 20. integer

10-7. Answers may vary. Possible answers include the following. 2. 4, 3
3. 1, 4 4. 3, 5, 2 5. –2, 5 6. 3, 3, 1 7. $\frac{1}{2}$, 2, –3 8. 7, 5, –1 9. 5, 5,
10, 3 10. 2, 3, 1 11. $10 \times 10 + 3 = 103$ 12. $(82 - 2) \div 10 - 2 = 6$

10-8. Accept reasonable vocabulary chains.

10-9. 1. E, $a + (b + c)$ 2. Q, $\frac{80}{2}$ 3. U, 3^1 4. I, –1 5. V, 1 6. A, 27 7. L, $ba - c$
8. E, $3 \times 3 \times 2$ 9. N, $12 - 3a$ 10. T, $ac + bc$ 11. E, 5^2 12. X, 0 13. P, 4^2
14. R, 3×3 15. E, $\frac{1}{2} \times n$ 16. S, $60 + 4$ 17. S, 7,300 18. I, 3×11
19. O, $\frac{1}{2}a$ 20. N, 4 21. S, 12.5×10 <u>Equivalent expressions</u> may have
different names.

10-10.

10-11. Accept reasonable lists of algebra words.

10-12. Answers may vary; possible answers include the following.   2. $ab + c = -2$ 3. $bc \div a + d = -5$ 4. $-c(-a + b) = -20$ 5. $abc = -24$ 6. $-abc - d = 23$ 7. $-(b + c) + d = -6$ 8. $bc - d = 11$ 9. $bc - a + d = 15$ 10. $c(b + d) = 16$ 11. $-ac + d = 9$ 12. $-bc + a = -14$ 13. $ab(c + d) = -30$ 14. $ca^{b} = -32$ 15. $b + c + d = 8$

10-13. The following statements are true: O, V, A, R, B   <u>Bravo!</u>

10-14. 2. beetles   3. 2.5   4. 100   5. 4,168   6. 3,579,000   7. $-129°$ F   8. 113,200   9. 1.4   10. 370

10-15. 1. brackets [ ]   2. raised numerals for powers   3. i and e 4. < and >   5. factorial symbol !   6. ratio symbol :   7. $\pm$ 8. $\div$ 9. =   10. letters for unknown quantities   11. absolute value | | 12. + and $-$ signs

10-16. Accept reasonable problems.

10-17. 1. Indeterminate Equations   2. "New" Concept of Zero   3. Logarithms   4. Cartesian Coordinate System   5. Famous Triangle   6. i 7. Family of Curves   8. Differential Equations   9. Quaternion Algebra   10. Logic   11. Algebra and Topology   12. Infinite Series

10-18. 1. René Descartes   2. Maria Agnesi   3. George Boole   4. Rozsa Péter   5. Thomas Harriot   6. Robert Recorde   7. Johann Rahn   8. Raphael Bombelli   9. William Oughtred   10. ibn yanya al-Samaw'al   11. Leonhard Euler   12. Muhammad ibn Musa al-Khwarizmi   13. Qin Jiushao   14. Michael Stifel   15. Francois Viète   16. John Napier

10-19. Accept reasonable reports.

10-20. Accept reasonable essays.

Know the Rules

Directions: Match the example of the mathematical property with its name. Write the letter of the property on the blank before the example. Then write the letters in order, starting with the first one, to complete the message below. Be careful: Not all the properties provided will be used and some are not properties at all.

1. _____ $a \times b = b \times a$
2. _____ If $a = b$ and $c = d$, then $a + c = b + d$
3. _____ If $a = b$ and $b = c$, then $a = c$
4. _____ $(a + b) + c = a + (b + c)$
5. _____ If $a > b$ and $b > c$, then $a > c$
6. _____ If $a = b$ and $c = d$, then $ac = bd$
7. _____ If $a < b$ and $b < c$, then $a < c$
8. _____ $a + b = b + a$
9. _____ If $ab = 0$, then $a = 0$ or $b = 0$
10. _____ If $a = b$ and $c = d$, then $a - c = b - d$
11. _____ $(a \times b) \times c = a \times (b \times c)$

Properties

I. The Commutative Property of Addition
A. The Associative Property of Addition
Y. The Commutative Property of Multiplication
T. The Associative Property of Multiplication
O. The Addition Property of Equality
P. The Property of Integers
H. The Subtraction Property of Equality
E. The Multiplication Property of Equality
S. The Whole Number Property
G. The Zero Product Property
U. The Transitive Property of Equality
R. The Transitive Property of Inequality

— — — —   — — —   — — — — —.

Cracking a Code

Directions: Perform the indicated operations. Correct answers will match the letters of the alphabet; for example, 1 = A, 2 = B, 3 = C, and so on. Write the letter that corresponds to the answer of each problem on the blank before each problem. Finally, write the letters in order, starting with the first one, to reveal the message below. You will need to break the letters into words.

1. _____ $-100 \div -4 =$ _____

2. _____ $78 - 7(5 + 4) =$ _____

3. _____ $18 + 13 - (5 \times 2) =$ _____

4. _____ $2^3 - 2^2 =$ _____

5. _____ $\frac{1}{2} \times (2 \times 5) =$ _____

6. _____ $-3(-2 + 1) =$ _____

7. _____ $3^2 =$ _____

8. _____ $-8 - (-8) + 16 =$ _____

9. _____ $\frac{32}{2^2} =$ _____

10. _____ $7 + 55 \div 11 - (3 + 4) =$ _____

11. _____ $5^2 - (2 + 5) =$ _____

12. _____ $7(6 + 3) \times (4 + 8) \times 0 + 5 =$ _____

13. _____ $-28 \cdot 0.5 + (9 \cdot 2) =$ _____

14. _____ $45 \times 2 \div 5 + 2 =$ _____

15. _____ $2^3 =$ _____

16. _____ $5 \times 1 + 7 - (-3) - 10 =$ _____

17. _____ $3^3 \div 9 =$ _____

18. _____ $90 \div (2 \times 3) =$ _____

19. _____ $\frac{10^2}{400} \times 16 =$ _____

20. _____ $\frac{1}{5}(25) =$ _____

___ ___ ___ ___ ___ ___ ___ ___ ___ ___ ___ ___ ___ ___ ___ ___ ___ ___ ___ ___.

Simplifying Expressions

Directions: Simplify each expression. Match your answers to the phrases to which they correspond at the bottom of the page. Not all phrases will be used; however, each phrase that is used will be used only once. The first one has been completed for you.

1. $45 \div (5 \times 3) =$ ___**3**___   _numbers in an area_

2. If a = 25 and b = 10,

   $\dfrac{b^2}{a} =$ _____   _____

3. $-451.75 + 817 =$ _____   _____

4. $13^1 =$ _____   _____

5. If a = 3, b = −4, and c = −1,
   $(a \times b) \div c =$ _____   _____

6. $10{,}560 \times \dfrac{1}{2} =$ _____   _____

7. $10^3 =$ _____   _____

8. $2^5 \times (10 \div 5) =$ _____   _____

9. If a = 3 and b = 9, $b^2 \div a^2 =$ _____   _____

10. $-(3 \times 8) \times (4 + -5) =$ _____   _____

11. If a = −6, b = 4, and c = 10,
    $(a + c) \times b =$ _____   _____

12. If a = 3, b = 4, and c = 5,
    abc = _____   _____

Answer Phrases

seconds in a minute	digits in a ZIP Code
inches in a foot	numbers in an area code
pounds in a ton	small squares on a checkerboard
hours in a day	planets in the solar system
feet in a mile	arms on an octopus
ounces in a pound	millimeters in a meter
days in a year	items in a baker's dozen
cards in a deck	quarters in a dollar

Following Instructions

Directions: Follow the clues and write the word they describe in the blanks that follow. Then write the letters that the clue calls for in the blanks at the bottom of the page to complete the message. Be sure to break the letters into words.

1. Take the first three letters of a word describing a power.

   — — — — — — — —

2. Take the fourth letter of a word that describes addition, subtraction, multiplication, and division.

   — — — — — — — — — —

3. Take the seventh and eighth letters of the plural form of "matrix."

   — — — — — — — —

4. Take the first and last letter of the word that reduces expressions.

   — — — — — — — —

5. Take the second letter of the word that describes the position of a point on a graph.

   — — — — — — — — — —

6. Take the fourth letter of a word that means the same as the answer to a problem.

   — — — — — — — —

7. Take the last three letters of a word meaning the reciprocal of a quantity.

   — — — — — — —

8. Take the first letter of a word meaning straight.

   — — — — — —

9. Take the first letter of a word that describes A = L × W.

   — — — — — —

Algebra Teacher's Activities Kit

Copyright © 2003 John Wiley & Sons, Inc.

Following Instructions

10. Take the first letter of the set of the counting numbers and 0.

    __ __ __ __ __

11. Take the fourth and fifth letters of the word opposite in meaning to negative.

    __ __ __ __ __ __ __ __

12. Take the last letter of a word that "shows" a relationship between sets of numbers.

    __ __ __ __ __

13. Take the first and fifth letters of a term that describes the distance of a point from 0 on the number line.

    __ __ __ __ __ __ __   __ __ __ __ __

14. Take the fourth letter of the word that names the starting point of a graph.

    __ __ __ __ __ __

15. Take the second letter of the word describing a group of objects.

    __ __ __

16. Take the first letter of the word that describes an expression consisting of two terms connected by a plus or minus sign.

    __ __ __ __ __ __ __ __

17. Take the first two letters of the term describing this symbol: $\sqrt{\ }$

    __ __ __ __ __ __   __ __ __ __

    __ __ __ __ __ __ __ __ __ __ __ __ __ __ __ __ __ __

    __ __ __ __ __ __!

Following Algebraic Directions

Directions: Solve each problem in order and follow the directions to find a special number. Keep a tally of your answers along the right. The first problem has been completed for you.

                                                             Tally

1. Solve $3n = 21$. $n = $ __7__   __7__

2. Solve $n + 1.4 = 3.8$. If $n = 2.4$, subtract $n = $ _____   _____
   2.4 from your current tally. If $n \neq 2.4$ keep
   your current tally.

3. Solve $19.2 = n - 5.2$. If $n = 14.2$, add this $n = $ _____   _____
   to your current tally. If $n \neq 14.2$, keep your
   current tally.

4. Find a number, n, such that the sum of n $n = $ _____   _____
   and 27 is 43. If $n = 16$, add 16 to your current
   tally. If $n \neq 16$, keep your current tally.

5. Find a number, n, such that 12 times n $n = $ _____   _____
   is 96. If $n = 8$, subtract 8 from your current
   tally. If $n \neq 8$, keep your current tally.

6. Solve $27 \div n = 9$. If $n = 3$, divide your $n = $ _____   _____
   current tally by 3. If $n \neq 3$, keep your
   current tally.

7. Three more than a number, n, is 9. If $n = $ _____   _____
   $n = 12$, add 12 to your current tally. If
   $n \neq 12$, keep your current tally.

8. Solve $\frac{n}{0.2} = 1.8$. If $n = 0.9$, subtract 0.9 from $n = $ _____   _____
   your current tally. If $n \neq 0.9$, keep your
   current tally.

Following Algebraic Directions

		Tally

9. Solve 6n = 28.8. If n = 4.8, add 4.8 to your current tally. If n ≠ 4.8, keep your current tally.   n = _____   _____

10. Find a number, n, such that half of n is 0.7. If n = 0.35, multiply your current tally by 0.35. If n ≠ 0.35, keep your current tally.   n = _____   _____

11. Find a number, n, so that 12 times n is 3.6. If n = 3, divide your current tally by 3. If n ≠ 3, keep your current tally.   n = _____   _____

12. Find a number, n, whose quotient is 10 when divided by 2.5. If n = 25, add 25 to your current tally. If n ≠ 25, keep your current tally.   n = _____   _____

13. 15 less than a number, n, is 19. Find n. If n = 4, subtract 4 from your current tally. If n ≠ 4, keep your current tally.   n = _____   _____

14. Solve n − 8 = 10. If n = 18, subtract 18 from your current tally. If n ≠ 18, keep your current tally.   n = _____   _____

15. Solve $\frac{1}{2}$ n = 7.5. If n = 15, subtract 15 from your current tally. If n ≠ 15, keep your current tally.   n = _____   _____

Special Number = _____

Why is this a special number? (Hint: What happens when another number is multiplied or divided by this special number?)

_____

_____

_____

Scrambled Algebra

Directions: Unscramble the common algebra terms that follow.

1. orfcta   _____

2. esiivtop   _____

3. arhpg   _____

4. naqutrda   _____

5. noilmmoa   _____

6. cdarlai   _____

7. arlebvia   _____

8. repriclaoc   _____

9. loteubsa uleav   _____

10. isnepxerso   _____

11. lseop   _____

12. odrcteinoa   _____

13. roropniot   _____

14. uaersq otor   _____

15. agveitne   _____

16. nypomaliol   _____

17. irgnio   _____

18. nufcoitn   _____

19. nonpexet   _____

20. gretnie   _____

Algebra Teacher's Activities Kit

Getting from A to B

Directions: Identify the steps to proceed from the first number to the second. Fill in the blanks with the correct number to make the equation true. Use the Order of Operations. There may be more than one correct answer for each problem. The first one has been completed for you.

1. To go from $9 \rightarrow 5$ ... $9 \div$ __3__ $+$ __1__ $= 5$

2. $7 \rightarrow 31$ ... $7 \times$ _____ $+$ _____ $= 31$

3. $17 \rightarrow 4$ ... $(17 -$ _____$) \div$ _____ $= 4$

4. $7 \rightarrow 56$ ... $(7 \times$ _____$) \times ($_____ $-$ _____$) - 7 = 56$

5. $11 \rightarrow 33$ ... $11 \times ($_____ $+$ _____$) = 33$

6. $9 \rightarrow 24$ ... $9 \times$ _____ $-$ _____ $\times$ _____ $= 24$

7. $72 \rightarrow 15$ ...   _____$(72) \div$ _____ $+$ _____ $= 15$

8. $57 \rightarrow 9$ ... $(57 -$ _____$) \div$ _____ $+$ _____ $= 9$

9. $15 \rightarrow 107$ ... $[$_____$(15 +$ _____$)] + ($_____ $-$ _____$) = 107$

10. $140 \rightarrow 32$ ... $[(140 \div$ _____$) \div 2] - ($_____ $\div$ _____$) = 32$

Write procedures of your own.

11. $10 \rightarrow 103$ ...   _____

12. $82 \rightarrow 6$ ...   _____

Building an Algebra Vocabulary Chain

Directions: Work with a partner. Choose an algebraic term to start a chain of algebra vocabulary. The rules are simple: The last letter of a term must match the first letter of the next word, and the words must relate to algebra. See how many words you can generate. An example is shown.

Algebr<u>a</u>
<u>A</u>ssociative Property of Multiplicatio<u>n</u>
<u>n</u>egative number<u>s</u>
<u>s</u>olutio<u>n</u>

_____

_____

_____

_____

_____

_____

_____

_____

_____

_____

_____

_____

_____

Finding Equal Values

Directions: Write the letters of the expressions on the right in the blank before their equivalent expressions on the left. Then write the letters in order, starting with the first one, to complete the statement below.

1. _____ $(a + b) + c$

2. _____ $4(3 + 7)$

3. _____ $\frac{1}{2}(10 - 4)$

4. _____ $-(4 - 3)$

5. _____ 10^0

6. _____ 3^3

7. _____ $ab - c$

8. _____ $4(3 - 2) + (2 \times 7)$

9. _____ $3(4 - a)$

10. _____ $(a + b)c$

11. _____ $4^2 + 3^2$

12. _____ $3 \times 2 \times 0 \times 5 \times 4$

13. _____ $(2 \times 16) \div 2$

14. _____ $\sqrt{81}$

15. _____ $0.5n$

16. _____ 8 squared

17. _____ 7.3×10^3

18. _____ $\frac{1}{3}(99)$

19. _____ $\frac{a}{2}$

20. _____ the square root of 16

21. _____ 5 cubed

I. 3×11

L. $ba - c$

R. 3×3

S. $60 + 4$

U. 3^1

P. 4^2

E. $\frac{1}{2} \times n$

Q. $\frac{80}{2}$

T. $ac + bc$

I. -1

V. 1

O. $\frac{1}{2}a$

E. $3 \times 3 \times 2$

N. 4

A. 27

X. 0

S. 12.5×10

E. $a + (b + c)$

S. $7,300$

E. 5^2

N. $12 - 3a$

_____ _____ _____ _____ _____ _____ _____ _____ _____   _____ _____ _____ _____ _____ _____ _____ _____ _____ _____ _____ _____

may have different names.

10-10

Finding Algebra Words

Directions: Find sixteen words related to algebra in the word search below. Write the words on the lines that follow the puzzle.

R	X	T	W	E	Q	V	S	O	L	U	T	I	O	N	E	U	T	I	S
A	W	E	O	P	B	R	Q	X	T	Y	U	A	B	M	W	O	R	R	P
N	E	S	A	B	Q	E	U	M	P	T	R	V	B	W	E	D	G	R	O
G	A	W	Q	C	Z	N	A	J	L	E	T	R	I	N	O	M	I	A	L
E	W	I	O	B	D	I	R	E	C	M	N	E	I	P	L	K	Y	U	Y
Z	L	A	B	I	E	G	E	E	W	R	C	D	I	J	M	R	T	Y	N
D	R	G	K	N	D	G	R	Y	P	M	K	G	H	Y	R	F	D	E	O
V	E	W	D	O	R	C	O	E	F	F	I	C	I	E	N	T	V	B	M
Y	U	I	E	M	F	V	O	W	E	M	I	O	T	R	F	F	V	D	I
C	G	R	T	I	D	F	T	N	E	L	A	V	I	U	Q	E	A	T	A
N	F	R	O	A	T	B	N	F	W	S	F	U	I	G	C	D	R	S	L
Z	U	S	M	L	F	R	E	F	V	C	O	Y	J	K	G	R	I	R	B
V	N	J	T	E	L	B	K	U	H	T	E	P	O	L	S	D	A	E	Y
K	C	T	C	R	A	W	O	U	B	N	R	F	D	U	Y	B	B	W	R
V	T	H	R	T	C	P	R	O	P	O	R	T	I	O	N	D	L	U	I
C	I	V	R	I	I	E	D	V	M	I	R	T	S	I	X	F	E	G	H
P	O	R	F	T	D	U	I	R	V	B	E	N	N	T	I	E	E	Y	M
X	N	Q	Y	I	A	X	I	R	T	A	M	C	B	A	P	J	R	T	B
O	P	M	R	T	R	E	R	C	W	R	I	O	N	R	E	R	V	Y	O
V	W	Y	I	O	V	W	D	S	X	U	I	O	K	R	F	V	E	I	L

_____

_____

_____

_____

_____

_____

Algebra Teacher's Activities Kit

10-11

The Words of Algebra

Directions: Write words that relate to algebra from the letters of the statement below. An example has been completed for you.

It is quite correct that expertise in algebra was never more important than it is today.

solution _____

_____

_____

_____

_____

_____

_____

_____

_____

_____

_____

_____

_____

_____

_____

_____

Creating Equations with Variables

Directions: If a = –2, b = 3, c = 4, and d = 1, write equations using variables to equal the given answers. Remember to use the Order of Operations. You may not use any other numbers. You must use at least three of the variables in each equation. The first one is completed for you.

1. _____ bc – a _____ = 14

2. _____ = –2

3. _____ = –5

4. _____ = –20

5. _____ = –24

6. _____ = 23

7. _____ = –6

8. _____ = 11

9. _____ = 15

10. _____ = 16

11. _____ = 9

12. _____ = –14

13. _____ = –30

14. _____ = –32

15. _____ = 8

Algebra Teacher's Activities Kit

Is It True or False?

Directions: Read the statements below. Write "true" if the statement is correct and "false" if it is not. When you have finished, write the letters of the true statements in order from *last to first* in the spaces at the end of the worksheet. If you are correct, you will spell a word that indicates you are right.

S. _____ The number set {0,1,2,3,4, . . .} is called integers.

U. _____ A radical is an expression in the form of a or b.

O. _____ The number paired with a point on a number line is called a coordinate.

G. _____ A numerical coefficient refers to an invalid number.

E. _____ A variable is a number whose value is not constant.

V. _____ A trinomial is a polynomial that has three terms.

I. _____ "Exponent" is a term that means a number must be multiplied by 2, 3, 4, and so forth.

A. _____ A solution is a value of a variable that makes an open sentence true.

R. _____ The Multiplicative Property of Zero says that for all real numbers a, a × 0 = 0 and 0 × a = 0.

H. _____ A null set and an empty set are two different sets.

B. _____ A monomial is a numeral, variable, or a product of a numeral and one or more variables.

C. _____ A quadrant is a number divided by 4.

___ ___ ___ ___ ___!

Algebra and Interesting Facts

Directions: Each sentence below is missing an important fact that makes it true. Two possible answers are provided for each sentence. Each answer in turn is followed by a statement. You can identify the correct answer by determining which statement is true. Place a check beside the true algebra statement and then complete the sentence. The first one has been completed for you.

1. At its longest length in the past, the Great Wall of China stretched about ___1,500___ miles.

   $$1,150 \quad \text{\_\_\_\_} \quad x^2 \cdot y^3 \cdot x^4 = x^8 y^3$$
   $$1,500 \quad \checkmark \quad x^2 \cdot y^3 \cdot x^4 = x^6 y^3$$

2. With more than 290,000 separate species, there are more different kinds of _____ than any other creature on Earth.

   ants   ___ A horizontal line has no slope.

   beetles   ___ A horizontal line has a slope of 0.

3. Many dinosaurs were big, but based on the sizes of their brains, it is doubtful they were very smart. For example, the stegosaurus was twenty feet long, weighed several thousand pounds, but had a _____ -ounce brain.

   $$6.4 \quad \text{\_\_\_} \quad 3x - 2y = 7 \text{ is the same as } 2y = -3x - 7$$
   $$2.5 \quad \text{\_\_\_} \quad 3x - 2y = 7 \text{ is the same as } 2y = 3x - 7$$

4. The average lifespan of a box turtle is _____ years.

   $$100 \quad \text{\_\_\_} \quad (-2)^4 = 16$$
   $$57 \quad \text{\_\_\_} \quad (-2)^4 = -16$$

5. The Nile River in Egypt is the longest river in the world, measuring _____ miles.

   $$4,168 \quad \text{\_\_\_} \quad x = 8 \text{ is the equation of a vertical line.}$$
   $$3,724 \quad \text{\_\_\_} \quad x = 8 \text{ is the equation of a horizontal line.}$$

Algebra Teacher's Activities Kit

Algebra and Interesting Facts

6. With an area of about _____ square miles, the Sahara Desert is only about 40,000 square miles smaller than the entire United States.

   4,897,000   ___ If x = –4, then $3x^3 = 192$

   3,579,000   ___ If x = –4, then $3x^3 = -192$

7. The coldest temperature ever recorded on Earth was at Vostok Station in Antarctica. It was _____.

   –82° F   ___ The point (0,4) is on the x-axis.

   –129° F   ___ The point (0,4) is on the y-axis.

8. Aside from the sun, the star nearest to Earth is Proxima Centauri at 4.2 light years away. That is so far that a spaceship traveling at 25,000 miles per hour would need about _____ years to get there.

   113,200   ___ The slope of a line whose equation is 2x + y = 7 is –2.

   113.2   ___ The slope of a line whose equation is 2x + y = 7 is 2.

9. The largest diamond ever found was the Cullinan Diamond, weighing _____ pounds.

   0.8   ___ $-\sqrt{144} = 12$

   1.4   ___ $-\sqrt{144} = -12$

10. Members of a species of eucalyptus tree are among the tallest trees in the world. These trees, found in Australia, can grow to be _____ feet high.

    370   ___ $-3(x - 5) = -3x + 15$

    325   ___ $-3(x - 5) = -3x - 15$

Who Used It First?

Directions: Each mathematician below is credited with having originated a mathematical symbol or notation in the form we use in algebra today. Match each mathematician with his contribution. Write the answers in the spaces provided. You may wish to consult math reference sources.

1. Raphael Bombelli (1526–1573) _____

2. René Descartes (1596–1650) _____

3. Leonhard Euler (1707–1783) _____

4. Thomas Harriot (1560–1621) _____

5. Christian Kramp (1760–1826) _____

6. Gottfried Wilhelm Leibniz (1646–1716) _____

7. William Oughtred (1574–1660) _____

8. Johann Rahn (1622–1676) _____

9. Robert Recorde (c. 1510–1558) _____

10. Francois Viète (1540–1603) _____

11. Karl Weierstrass (1815–1897) _____

12. John Widmann (1462–1498) _____

Symbols and Notations	
absolute value | |	i and e
raised numerals for powers	=
ratio symbol :	< and >
brackets [ ]	÷
factorial symbol !	+ and −
letters for unknown quantities	±

Algebra Stumpers

Directions: Create five problems or questions on the algebra topic provided by your teacher and try to stump a friend. Write your "stumpers" on the lines provided, then share your work with a friend. Be sure to include the answers to your stumpers on the back of this sheet.

1. _____

_____

_____

2. _____

_____

_____

3. _____

_____

_____

4. _____

_____

_____

5. _____

_____

_____

Famous Mathematicians and Algebra

Directions: The mathematicians below contributed in one way or another to the study and advancement of algebra. Research each one and match his or her contribution with the topics that follow.

1. Diophantus of Alexandria (about 250 A.D.)

   _____

2. Muhammad ibn Musa al-Khwarizmi (about 780–850)

   _____

3. John Napier (1550–1617)

   _____

4. René Descartes (1596–1650)

   _____

5. Blaise Pascal (1623–1662)

   _____

6. Leonhard Euler (1707–1783)

   _____

7. Maria Agnesi (1718–1799)

   _____

8. Pierre-Simon Laplace (1749–1827)

   _____

9. William Rowan Hamilton (1805–1865)

   _____

10. George Boole (1815–1864)

    _____

11. Emmy Noether (1882–1935)

    _____

12. Srinivasa Ramanujan (1887–1920)

    _____

Famous Mathematicians and Algebra

Topics		
Family of Curves	Logarithms	Famous Triangle
Differential Equations	Infinite Series	Logic
Algebra and Topology	Quaternion Algebra	*i*
"New" Concept of Zero	Indeterminate Equations	Cartesian Coordinate System

Who Wrote It?

Directions: Since ancient times, mathematicians have been writing about algebra and other branches of mathematics. A few of the men and women who contributed to the understanding of algebra are listed at the end of the activity. Research these mathematicians and match them with the books they wrote.

1. *Discourse de La Méthode* (*Discourse on the Method*), 1637

2. *Analytical Institutions,* 1748

3. *An Investigation of the Laws of Thought,* 1854

4. *Playing with Infinity: Mathematical Explorations and Excursions,* 1961

5. *Artis Analyticae Praxis* (*Practice of the Analytic Art*), 1631

6. *The Whetstone of Witte,* 1557

7. *Teusche Algebra,* 1659

8. *Algebra,* 1550

9. *Clavis Mathematicae,* 1631

10. *Al-Bahir fi'l-hisab* (*The Shining Book of Calculation*), 1144

Algebra Teacher's Activities Kit

Who Wrote It?

11. *Complete Introduction to Algebra,* 1770

_____

12. *Hisab al-jabr wa'l-muqabala (The Science of Reunion and Reduction),* about 825

_____

13. *Shushu juizhang (Mathematical Treatise in Nine Sections),* 1247

_____

14. *Arithmetica Integra,* 1544

_____

15. *In artem analyticem isagoge (Introduction to the Analytic Art),* 1591

_____

16. *A Description on the Wonderful Law of Logarithms,* 1614

_____

The Authors		
Maria Agnesi	Muhammad ibn Musa al-Khwarizmi	
ibn yanya al-Samaw'al	René Descartes	
Thomas Harriot	George Boole	John Napier
Raphael Bombelli	Leonhard Euler	William Oughtred
Francois Viète	Rozsa Péter	Michael Stifel
Robert Recorde	Qin Jiushao	Johann Rahn

An Algebra Research Paper

Directions: Select one of the major contributors to the advancement of algebra listed below, conduct research, and write a report. Be sure to include the individual's most notable accomplishment in algebra. Use a variety of sources, including biographies, math reference books, articles, and material posted on the Internet. Research your topic thoroughly, organize your information logically, and write clearly. Include a complete bibliography.

Possible topics include the following:

- Diophantus and Indeterminate Equations
- Apollonius and Conic Sections
- Muhammad ibn Musa al-Khwarizmi and His Overall Contributions to Algebra
- Brahmagupta and Negative Numbers
- Aryabhata and Quadratic Equations
- René Descartes and the Coordinate Plane
- Blaise Pascal and Pascal's Triangle
- Francois Viète and the Notations We Use Today
- Leonardo Fibonacci and the Fibonacci Series
- John Napier and Logarithms
- William Rowan Hamilton and Quaternion Algebra
- George Boole and Boolean Algebra
- Evariste Galois and Group Theory
- George Cantor and Set Theory
- Rozsa Péter and Recursive Functions
- Leonhard Euler and the Number e
- Emmy Noether and Abstract Algebra
- Maria Agnesi and the Family of Curves

Algebra Teacher's Activities Kit

Copyright © 2003 John Wiley & Sons, Inc.

An Algebra Essay

Directions: Think about your opinions and feelings about algebra and write an essay explaining why (or why not) you believe students should study algebra in school. Be sure to support your writing with facts and examples. Use the back of this sheet if you need more space for your essay.